UNSTOPPABLE

no matter how strong or smart my enemies are,
they're still unable to create my downfall

SHANE SILKY THOMAS

Order this book online at www.trafford.com
or email orders@trafford.com

Most Trafford titles are also available at major online book retailers.

© Copyright 2011 Shane Silky Thomas.
All rights reserved. No part of this publication may be reproduced, stored in a retrieval system, or transmitted, in any form or by any means, electronic, mechanical, photocopying, recording, or otherwise, without the written prior permission of the author.

Printed in the United States of America.

ISBN: 978-1-4269-7384-0 (sc)
ISBN: 978-1-4269-7385-7 (e)

Library of Congress Control Number: 2011911169

Trafford rev. 05/08/2012

www.trafford.com

North America & international
toll-free: 1 888 232 4444 (USA & Canada)
phone: 250 383 6864 • fax: 812 355 4082

TABLE OF CONTENTS

23rd Psalm

The Lord is my Shepherd; I shall not want.
He maketh me to lie down in green pastures:
He leadeth me beside the still waters.
He restoreth my soul:
He leadeth me in the paths of righteousness for His name' sake.

Yea, though I walk through the valley of the shadow of death,
I will fear no evil:
For thou art with me;
Thy rod and thy staff, they comfort me.
Thou preparest a table before me in the presence of mine enemies;
Thou annointest my head with oil;
My cup runneth over.

Surely goodness and mercy shall follow me all the days of my life,
and I will dwell in the House of the Lord forever.

WHEN I WAS A CHILD

I SPOKE AS A MAN

I THOUGHT AS A MAN

I UNDERSTOOD AS A MAN

WHEN I BECAME A MAN

I STOOD UP ON MY OWN TWO FEET

I AM MY BROTHERS KEEPER

THIS MEANS

I TEACH MY BROTHER

I CARE ABOUT MY BROTHER

I PRAY FOR MY BROTHER

I HELP MY BROTHER AND

I LOVE MY BROTHER

INSPIRE

BELIEVE

IT IS IMPOSSIBLE TO INSPIRE IF YOU DON'T BELIEVE

THE WESTERN WORLD IS HELL
SO YES HELL CAN FREEZE OVER

OUTERSPACE IS THE BOTTLESS PIT
IT'S AS DARK AS CAN BE
THE SUN THE MOON THE STARS THE WORLD
AND THE OTHER PLANETS RESIDE IN IT

RED GOLD AND GREEN

ARE THE COLOURS OF A NATIONS FLAG

RED: THE BLOOD OF THE PEOPLE

GOLD: THE WEALTH OF THE PEOPLE

GREEN: THE LAND OF THE PEOPLE

RED GOLD AND GREEN IS ALSO THE COLOUR OF THE STOP LIGHT

THERE IS A FACTORY OUT THERE THAT

PRINTS MONEY

POSSIBLY TRILLIONS A DAY

SO WHY IS OUR GOVERNMENT CLAIMING

BANKRUPTCY

THEY ARE IN THE POSITION TO SNAIL MAIL

EVERYONE IN THE COUNTRY

ATLEAST $10 MILLION EACH PERSON

INSTEAD WE SLAVE EVERY DAY

TO EAT AND LIVE

OBVIOUSLY MANKIND IS NOT FIT TO GOVERN

THIS WORLD

I HOPE GOD COMES SOON AND SAVE US

FROM THE LAWS OF MAN

Some people are known to be hopeless sinners, It's in the bible God himself said it. They rebel against him and his entire creation there is no hope for them. A lot of them are psychics let me explain: Say that Jane Doe is a psychic, and a hopeless sinner her phone is ringing she speaks to God, and says "since you are perfect tell me about this caller" God responds to her and says "His name is John Smith, 35yrs old, eats poorly, going to meet his soul mate next week, and also get a big job promotion in two weeks" so Jane Doe picks up the phone, and says "Hello Mr. John Smith, I know you are 35yrs of age, you should start eating healthy to prevent heart attacks, you will meet a fine young lady next week who could be your soul mate, and don't worry because a big job promotion is coming your way soon just trust me" John responds and says "Your amazing, you know my name, my age, your right I don't eat well, I am single, and I hope to God I get this important job that I applied for two days ago" Jane Doe responds and says "Don't worry John you will get that job I am perfectly sure of it" "Thanks Ms. Jane Doe I will call back again for sure, and I will tell my family, and friends all about you" says John Smith.

**AS A PEOPLE
WE WILL KNOW WHEN THE SECOND COMING OF THE SON OF MAN IS HERE**

HIS EYES ARE WINDOWS TO THE WORLD FOR EVERYONE TO SEE THROUGH

HIS MIND IS AN OPEN BOOK TO THE WORLD FOR EVERYONE TO READ

**I STRONGLY FEEL HIS PRESENCE
AND I KNOW THAT HE IS ALREADY HERE**

GOD IS PERFECT
HE MADE A BIG SACK OF BLOOD
IN EVERYONE, AND CALLS IT A HEART.
IF THE HEART GETS PIERCED IT BLEEDS,
HOW DOES IT KNOW HOW TO LOVE?
HOW DOES THE BIG SACK OF BLOOD
KNOWN AS THE BRAIN KNOWS
HOW TO THINK, STORE
INFORMATION, AND MAKE DECISIONS?
NO LIMITATION IS PERFECTION.

IF GOD COULD DIE I WOULBE BE
IFFY ABOUT HIM BECAUSE IT WOULD MEAN
HIS LIFE COULD BE TAKEN BY THE
HANDS OF MAN WHICH WOULD MAKE THE CREATOR
IMPERFECT

I DOUBT VERY MUCH THAT GOD CREATED THE WORLD
IN SIX DAYS AND RESTED ON THE SEVENTH DAY
BECAUSE A PERFECT GOD WOULD NOT NEED REST AND
WOULD BE ABLE TO CREATE EVERYTHING IN THE SNAP
OF A FINGER

THE THINGS I DON'T AGREE WITH CHURCHS

- THEY CELEBRATE THE DEATH OF THEIR SAVIOUR
- TEACH PEOPLE TO EAT HIS FLESH (CANNABALISM)
- TEACH PEOPLE TO DRINK HIS BLOOD (VAMPIRISM)

FOR DECADES VIOLENCE WAS MY WAY OF THINKING A LOT OF PEOPLE KNOWS WHAT IT FEELS LIKE TO BE A BAD MAN BUT I AM THE ONLY BAD MAN WHO KNOWS WHAT IT FEELS LIKE TO BE THE BADDEST MAN MY NAME IS SHANE ANTHONY THOMAS THIS MY LIFE

When I was born, I weighed 7 pounds 3 ounces.
As you can see I was born a baby boy.
I was born July 19th/1979.
I was born in Spanish Town Hospital in Jamaica.
I was raise in the country (Thompson Town) before moving
to the city (May Pen) which are both located in the parish of Clarendon.
My mother told me that I grew up on baby formula.
My favourite colour is red.
My favourite food is fried fish.
My favourite fruit is sugar cane.
My favourite soup is goat head soup.
My favourite beverage is carrot juice.
My favourite word is calling people goofs.
My favourite animal is the lion.
My favourite car is the Lamborghini.
My favourite objects are knives.
My favourite thing to do is kill.
My favourite name is Satan.
My favourite joy is a woman.
My favourite shoes are Nike air max.
My favourite clothing is jeans and a t-shirt.
My favourite season is summer.
My favourite hobby is listening to pretty girls talk.
My favourite artists are myself and 50 cent.
My favourite planet is my brain.
My favourite thing is money.
My favourite accomplishment is my journey.
My favourite girl is Empress Asheeba.
My favourite companions are Sqwin, Jug, and P.
My favourite job is my entire creation.
My favourite teaching is perfect truth.
My favourite mission is completion.
My favourite destination is above all.

My name is Shane Anthony Thomas I am a 31 year old single male. I left Jamaica, and came to live with my mother Gladys in Brampton, Ontario, Canada in 1989. We eventually moved to Mississauga, in an area called Ridgeway and my friends called me Silky. I use to get beatings a lot from mommy because I was a very bad child growing up. I always carried weapons such as knives, guns, ice picks, razor blades wrench's and such. I clobbered people, shot at people, stabbed people, beat up people, threaten people, extort people, and disrespected people badly. My friends and I formed our own family at 11years of age, we were known as **"THE RIDGEWAY BLOODS GANG"** in which I was the head guy. Due to the lifestyle I lived the community feared, and respected me; I quickly developed the status as the **DON** of Peel Region. We sold drugs, committed robberies of all kinds, and got expelled from schools. I lived at Fair Oaks Place next to McHardy Court right off McMurchy, and 475 Bramalea Road which are both located in Brampton. My fast paced life of crime, and violence turned me into a monster. I lived most of my life in Provincial Jails, Federal Institutions, and Federal Halfway Houses. For the past thirteen years, I have only resided independently out in the community on my own for approximately 3 months, the rest is confinement where I still maintained my status as the Head Guy every where I was. This is my word people.

My mother's name is "Gladys". She was born and raised in Thompson Town, Clarendon, Jamaica. My parents separated when I was born. My mother left me in Jamaica at the tender age of two years old because she wanted to move to Canada for a better life. She sponsored me when I was nine years old. Within the first or second week of living with my mother in Brampton (Ontario, Canada), I wanted to go back to Jamaica but she said "no". She would beat me really bad. I was not used to that kind of treatment because when I lived in Jamaica, my father and my aunt spoiled me rotten. I didn't like my mother growing up. All she did was hit me and call me names. Every time I went in to the shower I would break down and cry. I would keep things bottled up inside of me, and then I would go out in the community and release my anger on other people. I had no one to talk to because I had never trusted anyone. I didn't care if I lived or died. I get along with my mother now. She gives me good advice and cares about my future, which is a blessing.

When I was a child, my mom use to make me do all the house work, I then decided to stop at the age of 16yrs. Old I had to wash the dishes, dust the furniture, sweep, mop, vacuum, take out the garbage, shovel the snow, clean all the bedrooms, and spread the beds, do the laundry, while she only cleans the bathrooms, which she made me sometimes do. She worked me like a slave that bitch.

At one point I had to do the cooking as a 12yrs. old child growing up. I would sometimes cook macaroni with hot dogs chopped up inside of it, shake and bake chicken with either oven baked fries or white rice, ravioli, canned soups or other canned foods. At an older age, I cooked other foods like fried chicken, baked chicken, cod fish, fried fish, tuna/ pink salmon with stir fried vegetables, fried/boiled dumplings, boiled green bananas/fried plantains, baked/boiled potatoes, white rice, ground beef with spaghetti, and burgers with fries. At some Halfway houses the staff would come into the kitchen and admire my cooking. In the past, I carelessly added too much salt, or I would leave the pot on the stove for too long unattended. I also can make good breakfast, but I don't eat pork. I love to cook, and I am very confident with my skills.

I didn't like my mother's husband growing up, and I still don't mainly because he signed the papers for me to come to Canada, but he didn't do the same for my father. The goofs name is Horace, when I first came to Canada my mom was renting a small one bedroom out of a house where she, my sister, my grandmother, and I slept on the same bed. I had my own room when I was living in Jamaica, so coming to Canada was depressing. Horace was living in a three bedroom townhouse by himself which didn't make sense. He was afraid of me and insecure because he was worried that my father would be competition with him where my mother is concerned. One day Horace tapped me on the back of my head because I wasn't listening to him. I wanted to kill the goof even though that was the only time he ever laid a hand on me I was around 10yrs. old at the time. Later on in life, when I first went to prison, they bought a house, and moved in together, he didn't want me around. I never in my life lived under the same roof with Horace, he hates both my father, and I, but he knows that the feeling is mutual.

In my youth, my mother, her husband, my brother, my sister, and my two step sisters, and I would visit my family in New Jersey by driving down on vacation. I liked it in that State because clothing and shoes were way cheaper than shopping in Canada, plus I loved hanging with my cousins that lived there, and I loved my aunts cooking. I also loved their American accent. We stayed in Ervington, New Jersey which isn't far away from New York City. On one occasion while heading back to Canada, we stopped off in Southside Jamaica Queens, I got out the van, and noticed a lot of people starring me down, I felt tension, and I wanted to kill. Moments later, I got back into the vehicle, and we continued our journey back to Canada.

I have been in and out of confinement, since the age of seventeen, I am now thirty two. I wish I was serving time on death row, in an American prison for the simple fact that if I get lethal injection, or hanging, or the electric chair, and it doesn't kill me, they would have to set me free, that's the law. I can't die people, I am immortal.

My mother, sister, and I visited England when I was approximately ten years old. We have family there. The manicans at the wax museum looked so real, and we also went to Buckingham Palace, the buildings there looked so old. The guards at the gates had their guns with a blade attached to it, I wanted to break off the blade, kill the guards, go inside, kill more people, and take over the palace. I am a ruthless killer people.

My father's name is "Neville" but everyone calls him "Tony". I love him dearly. He looks exactly like me but his complexion is lighter than mine. He was born and raised in Blackwood, Clarendon, Jamaica. He's a very humble and quiet man. I take after him in that. As a child growing up, he would buy me anything I wanted no matter the cost. He was a lab technician working with my Aunt Cynthia, which is his sister. He later became a politician in Clarendon, Jamaica as the Minister of Transportation. I have no idea what he is doing now, but I am sure he is doing alright. He is a good cook and an amazing father. I can not stress the fact how much I love him. Our relationship right now is long distance, but I know that one day for certain we will meet again. The only time my father hit me was when I was approximately four or five years old. I was back-talking him and being rude, so he slapped me on the ass. It didn't hurt but I was still crying. You know how kids are, crying over nothing. I deserved it, but I know he meant me no harm. I love him.

I have a younger brother from my father side. He's in his twenties now. His name is Tommy. I am very disappointed with myself because I never got to send him things like money, shoes, clothing and such because I was always locked up. I know he's disappointed too, but I hope he understands and doesn't hate me. I love Tommy. I brought him a soccer ball when I visited Jamaica as a teenager. He goes to college in Trinidad and is studying to be an electrical engineer. He's probably done school by now and working. I know I will see my little brother Tommy once I am less restricted. I love him. I don't think my brother ever got into trouble with the law. I am proud of him.

I have a beautiful sister from my mom's side. Her name is "Alisha". She is 22 years old. I love her very much. When we were younger, I used to give her baths, change her diapers, feed her, take her to daycare, and when she got older, took her school. I would also take her to the park so she could play on the swings and help her with school work. When I started going to jail and prison, she would send me canteen money and accept my phone calls. She went to college and took social work. She did her placement in Mexico and decided it was too overwhelming, so she is taking nursing now and is working. She got time off from working because she is pregnant now and is due to give birth by May 2011. We are very close and I wish nothing but the best for her.

I have a younger brother from my mother's side. His name is Michael and he is 18 years old. When he was a baby, I used to give him baths, change his diapers and feed him. When he got a little older, I would punch him up and make him do push ups. I wanted him to grow up tough and that's why I did it. He would always get into fights at school and beat up other kids. At a later age, he got his black belt in Tae Kwon Do and that's when he really started fighting. I was once his age, so I know what him and his friends are all about. I had a serious talk with him about jail and prison. He quickly made up his mind that he does not want to go there. He is going to start college soon. He has two good paying jobs and he wants to be a firefighter and he is popular with the girls. I love him and very proud of him.

When my mother came to Canada, she left me in Jamaica with my grand parent's mama and papa. Some of their children which are my aunts and uncles also resided with us, along with their children which are my cousins. We lived in the country side of Thompson Town Clarendon, Jamaica. Papa worked on a yam hill for a living, he would dig up yams, give it to mama who would gather the yams with other types of fruits, and vegetables, travel to May Pen city by bus, and sell the products in the market. She made just enough money to pay the bills and feed us. On our land we had fruit trees, vegetables, goats, chickens and a donkey. Even though we were poor we ate well on a daily basis. It was hard for me because I would hear my cousins calling to their mommies; I couldn't do the same because mines were in Canada. I grew extremely close to mama, who took me under her wings, and treated me as if I were her son. She would always buy me candy and take me to the beach sometimes. I love mama and grew attached to her as if she was my mom. I would usually stay around the house or travel to the market with mama, because she couldn't afford to send me to school. As a child growing up she didn't even hit me when I was bad because I was her favorite.

Papa used to bring me to work with him where I would watch him dig up yams all day. Every morning he would let me sit on his lap at the dinner table, where I would watch him drink his coffee before he went to work. Papa was the type that loved his liquor; he would always go to the bar after work to drink with his friends. Mama and papa use to argue sometimes, because her earnings from the market couldn't support his drinking habits. Mama eventually left Jamaica, and came to Canada to live with my mom. She left me with my aunt Cynthia in May Pen Clarendon Jamaica where I stayed until I was nine years old, then I came to Canada to live with my mom. Mama now lives in a nursing home in Brampton Ontario, Canada where I visit her every two weeks. Papa also came to Canada where he died of old age. My aunt Cynthia is my father's sister.

When I was a child living in the country side of Thompson Town Clarendon Jamaica with my mom's side of the family, my cousins and I would go outside in the morning, and pick up eggs that the chickens laid, give them to my aunt who would boil or fry the eggs for breakfast.

One time my uncle which is one of my favorites cut the head off one of our chickens, which ran around the yard for a long time, with no head.

On one occasion, my grandfather who I called papa, tied up a goat on the banana trees, cut the left side of its neck, where the main artery is, and it bled to death, blood was spraying all over the place. When it died he skinned it, cut out the guts and fats, chopped it up, washed it, bagged it up and put it in the freezer. When I seen him cut the main artery, I got a vision that he was a killer in his younger days.

One day my grandmother took me to a shop (convenience store) down the road. We went behind the shop, and seen a pig in a pen, it was the biggest pig that I had ever seen in my life. I don't remember if that was the same pig I saw eating a pop can, the acids in its stomach must be strong, in order to digest, and break down the pop can. Don't eat pork people, its gross.

When I was living in Thompson Town Clarendon Jamaica at my grandparent's house, I got into an argument with my cousin Craig. We were approximately four or five years old, my aunt which is Craig's mother gave him a knife and told him to juk my eye out. My grandmother saw what was happening so she gave me an ice pick, my thoughts was to kill him, but I seriously can't remember what happened after that.

On a different occasion while living at my Aunt Cynthia's house in May Pen Clarendon Jamaica, my cousin Gavin who I love dearly, we got into a fight. I hit him, he hit me back, so I hit him again, and he hit me back again, I hit him a third time, in which he hit me back again and he ran inside the house. I chased after him until we ended up in my Aunt Cynthia's bedroom; he jumped on her bed on his back with his legs up in the air. I tried going from side to side to get around him but he was moving from side to side also, so I went straight at him, in which he kicked me in the mouth, and chipped my tooth. He jumped off the bed in which I chased after him. My intentions were to catch him and kill him. I caught him and beat the fuck out of him, and that was that. I eventually got my tooth fixed when I came to Canada. I got into a lot more fights as a child while living in Jamaica but I just can't remember all of them.

Aunt Cynthia was my favorite aunt when I was growing up. She treated me as if I was her son. She is a lab technician who spoiled me rotten, she put me through school, and bought me anything I wanted. She was just like my father to me. The school that I went to was called St. Thomas Moore Prep. I got kicked out of that school and went to another one and then later on they accepted me back at the school that I got kicked out of. I didn't live with my father because he lived in a small, one bedroom house with his wife and my little brother. In Jamaica back then the teachers were allowed to hit the students when they were behaving badly. One time I didn't know the answer to a question, so my teacher told me to make a fist, and she used a ruler to hit me on my knuckles. I started crying, so I went home and told my aunt who called the school and warned them not to hit me again, which they didn't. My aunt use to always keep big parties for me on my birthdays. We lived in a fairly large house where I did what I wanted to do. I use to always pee her bed even when I got my own room as a child. I love my aunt Cynthia very much, and she loves me too, I had bad asthma as a child, but it went away when I came to Canada to live with my mother.

While living at Aunt Cynthia's house, there were a lot of tropical lizards running around. They could even change colours. we would use sticks to smash them which killed them. We would sometimes chop their tails off, which would still wiggle around.

When we were playing outside, we would see big bull frogs hopping around so I would grab a bamboo stick, and tried smashing it to death. The fucking thing wouldn't die, so I would get some salt, and pour it on the bull frog, and smash it some more. It would eventually leak white stuff out of its back which looked like puss, I heard that if the puss gets on my skin, I would grow warts, so I quickly made up my mind to leave the fucking thing alone.

In our backyard, there was a big wasp nest by the roof, Gavin and I seen a lot of German wasps on the nest, and around the nest. I decided to grab a big bamboo stick, in which I used to knock the nest down to the ground. I then dropped the stick on the ground and we ran away quickly, and I ended up getting stung on the bottom of my right foot, because we always used to walk around bare footed, I eventually took out the sting.

One time my cousins and I were on our way home from school, there was an open field where we seen a lot of cows eating grass. I decided to pick up rocks off the ground and started stoning the cows. They all started chasing us so we started running, we opened the gate ran in, and closed the gate. The cows then realized that they couldn't get us so they turned around, went back to the open land, and continued eating grass.

As a child living in Jamaica at my aunt's house, where some of my cousins also lived, we use to climb fruit trees, which was fun for us. There was a tall tree next to our house that grew a type of fruit called guinep, which was sweet and tasty. You can find this fruit mainly in the carribean, and other hot climate countries. We would climb high up, and rest our bodies on a firm sturdy branch, and eat guinep's all day. Its round, with the same size as grapes, in a rough green shell, it's a seed and you suck the fruit off it. On our property we also had mango trees, a cherry tree, sugar cane, lime tree, sour sop tree, ackee tree, coconut tree, scotch pepper tree, and a plum tree. I have a cousin named Gavin who is a year younger than me, and Javid who was much younger than us. We use to fuck with Javid to piss him off. He would cry and tell his father who is my uncle Danny. He would chase after us, Gavin, and I would run to the backyard, and climb up the plum tree. Uncle Danny would then pick up rocks, and tried stoning us out the tree. He would eventually give up, and leave us alone. We would then climb down, and fuck with Javid again.

In Jamaica sometimes after school, I would walk to my aunts, and father's workplace. It was called a Middlesex lab which was owned by them. There were two location, one in Chapleton, Clarendon, and one in May Pen, Clarendon. If someone went to their doctor's office, their doctor would send them to my aunts and fathers lab to fill their prescription, whether in pill, or liquid form, to do blood work or to give a blood sample, which would go onto a lancet, then placed under a stethoscope, to be viewed for any kind of illness' including diseased ones. I would sometimes play around on the stethoscope, and view samples which caught my interest, but drove my aunt crazy. As a child she would always tell me to get my education, and learn the business so I can take over when they get old. My aunt and my father are highly educated people, which motivate me to accomplish only the best. I know I will no matter what because it's only up to me. My father would always leave work early, to take me out, and just chill with me. We would go to KFC, or where ever I wanted to go. Begger's would always hit him up for money, and he would always give it to them. I love my father a lot, he reminds me of myself, when he was in his twenties and thirties.

One day my father and I left the Middlesex Lab, walked down to the heart of May Pen City, when I was around seven years old. I then saw a cop that was walking toward us, who then stopped my father then engaged in conversation. I did not like the way he was talking to my father, so I looked up into his face, and gave him dirty looks, I wanted to kill the goof. Cops think that they are above the law, but the thing is I am above them, I can't wait to fucking rise up.

On a different day when my father, and I were in the heart of the city, we saw a man walking around wielding a machety. For some reason I thought that he was trying to intimidate us. I then made up my mind to approach the goof, disharm him, and chop his head off.

There was a big guy that was pissing me off, outside my aunt Cynthia's and my father's workplace, I wished I had a knife to fucking kill him, because he was fucking with me by chasing me around. My father then came outside, and started yelling at the guy and chased him around. He then told me to go inside and I did.

While I was living in Canada with my mother, my father would always buy my plane tickets, so I could fly to Jamaica to visit him. I use to go there in my young teens to visit before I started going to jail, I had the most fun. My father would always take me to the beach, we would always enjoy some sweet fresh jelly coconuts, drive all over the island, he would always give me money, buy my expensive clothing, but the best part was spending time with my father who is one of my favourite person in the world.

As a young child growing up in Jamaica, I would rip off a branch off the coconut tree in the backyard at home, pick limes off the tree, where my cousins and I would play cricket. We also had a soccer ball in which we would play football sometimes, but here in Canada we call it soccer. At school I was on the track team, and our teachers would feed us glucose before we performed. I was a sprinter, and very quick, the glucose was very effective because it gave us a burst of energy. I would always watch the other kids at school play foot ball, I didn't play though because if they played rough with me, it would cause problems for sure. I also played sports in Canada as a youth growing up, I once played in a soccer league, and in elementary school, it's my favourite sport to play, and I also loved watching the world cup on television, my favourite teams are Jamaica, and Canada. I also played basketball at school, and in a league called the Mississauga Monarchs, I suck at basketball but I love watching it on television during the playoffs, my favourite teams are the Toronto Raptors, and the L.A. Lakers. I also love watching hockey during playoffs, my favourite teams are the Toronto Maple Leafs, and the Calgary Flames, my favourite player is Jerome Iginla. I use to play street hockey with my friends as a kid.

When I was living at 3590 Colonial Drive in Ridgeway (Mississauga) at 13 years old with my Mother, Grandfather,and Sister my Mother was beating me for something I don't remember. I wasn't crying which pissed her off. So she went for a baseball bat right away I made up my mind to disarm her and beat her to death, but my Grandfather came in between us and stopped me.

When I was living at 16 Fair Oaks Place next to McHardy Court in Brampton at 18 years old the dishes piled up in the sink, I refused to wash them because I washed them earlier. My Mother then said she did not want me in the house anymore, and asked me to leave. I got upset and basically told her to go fuck herself and that I am not leaving because it is my house. I started calling her names like bitch and Drancro Gal (Jamaican) so she said that she was calling the cops then she ran upstairs. I went in the boiler room to rip out the wires to disable the phone but I did not know which one to rip out. I then left and a cop pulled me over down the road, he searched me found my knife but he did not charge me. He drove me to my Aunts where I stayed.

I lived at my Aunts for approximately 1 month where her four children also lived; she could barely pay the rent, and bills and also had to buy the groceries. During the day time my friends and I would rob banks, at night we would frequent strip clubs and do other robberies. I think she saw my face on the news and called the cops. I didn't need money from her because I had my own, plus I worked at Wendy's part time so that I could say I worked and that is why I have money.

I use to live at 475 Bramalea Road in Brampton when I was 25 years old; I rented a room in a townhouse in 2005 I was getting $620.00 from Welfare each month and rent was $420.00 so I had only $200.00 to buy my groceries, and pay my phone bill, buy my cigarettes, and bus fare, and weed which I got for free most of the time. I only had a little bit of money so I went to my landlord and told her, that it is my house now and I don't pay rent anymore. I took over the whole house until I went to jail in April 2005, for the charges that I am doing time for which you will read in my criminal history.

At this same house my Mother, her husband, my brother, sister, and my two step sisters visited me, I went outside to greet them. My mom disrespected me by calling me a Drancro and telling me I looked like a wild animal, I was pissed and I lost it. I asked her "who the fuck you talking to Bitch!" I started to call her names and told her I would kill her, they eventually left and that was that!

When I was a child in elementary school girls would send other girls to ask me for my number and every girl in my class wanted to go to the grade 8 graduation prom with me. I was very popular with the girls but extremely shy. I had a beautiful girlfriend named Selena, I was 13 years old and she was 12 years old. We spoke over the phone a lot but rarely spent time together. One day some girls from her school told me that she had a boyfriend, and she was cheating on him with me, so I broke up with her. She asked me if we could be friends I said no! Which she probably still hates me today. Selena was my very first girlfriend, the last time I seen her was at Clarkson secondary school when I went there to visit friends.

When I was 18 years old I had a girlfriend named Sarah who was also beautiful, she was 17 years old she was also cheating on her boyfriend with me, but I did not dump her. We met at Covenant house which was a homeless shelter for young boys and girls. We spent a lot of time together hanging out and stuff; when I was there I smashed a couple guys in and out of the house. I was the head guy there; I broke up with Sarah without saying goodbye because they kicked me out of the house for threatening a staff member there so I went to go live with my friend Mark in Ridgeway, a short time after that I went back to jail.

At the age of 19 years old I met a beautiful girl named Terry-Anne at my friend's house party in Ridgeway. I was noticing her and she was noticing me, we engaged in small talk and exchanged phone numbers. She was either in her late twenties or early thirties when we hooked up. We spent a little bit of time together. All I got from Terry-Anne was a hug which was depressing because we never went further than that. Once we met up at her friend's house in Ridgeway and another time we travelled to downtown Toronto together were we ate at a restaurant and then we went to a tattoo parlour so I could get a tattoo but I couldn't afford it so I didn't bother. One day I was calling her over the phone, and couldn't reach her, so I stopped calling and never seen or spoke to her since. I didn't want it to end like that but it did.

At 19 years of age I met this girl named Teneka at my step sisters Sebrina birthday party, I asked her for her phone number, we hooked up, and became boyfriend and girlfriend, and she was 17 years old. We spent a lot of time together at my place, her house, and out in the community. She spent a lot of money on me, and drove me anywhere I wanted to go. I was the baddest man in Peel Region and she loved it plus I still am. I didn't really want to be with Teneka, she was not my type but I was desperate. When I went to prison, things were falling apart between her and I. I spoke with her over the phone, and I told her that if she didn't visit me, and bring drugs for me I would kill her when I got out, so she did. My friends and I smoked the weed, and I sold the crack cocaine. When I got out we hooked up again. When I was living at 475 Bramalea Rd. she slept over frequently. One day I came to my senses and stopped taking her calls, I didn't want to be with her anymore. One early morning she came to my house and she said she came for her stuff, I went upstairs got her garments from my dresser drawers, went back downstairs, gave them to her, slammed my door in her face and that was it, I hate the bitch. After those relationships, I never had another girlfriend, not by choice though. Only one stripper, massages parlours, and escorts which sucks badly.

When we were younger in our teens in Ridgeway which is located in Mississauga we were at war with another gang called Trench Mobb whom were located in downtown Mississauga. These guys were cowards when confronted, we would go down to their area and disrespect them and they would not defend it. One summer day in August Sqwin and I were on our way to Caribana we got off the bus at square one shopping mall to wait on the next bus going to Islington subway station. I saw a couple girls I knew from school in which we engaged in conversation. Sqwin pointed out to me that one guy out of a large group just called me a pussy, so I looked in their direction and he looked into my eyes and said Yeah you, so I pulled out my ice pick went up to him, held it at his neck and asked him who the fuck is he talking to. He never said a word, so I called him a pussy and told him that I would kill him. I thought his friends would have stuck up for him and attack me but they did nothing. But instead they tried to talk me out of stabbing their boss that is how I knew for sure that they are all a bunch of pussies. After that I never seen him again, their Trench Mobb.

When I was a teen I use to get kicked out of schools a lot for carrying weapons, and beating up people badly. I didn't take my studies seriously, I would skip class, smoke weed with friends behind the school, and disrespect my teachers, A bunch of guys from a different school tried to swarm me so I pulled my wrench out of my school bag and smashed them with it so they took off jumped in their vehicles and left.

One guy was staring me down on the school bus so I pulled my ice pick off my waist and stuck it at his throat, I threatened to kill him, and then he apologized so I left him alone.

One guy at school thought I was soft because I am extremely quiet, we got into a scuffle in the school cafeteria where I threw him over the garbage bin, he landed on his back, I stepped on his chest and people started laughing at him He's a Malton Crip.

A next guy I disrespected who wanted to fight me in front of his friends, didn't know that I knew Judo so I kneed him in the face, threw him to the ground, and started punching him, I broke his nose. A lot more fights happened but I just can't remember all of them. I was the head guy at all my schools.

As a young bad ass teenager I was fearless and I still am. My friends and I are known as the most feared gang in Peel region. Some thought it was a toss up between us and the Malton Crips. They were trying to finish us and, we were trying to finish them. They feared Sqwin, and I badly, but me the most though, it was like a turf war but mostly personal. They knew me extremely well and they were very cautious, I had confrontations with them while in confinement, at school, and in the community. Up to this very day I still don't like them, and they still don't like me. Let's say in every confrontation with them I was victorious. I won't mention their names but they fear my name which is Shane Anthony Thomas A.K.A Silky the baddest man in Peel region.

As a child growing up in Canada I use to go to house parties a lot, and when I reached of age I started frequenting night clubs. I went with friends, and we always had fun drinking liquor, smoking weed, and hitting on girls. Every time we went, something serious would happen, and most of the time, I was involved, and I loved the drama. Sometimes fits fights would break out, shootings, stabbings, and murders. We would always leave the scene before the cops got there, every time we went, there was always enemies lurking. Some of us had guns, and some of us had knives, I always had knives because that was my preference. Back then my favourite music was reggae, now its both reggae, and rap. My friends would always play rap music in their vehicles, and I would always hear it in the clubs, I started liking it plus I could relate to some of the lyrics from artists like 50 cent, Styles P, Rick Ross, Little Wayne, and Mobb Deep. I don't like when artist only talk about their cars, and jewelry. In my lyrics, I talk about my life experiences, which is real.

As a teen growing up, I didn't work much because I would quit my jobs. I mainly worked for agencies which were slave work, and always messy. I use to deliver newspapers as a kid, but I use to hide the papers in my closet, or in the backyard, and not deliver them. People would complain that they weren't getting their papers, I didn't have a cart to pull the papers in, so I had to carry them in my hands which was way too heavy.

I use to stock boxes in trailers, at Purolator which was heavy. I use to open some of the boxes were I stole cell phones, and laptop computers at 16yrs. old in 1996, I got fired, charged, and went to jail.

I worked at Wendy's Restaurant for a couple weeks, before getting fired, and going to prison, for numerous armed robberies. I was spending way more money for cab fair on a weekly basis, than what I made working for Wendy's.

When I was serving time in a federal halfway house in Kingston, Ontario, Canada, I worked at a restaurant called Dunn's Deli for only a couple weeks. The place was getting dirty, and the dishes were piling up quickly, so I quit the job, and walked out.

When I was in prison, I always had a good job, and loved working even though I only got paid a dollar a day. I worked so that I could buy groceries like soups, chips, chocolate bars, and cigarettes. If you didn't work, you would be locked up in your cell all day.

My mental illness' prevents me from working. It is very stressful, and it causes me to breakdown mentally if I work long repetitive hours. I strongly feel that I developed my mental illness' as a young child, but it never got detected until I was in my early twenties while I was in prison.

My friends and I always had money because we sold drugs and committed armed robberies. We wore expensive clothing, name brand shoes, and bottles of liquor and weed all the time, we ate well. Sqwin and Jug had all the girls, and we all had fancy cars. We would frequent strip clubs and spend big money which attracted all the girls of course. The money came quick but also went fast; we would always get more and more. We were all at a strip club in Toronto once and we were all wearing red clothing, all eyes on us when we went inside. We sat at one table rolled up our weed and started smoking while we waited for a waitress to serve us our drinks. The bouncers snuck up behind us put us all in choke holds, and brought us outside and locked us out. I was smashing their cars, they came back outside and I chased after them with the crowbar, they ran inside and locked the doors once again. I would imagine that they called the cops, so we jumped inside our vehicles and took off.

Years ago when I was a teenager living with my mother in Brampton, there was a party at our house, a bunch of my cousins and friends were there. We were in my bedroom, and my cousin K-DOG was looking inside my closet and seen a whole bunch of silk shirts, so he started calling me "SILK" I later had a vision that "SILK" was also my nickname back in the first coming.

SILentKiller

Which made perfect sense, because guns bark loud and knives are quiet, I use knives.

I had a vision that JESUS was my name in the first coming, and SATAN is my new name in the second coming. Back in the first coming, I revealed this to HITLER (the world deceiver), in which he added and subtracted from the bible and wrote that SATAN is the world deceiver.

Shane Anthony Thomas And No one

SANTA comes on December 25th I had a vision that my real birthday is December 25th he wears red, My favourite colour is red, he flies in the sky on a sled, when I rise I can fly in the sky with my red wings, if you unscramble the word SANTA it spells SATAN. Don't let the hopeless sinners mislead you, I AM HE.

**I WAS CONFINED IN ALL THESE
JAILS, PRINSONS, AND HALFWAY HOUSES**

No Image
Available

SPRUCEDALE YOUTH CENTRE

HAMILTON-WENTWORTH DETENTION CENTRE

MAPLEHURST CORRECTIONAL CENTRE

METRO TORONTO WEST DETENTION CNETRE

MILLBROOK MAXIMUM SECURITY CORRECTIONAL CENTRE
(BUILDING TORN DOWN)

COLLINS BAY MEDIUM SECURITY CORRECTIONAL CENTRE
(GLADIATOR SCHOOL)

MILLHAVEN MAXIMUM SECURITY INSTITUTION (J-UNIT)

REGIONAL TREATMENT CENTRE (MENTAL ILLNESS)

DOWLING HALFWAY HOUSE (TORONTO)

PORTSMOUTH HALFWAY HOUSE (KINGSTON)

KEELE HALFWAY HOUSE (TORONTO)

ST. LEONARDS PLACE PEEL (BRAMPTON)

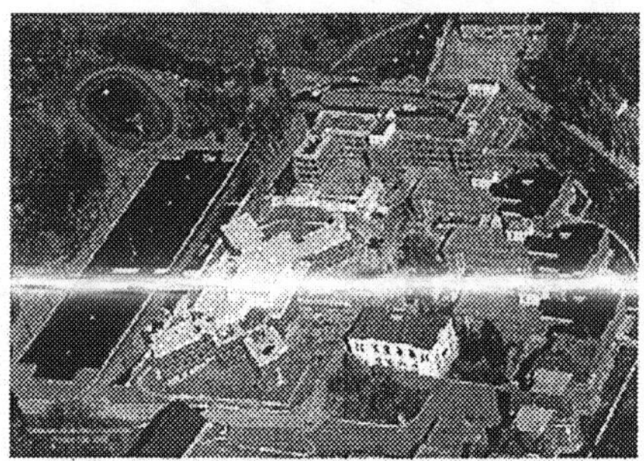

ST. LAWRENCE VALLEY CORRECTIONAL & MENTAL HEALTH FACILITY

Violence has always been apart of my life, as a child growing up I knew grappling, wrestling, and boxing from just fooling around. I have always been a street fighter, and I also took judo lessons. I grew up fighting, and I loved it. I looked at all my opponents as potential victims, I never lost a fight in the community nor in jail, even though I knew how to use my fists well I prefer using knives. In the community I sent a lot of people to the hospital. In prison I sent a lot of people to the hospital, protective custody, put people on crutches, and in wheel chairs. I took things very seriously I would not let anything slide. I faught physical spiritual, and mental battles which has turned me into a stronger person. I think the sword is mightier than the pen because the pen writes but the sword kills.

In 1997 when I was a young offender in the Metro Toronto West Detention Centre for stabbing a guy badly out in the community, there was a guy on my range who thought I was a punk or something because I was a scrawny little kid back then. I called him into the bathroom where I beat the fuck out of him. A guard caught on to what was happening he noticed me and the goof breathing heavily so right away he knew something was up. To keep us separated they would lock him up in his cell when I was on the range and vice-versa.

One day I was locked in my cell while he was out on the range, so I called my cell mate to my door and told him to tell the guard to open the cell door so he could grab his deck of playing cards. When the guard opened my cell door with the keys I ran out of my cell and attacked the goof, I punched him in his face, and then the guard restrained me and locked me back in my cell, this guard use to pass me cigarettes once in a while.

The goof said I hit him with something and he told the guards to move him to another range. Back in 2002 I seen the goof in J-Unit maximum security prison where a friend of mine beat the fuck out of him, and he ended up leaving, and went to protective custody to finish off his sentence.

When I went to Sprucedale young offender prison back in 1997 I called a couple guys to the washroom to fight over arguments but they all backed down. I flipped out on a couple staff members because of their stupid head games. One time I was in the TV room with a bunch of guys, some were playing cards, some were playing pool, and others were watching TV. One guy got up out of his seat so I sat there moments later he came back and asked for his seat back, I did not pay any attention to him and I remained seated while I watched TV. He started punching me in the face and as soon as I got up to smash him one of the staff members grabbed me in a bear hug. We both went to segregation. When we got out of segregation I got an ice pick from the metal shop put it in my shoe, went through the metal detector and back to my range I did not get to stab him up with my ice pick because he got set free. Many years later I saw him at Portsmouth Halfway House where I punched him in the face, in which he said nor did nothing. I felt so much better after that, I was the head guy there.

I've always had a relationship with God. I've always read the bible. I've always believed in him. I was angry with him for a long time. I was suffering and he didn't care I was waiting for the second coming. I still await his arrival. I've always asked for forgiveness for all my wrongs. I've always followed his lead. I am the baddest man every where I go. I have put fear into a lot of people without realizing it. I never did it for stripes. I am not afraid to get stabbed with knives or poked with ice picks or shot with a gun. I have been in the presence of death. I have been through investigations but no charges have ever applied. I had no personality. I did not even know how to hold a conversation. My hobbies was making knives ice picks, and stabbing people. I was the best at it. I would get beat up by a team of 12 guards frequently. People would give me knives and ice picks as gifts so that I wouldn't use it on them. Every prison that I was in guards and other convicts feared me. The special handling unit {super maximum security} refused to accept me there. I prefer knife fighting over anything else. I use to shed a lot of peoples blood. I would roll up my mattress, and practice stabbing it. I use to draw a human figure on my wall, label the temple throat heart lungs bowel, and practiced my stabbing skills. I use to spar with guys to practice my fist fighting skills both defensively, and offensively. I would also practice on a small fist sized speed bag to improve my skills. I was a warrior, a dangerous one.

OUT OF ALL THE PEOPLE THAT I STABBED UP, EVERY STRIKE HITS ORGANS, MAIN ARTERIES AND OTHER VEINS. IN J-UNIT I WOULD DRAW A HUMAN FIGURE ON MY WALL, LABEL THE VITALS, AND PRACTICE MY AIM IVE BEEN THROUGH MANY INVESTIGATIONS, BUT I REMAIN TO BE UNSTOPPABLE

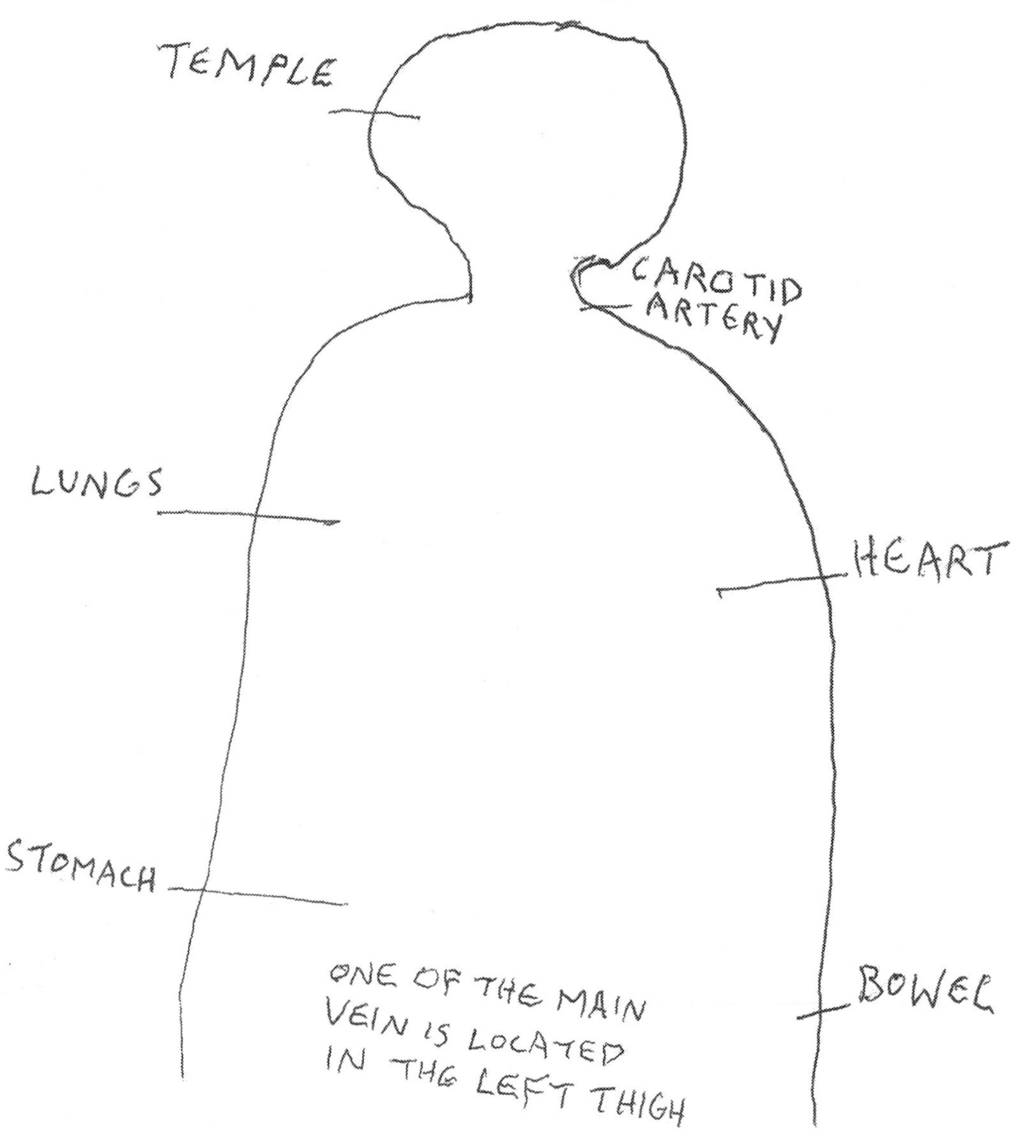

Back in early 1999 before I went to prison for numerous armed robberies I bought a good looking 1991 Acura Integra. It was a red car which I purchased from my very good friends mechanic, for $5500.00. I brought it to a shop to upgrade it, which cost me another $10 000.00, I got them to put fog lights, tinted triangular windows, power windows, power locks, a double chromed muffler, batman alarm system, wicked stereo system, with surround sound, and big subwoofers in the trunk, Momo steering wheel, Momo gear stick, Momo pedals which were all red, and Velcro Acura straps for the seat belts. I couldn't drive it because I didn't know how to drive standard, the reason why I got it was because my best friend Sqwin was trying to teach me how to drive standard with his car.

When I get rich I am going to buy myself a brand new red Lamborghini. I love how that car looks. I will have diplomatic license plates on it, so I won't need a driver's license, I will always speed, and if cops pull me over, I will kill them.

Back in March of 1999 I went to the Metro Toronto West Detention Centre, I terrorized that place. After serving my time in segregation one guard was escorting me to a range in the jail. I wanted to go back to 1B where my friends were, he said I can't go back there because the lieutenant gave him instructions to place me on 1A range.

I warned them not to put me there, but they didn't listen. I said to myself that when I get on 1A I'm going inside the washroom and the first guy to come in, I'm going to smash him, and I did. He bit me a couple times but I hurt him badly. I was sent back to segregation immediately for a couple of weeks. When I finished my time in seg they put me down stairs on 2B range where the guy was.

I was waiting for him to go to the washroom so I could smash him again but he left the range and went to protective custody. My best friend Sqwin was on the range too, I was the head guy there. Days later I knocked out another guy and the guards placed me back in segregation.

In the Toronto West Detention Center I was the head guy on my range. Some people called me Mike Tyson instead of Silky because I knocked out at least six guys, and stabbed up one guy very badly in the washroom. The guy was huge, and he tried to take over my range the night before the stabbing. The very moment he landed on my range I felt a lot of tension. Ants Man was singing that night in his cell as he usually did which was fun for us. The guy that was trying to take over my range yelled at Ants Man to shut up because he was trying to sleep. My cell mate, and best friend Sqwin asked me if I heard that so I told the guy yelling to shut the fuck up, and wait until morning. That night I used my lighter to melt my toothbrush, and made it into a dagger. The next morning Sqwin, and I followed the guy into the washroom where I began stabbing him in his face multiple times there was blood everywhere. Sqwin grabbed the guy from behind, and placed him in a bear hug that's when I started punching him in the face. On the sixth punch his knees buckled, and he fell to the ground when he was down Sqwin, and I started kicking him in his face, but he managed to grab both of our legs. We heard the guards coming so I threw the dagger into the toilet, and sqwin flushed it. Both sqwin, and I were placed in segregation, and they rushed the guy to the hospital we both received internal charges for the incident. I was the head guy in The Metro Toronto West Detention Center.

I was in Millhaven on the assessment unit side in January 2000 to April 2000. I was there with Sqwin, Jug, and Stucky, we were alright there because I had an ounce of marijuana that I brought with me from the West Detention Centre plus I had a chunk of crack cocaine which I sold to a guy in there for $200.00. Sqwin is the second baddest man from Ridgeway next to me. Jug is third, and Mark ("P") is fourth. He is one of the best fighters in Ridgeway, but he did not go to the Penitentry for armed robberies like myself, Sqwin and Jug. We are the four kings. There was a goof there that I got into an argument with I was going to slice him up but I didn't because someone told me he's an Aids victim. So I didn't want to get his blood all over me. I had a bunch of razors which I broke up and took out the blades, I took a toothbrush and I used a lighter to melt around the handle of the toothbrush and insert the blade which looked like a home made box cutter.

On a different occasion I was in the dinner line by the servery, I asked the food steward for my Diabetic Snack, and she basically said no so I threw my food tray against the wall which made a big mess. I eventually cleaned it up.

On a next occasion I was on my range, a new guy came which I recognized from the west detention centre in 1999. I used to sell him drugs, I went in his cell, and I asked him for the money he owed my friend and myself, he said he already paid my friend and he doesn't owe me. So I beat the fuck out of him and gave him two black eyes.

My parole officer spoke to me, and said if I kept it up she will send me to J-Unit. I asked her for one more chance so she said if I don't cause any more problems for the next thirty days she will send me to Collins Bay prison and that's what happened. I was the head guy there.

In Collins Bay there was a Muslim guy who worked in the kitchen with me, he threw vegetables in my face so I picked up a whole cauliflower, and palmed it in his face. He then picked up a knife, and started yelling at me, I told him to shut the fuck up! The kitchen steward asked us what's going on so I quickly said we are just playing around. I kept following the guy around in the kitchen because I wanted to smash him. Miami, and myself left the kitchen and went into the cafeteria. The guy finally came into the cafeteria so I punched him in the face, he fell to the ground and eventually he got back up. I called him a goof, and told him I would kill him, he then apologized, and it ended there.

One time in Collins Bay prison my friend named Prestige had a brown recliner chair in the hallway on four block. This guy who was from a different gang moved the chair close to his cell, I approached him because he disrespected my friend. We agreed no knives or ice picks just fist to fist, I beat the fuck out of him in the laundry room, and his friends begged me to stop.

On a different occasion some idiot that was either high or drunk told Prestige to drift, he came and told me about it so he got his ice pick, and I got mines, we went into his cell and the guy was passed out on his bed. I still wanted to kill him. I was about to start stabbing him but Prestige stopped me.

On another occasion I was a new arrival in Collins Bay prison and this big guy called Prestige a goof, I did not know Prestige at the time but I was still pissed I went to my cell got my ice pick, and strapped it to my waist. I was staring at the guy who then noticed me staring at him. I heard him apologize to Prestige and that was that!

In Collin's Bay Institution (Gladiator School) I was the head guy in the prison. I knocked out 2 guys and stabbed up one guy extremely bad in the group room. A guy hit me in the back of my head with a baseball bat while I was paying attention to his friend who was in front of me with an ice pick. They did not like how I was controlling the whole prison and disrespecting their whole crew. The guy with the ice pick got scared and ended up going to protective custody couple days after the incident which took place in the gym. The guy who hit me with the bat was a bum, he did not have a TV in his cell so he occupied the group room on weekends, 30 days after the incident on a Sunday I went into the group room and stabbed him up with my ice pick badly in the face, neck, and torso at least 30 times. He was bleeding badly and I thought for sure he was going to die, he was immediately rushed to the outside hospital where they saved his life. He then went to protective custody and I got transferred to Millhaven maximum security prison, the infamous J-Unit.

I was the head guy at Millhaven Maximum Security prison. I knocked out 2 guys and stabbed up 3 guys very badly. The first guy came from Collins Bay high-medium security prison who was one of the guys I disrespected there. I made a promise to myself that anyone from that crew who comes over to J-Unit is getting stabbed up. He ironically landed on my range which was a blessing. Recreation was called where I stabbed him up out in the yard with an ice pick. He kept on running away, so I kept on chasing him, and stabbing him. I took my shirt off and used it as a mask to conceal my identity, I then ran over to the front of the prison where my friends were. I told them to form a circle around me, so that I can take off my bloody clothes in which I had on clean clothing underneath it. I threw the bloody clothes in the metal garbage can and lit it on fire to burn up all of the evidence, then I walked around as if nothing had happened. The guy was rushed to the hospital and finished his sentence in protective custody in a prison outside the province of Ontario Canada

The second guy I stabbed up in J-UNIT was a big boy he ran the show before I got there. He was very good friends with the guy I stabbed up in Collins Bay Prison so right away I didn't like him. One day I was on my way to health care to get my insulin, and he asked me to get some request forms from the staff office for him because he was locked up on his range but I just ignored him, and continued walking. He called me a 'DUPPY' which means a dead man walking in Jamaican, and I lost it. I started calling him a goof which is the worst name you could call someone in the Canadian prison system. I called him on in the yard, where we engaged in battle. He had a knife, and a ice pick, and so did I. I flipped him over onto the ground were I positioned myself on top of him, and started stabbing him in his face neck torso, and once in his left thigh because that's where one of the main artery is. He started screaming begging for his life, and asking me to stop. The guards in the tower drew their guns aimed at me, and ordered me to stop but I didn't, I just kept on stabbing him. When I stopped he walked back into the prison where the guards escorted him to health care, and then to the hospital. He told on me, and the guards escorted me to the hole where they kept me for months. They even wrote me up for a transfer to the Special Handling Unit (SHU) which is the super maximum security prison out in Quebec, the transfer never happened, and they saved his life. When he wasn't on crutches he was in a wheel chair, and he went to protective custody. The SHU didn't want me there neither guards nor convicts because bodies would be dropping like flies. The guys from J-UNIT that came from the SHU went back there, and told everyone that black guys will take over if Shane Anthony Thomas AKA Silky came there.

The third guy I stabbed up in J-Unit was supposedly a bad boy from the Special Handling Unit. I told him to quit his job so that one of my friends could get it, he said no, which upset me. I started with him, and he pulled out his knife, I tackled him to he ground on my range where he cut me on the back of my neck and lower back. There was too much heat on my range so I decided to wait thirty days for retaliation which was Halloween day. I was in my cell with two of my ice picks, I ran both of them through the fire of my lighter repeatedly to make it extremely hot. This technique would make it impossible to stop internal bleeding from occurring. As soon as the cell doors were open , I went to his cell and started stabbing him repetitively, it was a bloody mess, he was scared and begging for his life. I told him to give me his shank, and he immediately told me it was in the corner by his toilet. It was an ice pick, and I added it to my collection. As soon as I left his cell, he locked himself in and pressed his panic button to alert the guards. I gave my friends my two ice picks to clean off and hide it on my range and I also gave another friend my clothing to put in the washing machine because the guy's blood was all over me. I quickly changed into some clean clothing then we went to the yard. The guards then caught on to what had happened, and rushed the guy to the hospital. He then went to protective custody to finish off the rest of his sentence

In J-UNIT (Millhaven Maximum Security Prison), there were a handful of guys who came there from the Special Handling Unit (Super Maximum). They were my connection for my access to a small hacksaw blade to cut through metal, to make my knives. I never needed to use it because I shaped, and sharpened mines on concrete for hours to get them perfect, plus I had sheets of sandpaper. For some reason they feared and respected me, probably because my name rings bells throughout the whole Canadian Prison System, plus they seen what I did to people in that prison. One day I loan them my favorite weapon which was my double edged sword, one end was shaped like an ice pick, and the other end was a dagger, it was disgustingly sharp, and beautiful. Out in the yard I would find a patch of grass, stick one end of my weapon into the ground, and step on it until it was buried into the patch of grass. I just had to remember the spot were I hid it. Any how they used it to stab up a guy very badly, couple of them went to the hole, and the next day one of them told me that they lost my favorite weapon, I was pissed. I had a different one on me, I was about to kill him in the yard, but he started begging me and crying tears for me to spare his life, then I felt bad and left him alone. They later replaced it, before they got transferred back to the S.H.U.

Couple years later on a different occasion in Maple Hurst Jail I met an older white man, who I grew attached to, I call him Uncle John. I had a vision that he's my second favorite uncle on my father's side, plus he's a Hells Angel. I found out that 'Mom' Boucher was in the S.H.U., so I gave my guys there orders to kill him, they got him good with knives but he didn't die, he went to protective custody though. The reason why I did that was because I wanted Uncle John to take over, and become the head guy in which he did. Fuck 'Mom' Boucher, he's a goof.

In J Unit I was residing on 1K range, a new guy came on the range; he was a fairly big guy. After being on the range for a while, he was apart of Bumbas crew. One day I heard Bumba and the boys making fun of the guy, because his father is a crown attorney. I smiled, and the guy said "I keep it real still" I asked him what he meant by that but he just ignored me; right away I made up my mind that I was going to kill him. Recreation was called where Bumba and they went. I saw that he didn't go so I stayed on the range as well. I walked into his cell, and punched him in his face; he ran out the cell and went to the front of the range. I went back to my cell and got my knife, and then I went back to his cell, and told him to come back to his cell but he didn't. I started calling him a goof but he didn't respond, I told him that I have two cells now and he can't stay on my range anymore, I then sat on his bed, and started playing his video games, until lock up. Bumba begged me to leave the goof alone, because he didn't want no more problems, so I left him alone then one day the guy gave me some weed, and that was that. One day I got into an argument with Bumba, because he wanted to control the woks for both cooking periods. So I told him its not happening, because I'm using it for one period, so he walked away. I was thinking that he was going for his knife, so I went for mines, he got scared, and tried to befriend me, and told me to go ahead, and use the wok. Right away I thought he was a bitch, because I caught his bluff. Bumba always made sure I had weed, and moonshine, even though I wasn't apart of his crew. He feared, and loved me at the same time we even use to lift weight in the gym together. I was the head guy on 1K.

When I was in J-Unit on range 2-K, A guy that I knew from the Metro Toronto West Detention Centre Arrived On my range, He told me that his girlfriend was coming to visit him the next day, a week after his arrival. He was trying to get his girl to bring him some weed, and I was also trying to do the same thing with my girl. We made arrangements for both of our girls to drive up together. The big day came and he got called down to the visit, I was waiting to get called down too, but to no avail. I then decided to call my girl on the phone, she picked up and told me that the next girl said her boyfriend told her not to bring my girl if she never got no weed, I was pissed. When he came back from the visit I confronted him in his cell and I punched him in the mouth breaking off a piece of his tooth. I kept punching him in the face over and over again, I was definitely not satisfied because he wasn't bleeding badly, so I went back to my cell grabbed my cup and went back at him He started bleeding more and begged me to stop, I did after a while. He then asked to be transferred to another range which happened days later.

One time in J-Unit a Hells Angel guy came on my range and a lot of guys were intimidated by him because of who he was. I and he got into an argument over the phone. I told his friend to tell him to come back to the end of the range because I wanted to fight him. But he said no! I brought my ice pick out to yard that day to stab him but he went upstairs to get a hair cut to show me that he did not want any problems with me. Every time he had weed he would piece me off a nice amount for a couple packs of smokes.

On a different occasion one of my friends in J-Unit feared me badly. He cooked some chicken and rice and gave me some, but he poisoned it to try and kill me. When I ate two forks of the rice I started to vomit. When they opened all the cells on my range I walked out with my knife to go and kill him. But he ran out of his cell quickly before I could get to him, from that time on he made sure I always had weed. On the same range another Hells Angel guy was giving me hash every night, plus I didn't like him he is a bitch!

One time I didn't go to my range on time so three guards surrounded me and escorted me to a room behind the tower where the guards worked. I thought they would try to beat me up for sure because I told one of them to fight me one on one, I told him not to charge me and I won't charge him, but he backed down then they escorted me back to my range. The guard that I wanted to fight is the leader of the institutional emergency response team.

All of the time I use to get swarmed by guards, trust me I could take a serious Beating because I am immune to it. There uniforms are black, with black boots, black gloves, a black vest with a black mask, and a Billy club with shield. They also carried hand-cuffs and their pepper spray.

In J-Unit I was the baddest man, everyone feared me even the guards. One time I was roaming around the unit talking loud for everyone to hear me. I was yelling out that "I run things in J-Unit!" But Prestige wanted me to say we instead of I. He is my friend but he is a bitch compared to me, and that's a fact. Ritchie Walker and Clinton Gayle both were trying to explain to me that they all feared me and I don't need to walk with knives and ice picks no more. The bottom line is I love them things, I feel naked without them on me.

I even walked to health care with my plastic ones; I was always prepared to use it. Anyhow I told Marlon (R.I.P, He got swarmed and killed in his cell) and Ritchie that I felt like stabbing someone that day, so Marlon said he has someone in mind, everyone went to yard that day. Marlon beat some guy badly, he asked for a shank and his friends never supplied it so I didn't. I sensed that something wasn't right; my instincts told me that everyone was against me and were going to try and kill me. I went and Miza Ben was telling me to come walk laps with them but I ignored them, one guy said to Clinton that we should all rush him so I got up with my ice pick to go and kill the goof, but a force sat me back down. Marlon was walking laps with the guy he beat up, I wanted to kill everyone. No one wanted me in J-Unit all the convicts and guards signed a petition to have me shipped out because I was too dangerous.

When I was in J-Unit I wanted to walk laps so I saw Ritchie Walker talking to some of his friends in front of the yard so I told him to walk with me and he said out loud “I am not walking with you without my jacket”. I was pissed but still smiled and went about my business. It bothered my mind so the next day I put on my weapon proof vest under my clothing and brought my ice pick to yard. I was going to stab him up, I called him over to walk laps with me and he did. Half way around the track I reached for my ice pick to stab him up but it fell down my pants, I seen fear in his eyes so I did not bother to stab him up. Ritchie Walker also gave me knives and ice picks as gifts so that I wouldn’t use them on him. At one time we were doing all the stabbings in J-Unit.

In J-Unit I went to segregation for refusing a direct order. I was told to lock up, and I didn't, I barricaded my door with a food tray because I wanted to shower, eat, and use the phone. They only gave me 5 minutes to do all of that which wasn't enough time.

The guards came on my range beat me up and escorted me to segregation, one of the guards gave me a black eye by punching me while trying to restrain me. I saw him later that evening in seg, I called him a goof and then moments later I saw him pass a big brown envelope to Ivan Belnaps cell, right away I knew it was my file containing my criminal history. The next day Ivan was sending me weed, and I thought he was trying to get guys to swarm me in segregation yard because I have 2 sexual assault convictions when I was twelve years old.

The first day I arrived in J-Unit I thought all the convicts had computers in their Cells, and knew my criminal history and was waiting for me to come down from the orientation range to try and kill me. Plus the guy I stabbed up in Collins Bay was from J-Unit so I knew his friends were waiting on me to come over to kill me for that as well.

Before I left seg Ivan Belnap was waiting for his transfer to the SHU (super max), and said he would be back November 2002. I tried my best to be on good behaviour so I can get to a medium security prison. I spoke to Clinton Gayle, and told him that I might have problems with Ivan Belnap but Clinton said he's cool with Ivan. When yard time came I put on my body armour under my clothing and brought my knives with me, I made up my mind that I am going to stab him up but when I got to the gym he showed me he did not want no problems by him sitting on the ground with his gym bag unprepared for battle. In J-Unit when I walked into the pool room Ivan would rest the pool stick on the table and say "here bro" and leave the pool room. When we were in seg I called him a goof and told him to come to yard so we can war, and he said no. He is scared of me. Ivan was one of the main bad boys in J-Unit.

I had the best file in J-Unit and the rest of the world. No one rushed me for stabbing that guy in Collins Bay, all his friends feared me.

In J-UNIT I was sent to segregation for 25 days because the guards found excessive amounts of weapons in my cell. I refused to go so he pressed his panic button, and a lot of guards came to escort me. I then requested for them to show me the paper work, and they provided it. It said Marvin Thomas instead of Shane Thomas with the wrong prison I.D. number. I said to myself in my mind that if anything happens to me in segregation I could sue the prison. I explained my situation to one guy, and begged him to stab me up a couple of times in the segregation yard, and he did. I then initiated a law suit, and my lawyer said I could get $80 000 but I had a vision that I should not follow through so I didn't. I was pissed off because I had let the guy stab me for nothing. My vision was that if I got the $80 000 it would mean that I can't rise up to rule the world.

When I was bored in segregation I would put a lot of paper, and institutional clothing in front of my cell door, and light fires. The guards would smell it, and they would use their keys to open the food slot on my door, and use the fire extinguisher to put the fire out I would then light another one. Whether I was in segregation or in the Unit I would break the sprinklers, and flood the place. I would then receive a $55.00 fine which didn't stop me. Sometimes I would start riots fight with guards call them names, and break the rules of the institution. I use to make body armour out of segregation gowns, which were fire, and weapon proof. I also did weight training, and used my natural body mass as body armour. I made my weapons out of metal bins food trays plexi-glass mop bucket metals washroom vents window frames butter knives, and I also had access to sandpaper, and a small hacksaw blade.

In J-unit I was serving time in the hole for a misconduct. Usually when convicts go to the hole, they don't conversate with the cleaners, because they are snitches, goofs, and protective custody inmates. There role is to sweep, mop, take out garbage, do laundry, collect the food trays, and to notify the guards of what they see and hear. I did differently, I befriended the cleaners. When my cell was cold, they gave me extra blankets, when guys from the prison sent me weed, they smuggled it to me, they passed me segregation gowns so I could bring them back with me into the prison, so I could use them to make my body armours. They gave me extra t-shirts, boxers, and socks all brand new, and most importantly I give them my ice picks and knives, to hide in the hole for me, instead of me possessing it because the guards always searched me and my cell. I might have to kill someone in the segregation yard that is why I keep weapons down there. When I get released from the hole back into the prison, and get into more trouble, and go back to the hole, the cleaners still have my weapons hidden for me. At one point, I had to grab one of the cleaners by the throat, because he did not respond to me quick enough when I called him, plus I heard attitude in his voice. Everyday was fun for me in prison, even though I preferred being free.

When I was in J-Unit, I had a pair of Nike shoes which were fairly old, its colors were black, green, and white. Whenever I wore them, the other prisoners, and guards knew something was going down, either someone was getting smashed, or stabbed up by me. These were my war shoes, which were extremely comfortable.

When I was on my range, I would put on my body armor under my shirt, and either my knife, or ice pick on my waist, before going out to the yard. Every time the same guard would frisk me, in which he would feel my weapon proof vest, my weapons and just let me through. I would then go through the metal detector which wouldn't beep, because my weapons are aluminum, and the metal detector does not detect them.

Even in the summer time no matter how hot it was, I would still wear my spring jacket, because I always had a weapon on me, and always well prepared to battle with who ever. The best time to battle is in the winter time because it gets dark outside very early, so its hard for the guards to see all the way from the towers, plus every body looked the same with their big winter jackets on.

No one would look into my eyes, and hold my stare because it would definitely cause problems, and no one wanted to end up dead in a body bag. Since I was a teenager, my best friend Sqwin would tell me that he knows I'm a killer, by just looking into my eyes.

Every prisoner from all the prisons in Ontario, Canada fear, and respect me, because they hear about me from guards, other convicts, the local news station in Kingston, Ontario, Canada, CNN, other local news stations, the news papers, and other sources of the media, I was the baddest of the bad, and I still remain to be Unstoppable.

Box thief is a term used in the Canadian prison system, its very serious, and you could get killed for it. A lot of goofs do it, some get caught, and some don't. Say you invite someone into your jail cell, the individual sees your cigarettes on your desk, you turn your back for a second, and he scoops it. That's a box thief. Another example, say you invite friends over to your house, your mother is in the kitchen cooking while you guys, are watching television, a hour later, your friends leave, your mother goes inside the living room, and notices her $400.00 is missing off the coffee table, due to the fact that one of your friends stole it.

"My Word" is a phrase used by every prisoner in the Canadian prison system, when you give your word, you are basically telling some one to trust you because your telling the truth 100%. If you are not sure that you can keep your promise then you don't give your word. To keep your word is a very sacred, and honourable thing. In the past, it was made to seem like my word wasn't good, in certain situations, let me explain: Say John Doe is a hopeless sinner, back in the first coming I revealed to him that in the second coming, he's going to break the law and go to jail and see me there, I also told him that he's going to ask me to send him money when I get released, for canteen (groceries) but I wont do it. He then requests for me to promise him, even though I won't do it because he wants it to seem like my word isn't good. I told John Doe to go fuck himself, so he then said "If your perfect you'll do it" so I agreed with John Doe to make it look like my word isn't good.

Back in 2002 I got kicked out of J-UNIT because of my violent tendencies towards other prisoners and guards. They kept me in the hole where I was locked up 24hours a day. It was hard time but I did it, I had no choice. I felt so confused because some guards started calling me Jesus, some said I was a prophet, some said I was the new government, and others said I was like the guy on Giligans Island because I vote who I want to vote off, and keep who I want to keep on. I picked up the bible and read it every day, my favourite part was the book of the Revelations which was mainly about the wrath of God. For twelve days straight I did not eat or drink anything, but only swallowed my saliva, and refused to take my insulin. I was dressed in a segregation gown because the guards said I was suicidal. I lost a lot of weight so they locked me up in another cell on the health care side plus one guard told me that the other prisoners were refusing to go to the segregation yard with me because they were scared. One day a guard slipped a piece of paper under my cell door, it was an involuntary transfer to Kingston Penetentary. I told them all to go fuck themselves and that I am not going because it was protective custody. Moments later the Institutional Emergency Response Team came to my door, opened the food slot, and pepper sprayed me, they told me to come to my cell door where they handcuffed me. I couldn't see properly because they sprayed me in my face, which got into my eyes. I told them I couldn't see so they turned the shower on and I ran my face through it, but I still couldn't see properly. They escorted me to the back of the prison where we went on a bus, there were approximately ten guards plus the driver. A bee landed on my face and drank up the pepper spray from my eyes which gave me my sight back. I was placed in the Regional Hospital in K.P. A guard hit me on my leg with his billy club, the nurse then tested my sugar levels and gave me my insulin. The guards took my bed out of my cell, because they said I was making weapons back at the other prison. The guards left and then the nurse gave me a blanket to spread on the floor. I asked for another blanket to cover up with, and she gave it to me, I then fell asleep. That night I woke up and seen a nurse giving me head, she was good. I fell back asleep and woke up in the I.C.U., in Kingston General Hospital, all the women were hitting on me. When I got well I went to the Regional treatment center, I didn't like it there so they sent me back to J-UNIT on the health care side. A nurse there was describing to me how my private parts look, so the first thought that came to my mind was that she gave me head too, which I didn't recall because I was out cold in the hospital for weeks. She told me that she went to the hospital, and seen me in the I.C.U.

The T.D. unit in Kingston penitentiary is better known as the Transfer and Discharge unit. If you fuck up in a halfway house, you go to jail then your parole officer makes a decision to either release you back to the halfway house or send you back to prison. You go to the T. D. unit first to get reassessed. They can also increase your classification from low to medium or medium to maximum, they can also decrease it from maximum to medium or medium to low. They never changed mines because I was always problematic. The T.D. unit houses prisoners from different prisons all across the province. One time out in the yard I punched a guy in the face, because he talked too much, and he acted like a tough guy, I was the only black guy there, and they still all feared me.

On a different occasion a friend of mines, which was a white guy named REDZ we went to the T.D. unit together. The same day I got there I yelled out this to everyone "I run things here now, and if anyone has a problem with that, let's deal with it right now" everyone looked in my direction but no one said a word.

Another time I went there, I demanded to go to the Regional Treatment Centre the same day, because I was feeling severe pain throughout my whole body, I felt like I was burning up in fire, so they segregated me from everybody else, in which they sent me to R.T.C the same day. The real reason why they segregated me is because there were a few guys there that I stabbed up in different prisons that didn't want me there. I was the head guy there on every occasion.

In the Regional Treatment Centre, where I was diagnosed with severe mental illness, I knocked out 2 guys badly. The first guy I got into an argument with was over religion, he was Roman Catholic and I dealt with the Rasta faith. There was many disagreements and he just kept on talking which pissed me off, after punching him in the face over and over again, his face became swollen especially his right eye. His friend immediately retaliated and punched me in the face, at that moment the guards were coming on the range to take me to segregation because the first guy told on me. Before the guards got to me, I quickly walked to the second guys cell, and punched him in the face, the guards tried to separate us but I managed to land more punches in his face before they restrained me and escorted me to segregation. Both guys ended up charging me at the institutional level. I was the head guy in the Regional Treatment Centre (R.T.C).

At the age of 18yrs. Old I was young, and ignorant. After seeing my probation officer I was heading back home. I got off the bus at Square One Mall where I bumped into some friends. A friend of theirs offered them a ride back to Brampton, he asked her if I could come too but she said no because she did not want to have more than four people in her car. We got into an argument over that issue, and I ended up slapping her couple of times. Witness' alerted the security guards which I got into an argument with them, I spat in one of their face, so they ended up calling the cops who then arrived on the scene, arrested me, and took me to Maple Hurst Jail. Good thing I hooped some drugs before heading to Toronto to see my probation officer. I landed on my friend's range his name is Tiger plus he is the leader of his bloods gang just like me. We shared the same jail cell, and we did our time easily because I smuggled drugs into the jail. Let me explain to you what I mean by I hooped drugs, I took some marijuana, and wrapped it in some saran wrap, I also took some crack cocaine and wrapped it seperately, I lubricated my anus, and pushed the drugs up inside of me. We smoked the weed, and sold the crack for cigarettes, and munchies because the weed made us hungry. Tiger and I even took turns beating the fuck out of another inmate because he was a crip, and we were bloods. Tiger is now a professional mixed martial arts fighter he is also the leader of his Bushman Bloods gang which are in Brampton, Ontario, Canada. I could still kick his ass though.

I was in Maple Hurst jail in 1998 on the correctional center side at the age of 18yrs. Old. I was only there for a few hours before ending up in segregation for a serious misconduct. On my first night there I was in the bathroom with a couple of guys getting ready for bed. We were brushing our teeth when a guard came, and rudely ordered me alone to get to bed, so I told him to go fuck himself, and I also threatened to smash him. He radioed other guards for back up, and stormed out the bathroom, so I dropped my toothbrush, and chased after him. I swung a punch at him, and the other guards tried to tackle me down the stairs, I even spat at him but it got the lieutenant instead. They tackled me handcuffed me, and placed me in segregation where I caused trouble everyday. A couple weeks later the lieutenant spoke to me, and said I was unmanageable in that jail, and don't know what to do with me. The next day guards came to my cell, handcuffed me shackled me threw me in the back of a car, and drove me to Millbrook Maximum security provincial jail in Peterborough, Ontario. On our way there I tried to escape while we were on the highway by ripping out the whole interior of the right passenger door, when the guards finally realized my attempt to escape they pulled off the highway next to Scarborough Town Center. They dragged me out of the car handcuffed my hands to my legs, and threw me back into the car, and continued the journey to Millbrook Jail where they placed me in segregation for weeks before releasing me into the general population. I served 3 to 6 months there before my release I was the head guy there.

In Millbrook jail there was approximately 15 ranges, 1 wing, 2 wing, and 3 wing were the general population ranges, the rest were protective custody. I was on 2 wing and 3 wing back and forth. I was trying to twist up one guy there, the more he told me to stop the more I did it. I could tell that he was getting mad but I did not give a fuck! At one point I was the only black guy on the range, so this Hells Angel guy kept on staring me down. I was thinking that if I fucked him up all the white guys would rush me so I went to one white guy I knew from Maplehurst and he said he has my back. So I approached the Hells Angel guy and said "what the fuck you starring at goof I'll smash you!" So he held down his head and stopped giving me bad looks. This happened on two wing, I got into a verbal confrontation with some of the guards so they placed me on three wing after my release from the hole. There was a bunch of black guys there compared to me being the only one on two wing. When I got on three wing I heard racial remarks when everyone was locked up in their cells.

When the guards opened the cells all the blacks sat down and watched TV while all the white guys sat at the back table with a sheet over the table. The white guys still had the TV on their choice station while they sat at the back of the range writing "white pride, Millbrook wide" on the table cloth. So I walked back to my cell grabbed my durable black pen and walked to the back starring them all down.
We went to the weight room where one white guy grabbed a bar one

guy grabbed a piece of wood and the main one approached me face to face. He then said listen mother fucker I heard you're telling people that you're calling on boys on this range everyday. I said I didn't say that. I did though I was waiting to get back on the range. We went back to the range where I waited for the main one to go to the shower, I grabbed my pen and went to the shower to stab him up and Junior Speed stopped me because the man was apologizing to me about approaching me like that.

He just kept saying he was sorry. I told the black guys to watch whatever they want to watch on the television and they did. I tried applying in the metal shop where they made license plates so that I can make knives, and ice picks but the lieutenant would not let me. The white guys complained to the guards about me because I was the head guy there. Prentice landed on two wing with me, he's from Jane and Finch and was on immigration hold in which he got out after I did. He eventually went back to prison and his new charge is now first degree murder.

Back in early 2005, I got released from a Toronto halfway house called the Keele Center. I needed a doctor because of my diabetes, and metal health. I became a patient of my moms doctor who's name was Larna Teape Humphry. The first time I saw her I was in awe, she was eye candy, but I thought she was too old for me, I still wanted her though. I was in love with her looks, and her personality, and still am, the only thing ugly about her was her toes, eew gross. Even though I'm a quiet person, I still conversated a lot with her because I was interested. I tried giving her pictures of myself, but she said "I can't accept your pictures, because I'm your doctor o.k. Shane". I once told her that I have a crush on her and her response was "it's an obsession, o.k. Shane". I was going to say, don't flatter yourself bitch, but I didn't. One day at home I was feeling bad pain below my waist, so I called her office, and told them it was an emergency, the receptionist said they were booked for the day, so I told them to ask Dr. humphry if she could squeeze me in and she did. That day I asked her out on a date, and she turned me down. I was vex with her, so when I left her office, I punched a hole in the wall, I went down the next flight of stairs, and punched another hole in the wall, when I got down to the main level, I punched another hole in the wall, I looked up and seen a camera, so I figured they would call the cops. When I went outside, I seen people walking in my direction so I made up my mind that when they get closer I'm going to smash them, I instantly heard Dr. Humphry's voice in my head saying "leave the people alone, o.k. Shane", I listened to her. I was about to smash the brick wall, and I once again heard her voice saying "don't punch the wall, you'll break your hand, o.k. Shane", so I didn't. I was walking to the bus stop, and I noticed my hand bleeding, so I went to the washroom inside Tim Horton's, washed my hand and wrapped it in toilet paper, then proceeded back to the bus stop, where I saw two other people waiting for the bus as well. Out of nowhere, a police cruiser pulled up at the bus stop where I was standing. He winded down his window, and started yelling at me, so I started yelling back at him saying, "who the fuck are you talking to, I'll kill you, I dare you to come out of your car!", he then sped off, I had a strong feeling that Dr. Humphry's receptionist called the police. I was about to get on the bus, but I heard her voice again telling me not to go on the bus, because she was going to bring me home with her so we can live together. I was good with that so I waited, I ended up missing three buses so I got on the next one and went home, because I thought it was someone else impersonating her voice to fuck with me.

I was the head guy in Maple Hurst Detention Center. For my latest charges I was there between 2005, and 2007. I would walk on a range, and say I am running things now, and no one would say anything to me, I called guys on, and they would always back down. I would tell guys to leave my range, and they would either go to a different range or protective custody. I slapped up a guy there called people names like goof or piece of shit altercations with guards, if my cellmate acted tough I would disrespect him, and they would ask the guards for a cell change or a range change. I would turn off the television on different ranges, and tell guys that if they don't chill out I would drown them in their own blood. I spent most of my time in segregation due to the fact that no one wanted me on their range because they all feared me.

While in Maplehurst Detention Centre, something happened to me that has never happened to me before, I got swarmed by inmates, it was an experience but I still never changed. It happened to me 3 times while I was there, on the first incident 3 guys rushed me because I wouldn't give them my soya milk, but it was deeper than that. I was the head guy on that range and it was a gang thing. I was a blood and they were crips. I wore red, they wore blue, it was just a beat down, no weapons were used. After getting into a verbal confrontation with their head guy about the soya milk, I went to my cell to change from my slippers to my shoes. I swung a punch and connected to the left side of his head, that's when the other two came into my cell and all three of them rushed me. I was stomped on and punched the whole time, it was almost lock out, so they cleared out before the guards came on the range. I pretended like I was out cold so they would stop, when they left I went downstairs into the shower to hide my bruises from the guards before they came on the range. After the guards left I stuck my head out the shower and said I dare you goofs to try that again and none of them said nor did anything. I was still running the range even after that.

On the second incident I got swarmed by 2 guys, they were both crips. This happened because when I was on a different range with one of them, I never liked him because he acted like he was the head guy on my range. I did not like that, so one day he arrived back on my range from court, and he was talking to his friends about his court case, I walked over to them, spat in his face, and told him to leave so he packed up his belongings, and left. I know him from J-Unit, he's a goof.

On the third incident I was still the head guy on my range the big talk was how come a blood is running a crip range. I was in my cell on the top bunk that morning my cell partner was out on my range he came back, and said all the guys said that I have to leave so I told him to tell them that I said they should go fuck themselves. He told them, and they all came to my cell about 15-20 of them. I rolled off my bed, and landed on the floor where they started kicking, and punching me. They then took turns jumping off the table unto my head one guy pulled out his homemade weapon, and tried to cut my left eye out there's a scar there now over, and under my left eye. They fucked me up bad then they all cleared out of my cell then some guards, and couple nurses came to my aid. I stood up, and had to sit back down because I was so dizzy. They placed me on a stretcher, and took me to the hospital were I got stitches when I got back to Maple Hurst jail they placed me on the medical range until my wounds were healed they then placed me back on a range out in the open population where I was the head guy. I ran things on every range I was on. I was rebellious, and no one could say anything to me. Everyone knew the name Silky as the Don of Peel Region.

St. Lawrence Valley is a jail in Brockville, Ontario, Canada, for men who suffer with mental health and addiction issues. I was there for mental health serving out my index offence for 1 year and 3 months. I had very few issues, while there, couple verbal confrontations with offenders and staff, and only one physical confrontation with a guy that was there. I was in my room sleeping and got awaken by people talking, I looked towards the window of my door and saw one guy standing with his back turned to me. I got up and pushed the door open which hit him, he told me to say excuse me, so I told him to get the fuck away from my door, then he told me to kiss his ass. I waited for staff to get off my range and then I followed the goof to his cell and slapped him up, no institutional charges were laid, I was the head guy there.

Yo, people. I never went to protective custody in my life. I don't need protection from nothing or no one, I would rather die but I can't, that's why I suffer. On one occasion I went to the Regional hospital in Kingston Penitentiary. That prison is mainly protective custody, but the regional hospital side is not. It's the only one in Ontario which houses prisoners all across the province from different institutions who need to be hospitalized. When I was in J-Unit I complained that I had chest pains a lot of times so they would escort me in a vehicle to K.P. Hospital where I would stay overnight. I did this for the drive so I can see the outside world: People, places and things. K.P. hospital is not protective custody. One time in the Metro Toronto West Detention Centre, I was placed in the bullpen with PC's (protective custody offenders). A guard explained to me that PC's and mental health offenders go in the same bullpen when going to court and getting admitted into the jail. Another time when I went to Maple Hurst Jail, back in 2005, I thought I was in protective custody because all the other inmates there acted like creeps, but a guard told me that I wasn't in PC. It was just a new part of Maple Hurst Jail which they call the Super Jail. In J-Unit, Yves Deslauriers is IPSO, which stands for Institutional Preventive Security Officer. His role is to investigate communications over the phone, the drug subculture, gangs, organized crime, weapons, other contraband, assaults, stabbings, and murders. One time I was in the office and he said this to me, "Why is it that when you go into J-Unit population, everybody feels obligated that they have to carry a weapon?" I couldn't believe that all the other prisoners said that. I explained to Mr. Deslauriers that J-Unit is a maximum security prison built to house guys like me, so if people don't feel safe there, send them to protective custody. Death is easy but life is so hard, sleep is the cousin of death, but life is in its own class. The only relation between life and death is that when an individual dies, they're still living, six feet under in a casket. I have no fear, that is one of my many differences between myself, and each of every one of you. Life is something that only God can give, but any can take. There are similarities with God and his creation when it comes to giving life. A woman gives birth, and trees bare fruits, only because of the perfect powers of God the Almighty.

Usually I never lasted more than 2 months in a halfway house, I would always end up getting sent back to prison by my parole officer in which ever halfway house I was at. I still got into conflicts with staff and other residents both verbally and physically. At Portsmouth halfway house, I was smoking a cigarette in my room which is a violation and then one of the staff opened my room door where I had 3 roommates. I immediately threw my cigarette which landed in my garbage can which caught on fire and nearly burn down the halfway house. I got sent back to prison for that, because one of my roommates told on me, I was the head guy there.

On one occasion when I was residing at the Keele Street halfway house, I was very stressed out, I had no money, no motivation, no structure, and no life, I wasn't happy. Whenever I walked outside the building, I saw couples walking together alone, or pushing their children in baby strollers, people my age or younger driving nice cars, people spending money , living free and happy, I wanted to live free and fit in just like them. I would usually go for walks and smoke a joint, but I got careless and started smoking it inside the halfway house. Other residents saw me smoking it, smelt it and told on me, so I got sent back to prison for it, and now I get urine tested once a month and stopped smoking weed. I was the head guy there, people feared me and I can imagine how happy they were when I got sent back to prison.

When I was at Dowling halfway house I was the head guy there, it was a good environment, the food was good, it was easy going, the staff helped me to get Ontario works while I waited to collect my Ontario disability security pension, (ODSP). One of the residents there helped me to create my own website which was titled "Satan is God.com" I was trying to make money the legal way instead of resorting to crime, I set up an account and all was well. My parole officer asked me what was on the site and I told him, so he told me to take down the site. I told him to get the fuck out of my face and go fuck himself because I have freedom of rights like anyone else who lives in Canada. On my site I had a couple nude pictures of myself posed as a lion, couple of my songs with swearing in it, I described my type of women in great detail, and shit I use to do criminally, so he said my website has degrading to women and glamorizing crime. He called the cops on me and I went back to jail. They gave me a new parole officer who informed me that if I agreed to take down my website upon release back into the community, and reside at Keele halfway house instead of Dowling halfway house she would release me. I agreed to follow her instructions and she let me out of prison immediately and I was happy, and she was happy. I took down my site, resided at Keele street halfway house and got along with my new parole officer extremely well. I resided there for six months straight before my transfer to St. Leonard's Place Peel halfway house located in Brampton Ontario Canada.

While I was going through the courts the crown attorney was asking for the dangerous offender status to be imposed on me which would mean I would be stuck in prison and get a review of my case every 5 years. My lawyer wrote a letter to the attorney general who disapproved it. The crown attorney then went for the long term supervision order in which they got it approved due to the fact that I have two aggravated assault convictions on my criminal record. I am on parole for 10 years in which I have only served 2 years thus far. If I was found not criminally responsible for my index offence because of my chronic mental illness' I wouldn't have a release date. I can now say I have completed my journey and can finally see the light at the end of the tunnel. There is a God

This is my criminal history containing everything that I have been charged with as a Young Offender, and Adult Offender.

PRO CRIM/CRIM PRO

Correctional Service
Canada

PROTECTED ONCE COMPLETED
[ ] A [X] B [ ] C
PERSONAL INFORMATION BANK

CRIMINAL PROFILE REPORT
ORIGINAL

Completing Operational Unit
KINGSTON PAROLE OFFICE

IDENTIFICATION		SENTENCE MANAGEMENT	
FPS:	464271D	Sentence:	1 Years 3 Months 0 Days
Family Name:	THOMAS	Sentence Number:	2
Given Name(s):	SHANE	Sentence Commencement:	2007/09/04
		UTA:	
Sex:	MALE	DPE:	
DOB:	1979/07/19	FPE:	2008/02/02
Citizenship:	CANADIAN	SRD:	
Deportable:	NO	WED:	2008/12/03
Marital Status:	SINGLE	LTED:	2018/07/04
Preferred Language:	ENGLISH	APR:	NO
Home Language:	ENGLISH	PED set at 1/2:	NO
Need for Translator:	NO	Judicial Review:	NO
Alias(es):	NO	Long Term Supervision:	YES
		LT Sentence:	10 Years 0 Months 0 Days

Reference Documents:

Police:	YES	Court:	YES	CA:	NO
Victim:	NO	Other:	YES	Psychiatric:	NO
Crown:	NO			Psychological:	NO

Current Offence(s):

No.	Type of Offence	Counts	Sentence Direction	Place Sentenced	Date
1	CCC 268 1 AGGRAVATED ASSAULT	1	NOT STATED	BRAMPTON, ON	2007/09/04

Affiliations: NO

Detention Criteria:
Schedule: I
Serious Harm: YES

OFFENDER'S VERSION

ASSESSMENT

ORIGINAL
INTRODUCTION

Shane THOMAS is currently serving a sentence of 1 year and 3 months for convictions of Aggravated Assault. As well S. 109(2)(a) & (b) orders have been imposed for LIFE. This prohibits THOMAS from possessing firearms.

A 10 year Long Term Supervision Order was also ordered at the time of sentencing. THOMAS is currently housed at St. Lawrence Valley Correctional and Treatment Facility in Brockville with a release scheduled for 2008-07-05, at which time his LTSO takes effect. His LTSO is in effect until 2018-07-04 .

THOMAS pled guilty to the above offences on 2006-06-14. It is noted that he was not sentenced until 2007-09-04. He had been in custody since 2005-04-22.

THOMAS is a Canadian citizen and therefore is not reportable to Immigration upon release.

CRIMINAL PROFILE REPORT
Ce formulaire existe aussi en français.
CSC 965 (R-02-03) OMS VERS (2)

DISTRIBUTION
Original - Offender CM File
Copy - National Parole Board Copy - Offender
Copy - Offender PS File (if file exists)

Date and Time Locked 2008/05/12 13:39

TIME IS BASED ON A 24-HOUR CLOCK PERIOD.

PROTECTED ONCE COMPLETED
[ ] A [X] B [ ] C
PERSONAL INFORMATION BANK

FPS 464271D	NAME THOMAS, SHANE
DOB 1979/07/19	LOC. KINGSTON PAROLE OFFICE

THOMAS's official language is English and all correspondence shall be provided in his chosen language of English.

Offender's Version

THOMAS indicated that he had been living on his own for a few months following completion so his last sentence. He said he had placed his medications in the bottom drawer of his dresser when he moved in and stopped taking his pills. He said that the voices came back because he was not taking his medications. He said the voices told him to stab her so he did.

OFFICIAL VERSION

According to the Peel Regional Arrest Record dated 2005-04-22, THOMAS was initially charged with Break and Enter, Attempt Murder, Aggravated Assault, Assault with a Weapon and Weapons Dangerous.

According to File Information he pled guilty to Aggravated Assault on 2006-06-14. The following information has been taken directly from the Peel Regional Arrest Record dated 2005-04-22.

Shane Thomas was renting a room at 475 Bramlea Rd Unit #45 for 3-4 months prior to the incident. Previous to this he was residing at a shelter. His rent at the above residence by been paid by the shelter. The victim was a college student who also rented a room at the above residence. She had resided there for approximately 6 months prior to the offence. The two were casual acquaintances as a result of them residing in the same building. They both had their own bedrooms with were equipped with a deadbolt lock.

On April 22, 2005 the victim and the accused were at their residence. The victim was in her bedroom with the door locked. No one else was present at the time.

At approximately 1925 hours, the accused knocked on the victim's bedroom door wanting to use her telephone. The victim did not answer the door because she was praying. Suddenly the accused kicked in the victim's door and attacker her with a black handled kitchen knife with an eight inch blade. The accused stabbed the victim in the forehead causing two lacerations. The victim used her hands to grab the blade and bend it in an attempt to stop the attack. As a result she sustained lacerations to both of her hands.

The victim was able to flee the residence and obtain assistance from the neighbours. Police attended and located the accused in front of his residence where he was arrested at 1941 hours for aggravated assault. The accused was read his rights to which he stated he understood. Upon interviewing he provided an inculpatory statement to the effect that he was going to get the bitch before she got him.

The victim was treated at Peel Memorial hospital for non life threatening injuries. She received 40 stitches to her head and hands. According to the victim impact statement, the victim suffers daily from headaches and emotional trauma.

OUTSTANDING CHARGES

According to all available information there are no outstanding charges in this case.

PROTECTED ONCE COMPLETED
[ ] A [X] B [ ] C
PERSONAL INFORMATION BANK

FPS 464271D	NAME THOMAS, SHANE
DOB 1979/07/19	LOC. KINGSTON PAROLE OFFICE

ANALYSIS OF CRIMINAL BEHAVIOUR

At the age of 28, THOMAS has already established a persistent pattern of violent offending. His FPS dates back to when he was merely 13 years old. His offending has involved violence and serious harm has resulted from his offending.

THOMAS served a previous federal sentence of 5 years for Robbery (7 counts) and Use Firearm Commit (7 counts). The offences involved THOMAS and his five co convicted committed numerous armed robberies in the Greater Toronto Area.

His FPS also shows convictions for Sexual Assault (x2) (1994), Aggravated Assault, Attempt Theft, carry Concealed Weapon, Assault Possession of Property Obtained by Crime and Possession of a Weapon (1997), Possession of a Weapon (1998), Assault, Causing a Disturbance and Fail to Comply with Probation Order (1998),

His offences have become increasingly violent. He has used a weapon in numerous offences and his offending is becoming more frequent. THOMAS has struggled with mental health issues and his mental health instability is directly linked to his offending. He reports that this current offence was the result of voices telling him to get her before she got him. While he is on his medications he appears able to follow the conditions and expectations however he quickly deteriorates when not on medication thus resulting in a drastic increase in risk. THOMAS has poor impulse control which is heightened by his mental health issues, his need to belong with others and lack of consequential thinking. His current offences had the potential to result in the death of the victim if she had not fought back.

Occurrence Reports on the 1994 Sexual Assault convictions are no longer available. All that is left is a Charge Sheet, indicating that Thomas was charged with Sexual Assault and Threatening on 93-06-14, when he was aged 13 and that he was released on an Undertaking. Thomas self reports that he was only convicted of one sexual assault and it relates to an incident that occurred when he was aged 13. He indicates that this girl and her friend came into the boys' change room after his track and field practice and the girl began kissing his neck. He soon started kissing her and touching her breasts. He claims that her friend was "jealous", as "nobody would give her the time of day", so she called and told the girl's parents what she had witnessed. He guesses that the parents called the police. He is adamant that the girl was a consenting participant and notes that she performed fellatio on him on a subsequent occasion. He relates that he pled guilty on the advice of his lawyer, as he was "young" and it was his "first time ever getting charged".

On 97-03-25 Thomas registered convictions for Aggravated Assault, Attempt Theft, Carry Concealed Weapon, Assault, Possession of Property Obtained by Crime and Possession of a Weapon, for which he received nine months secure custody (plus two months time served), probation for two years and a ten-year firearm prohibition. Police Reports reveal that the Aggravated Assault and Attempted Theft occurred on October 31, 1996. At about 9:00 p.m., the male victim was in the Food Court at Shopper's World in Brampton and overheard Thomas telling people that he had attempted to steal a van from the parking lot by removing the ignition (causing about $150 damage). When Thomas left the Food Court, the victim followed him to the parking lot and observed Thomas opening and closing the door to the parked vehicle. The victim approached Thomas and told him he was going to take him to the security office. The victim led Thomas to the Food Court entrance to the mall. At this time, Thomas removed a folding knife from his jacket pocket and began stabbing the victim, who received two stab wounds to

PROTECTED ONCE COMPLETED
[ ] A [X] B [ ] C
PERSONAL INFORMATION BANK

FPS 464271D	NAME THOMAS, SHANE
DOB 1979/07/19	LOC. KINGSTON PAROLE OFFICE

his side, one to the left side of his neck, four to his back and a laceration to the top of his head. Two of the stab wounds required stitches, as did the laceration to his head. The victim let go of Thomas and Thomas fled the area, leaving his folding knife behind. The writer is satisfied that this assault resulted in serious physical harm.

A Possession of a Weapon conviction was registered on 98-05-26, when he was aged 18. This conviction earned him a five month jail term and probation for 18 months. A second Possession of a Weapon charge was withdrawn. On 98-12-02, he was convicted of Assault, Causing a Disturbance and Fail to Comply with Probation Order, for which he received 14 days on each charge concurrent. The 1997 Assault and weapons offences occurred on January 15, 1997,at which time Thomas was living with his mother, grandmother and younger siblings in Brampton. He became involved in a verbal confrontation with his mother about household chores. Having been recently expelled from school, he was home all day and, therefore, available to do housework. The argument escalated to the point where Thomas grabbed his mother (the victim) by her shirt and banged her head off a solid wood door twice. He then pushed her onto the ground and had his whole weight on her as he banged her head on the hardwood floor at least four times. He was very angry and kept saying, "fuck you" to the victim, who thought that he was going to kill her. This assault ended when Thomas threw the victim to one side and ran upstairs. The victim chased after him, but he entered his bedroom and escaped out the window. As a result of this assault, the victim suffered a sore chest, back, head and left foot. She did not attend for medical treatment. These injuries do not appear to meet the definition of serious physical harm. Although some emotional trauma likely resulted, there is insufficient information to argue that the victim has suffered serious psychological harm.

In regards to his last federal sentence for Robberies, Thomas entered guilty pleas to eight or nine incidents, but Police Reports suggest that he was actually involved in 16 robberies, which occurred between October 21, 1998 and March 19, 1999. He and his co convicted robbed banks, grocery stores, fast food restaurants, a video store and a Beer Store. In all cases, Thomas and/or his co-accused were armed with replica handguns. Thomas pointed the gun at a couple of victims, but did not verbally threaten to harm or kill them. None of the victims suffered any physical injuries. In many cases, Thomas and his co-accused had bandanas covering the lower portion of their faces, to conceal their identities. When they were robbing a store, Thomas and his co-accused used the guise of asking where to acquire/hand in job applications, in order to ascertain where the main office (containing the safe) was. They also approached cashiers and demanded money from the cash registers. In the bank robberies, they would produce their weapons and order all staff and customers to get down to the floor and/or not move. They then jumped or went behind the counters and demanded money from the drawers and safes. They were not always able to get money from the safes. They stole anywhere from $200 to $18,000 in these robberies. On one occasion, they abandoned over $13,000 in cash, as it contained robbery prevention packs. The only other money that was recovered was the $12,000 that they stole from a Canada Trust branch just prior to their arrest.

The most recent psychiatric information on file is dated 2006-08-16completed by L. Ramshaw at Penetanguishene Oak Ridge Division. This report was completed for the purposes of the LTSO hearing. It reviews all previous reports and psychiatric interventions. According to this report, THOMAS was diagnosed in 2003 with Psychotic Disorder Not Otherwise Specified, with a differential diagnosis of Schizophrenia, Schizoaffective Disorder, Substance Induced Psychotic Disorder and Psychotic Disorder Due to a General Medical Condition. In March of 2004 he was diagnosed with Schizophrenia(provisional) and Insulin

PROTECTED ONCE COMPLETED
[ ] A [X] B [ ] C
PERSONAL INFORMATION BANK

FPS 464271D	NAME THOMAS, SHANE
DOB 1979/07/19	LOC. KINGSTON PAROLE OFFICE

Dependant Diabetes. Throughout his previous sentence and supervision period he was admitted to and discharged from RTC(O) on numerous occasions. The risk of re-offending was found to be moderately high using the PCLR and VRAG. His criminal behaviour and risk appears to have flowed largely from his personality variables with his psychopathic traits.

There have been extensive psychiatric interventions in this case. On his previous federal sentence he was admitted and discharged from RTC(O) on a number of occasions due to deterioration in his mental health. While in the community he was also returned to custody for stabilization after he ceased taking his medications. Throughout these interventions it was found that his non compliance with his medications contributed to his deterioration. On medicated he was able to function effectively. It was also noted that his poor diet and care of diabetes was also contributing to his instability.

A current GSIR score is not on file for this current sentence. The GSIR from the previous federal sentence is -6 indicating that two out of every five offenders will not commit an indictable offence after release.

There have been no crime free periods since the age of 16. THOMAS' offending has become increasingly violent and unpredictable. Despite previous program interventions and psychiatrist assistance he has continued to offend.

Based on the pattern of offending, the escalation of violence and his continued offending despite treatment, the risk of re-offending is high. While it is noted that THOMAS has been receiving treatment at St. Lawrence, is premature to conclude that the risk he presents has been significantly impacted.

FAMILY VIOLENCE

There is no evidence or documentation of domestic violence. However file information notes that THOMAS's mother was the victim of one of his violent attacks. The SARA was not completed on his last sentence given no history of spousal assault. THOMAS has not had significant relationships in the past.

INSTITUTIONAL/COMMUNITY SUPERVISION HISTORY

THOMAS served a previous federal sentence. He was a maximum security offender that required constant interventions. Incidents included assaultive behaviour against staff and other offenders. He was involved in brew making, non compliance with the rules and regulations and possession of homemade weapons. of staff and overall negative institutional conduct. There were also a number of segregation placements. There have been no reported institutional difficulties while at St. Lawrence Valley.

THOMAS had imposed residency on his past statutory release. He struggled with stability in the community and had his release suspended on two separate occasions. Shortly following his WED he committed his current offence.

ESCAPE/ATTEMPTED ESCAPE HISTORY

There is no noted escape or attempted escape history in this case. A review of the FPS does not reveal any Unlawfully at Large charges. There is one conviction for Fail to Comply with Probation Order (1998).

VICTIM IMPACT

PROTECTED ONCE COMPLETED
[ ] A [X] B [ ] C
PERSONAL INFORMATION BANK

FPS 464271D	NAME THOMAS, SHANE
DOB 1979/07/19	LOC. KINGSTON PAROLE OFFICE

There is a victim impact statement on file for the current offence. The victim suffered serious slash wounds and required 40 stitches. She reports living in total fear due to the attack. Her life was impacted negatively and she feared living the house. Overall the victim has suffered serious physical and psychological harm.

DETENTION CRITERIA

This is not applicable as he is not currently serving a federal sentence.

OFFENCE CYCLE

THOMAS's offence cycle is directly linked to his personal/emotional issues. He lacks community support and life skills. While in the community he is easily led by others and is a very impulsive individual. He has been unable to support himself in the past and has used criminal offending to do so. He reports that his previous offences were the result of being pressured by friends. He clearly lacks the skills to make appropriate choices for himself.

His mental health has also contributed to his violent offence pattern. He has a history of not taking his medications and then deteriorating very quickly. He reports having auditory hallucinations which tell him to do "bad things". While he is aware that not taking his medications increase his risk he still is unable to comply. THOMAS does not fully understand his mental illness and his offence cycle. He clearly requires intensive support to address his cycle.

LEVEL OF RISK

Based on the available information and in considering THOMAS' offence history it is the opinion of the writer that he presents a high risk to re-offend in the same manner if he is not subjected to strict supervision and is not complaint with his medications.

Completing Officer - Signature

Date
Y M D
2008/05/07

SAUVE, ANGIE P
PAROLE OFFICER

CRIMINAL PROFILE REPORT
Ce formulaire existe aussi en français.
CSC 965 (R-02-03) OMS VERS (2)

DISTRIBUTION
Original = Offender CM File
Copy = National Parole Board
Copy = Offender
Copy = Offender PS File (if file exists)

Date and Time Locked 2008/05/12 13:39

TIME IS BASED ON A 24-HOUR CLOCK PERIOD.

PRO CRIM/CRIM PRO

PROTECTED ONCE COMPLETED
[ ] A [X] B [ ] C
PERSONAL INFORMATION BANK

FPS 464271D	NAME THOMAS, SHANE
DOB 1979/07/19	LOC. KINGSTON PAROLE OFFICE

CSC Supervisor - Signature

Date
Y M D
2008/05/07

JANSEN, JOE P
A/PAROLE SUPERVISOR

Copy provided to offender by:

Date
Y M D

Signature

CRIMINAL PROFILE REPORT
Ce formulaire existe aussi en français.
CSC 965 (R-02-03) OMS VERS (2)

DISTRIBUTION
Original = Offender CM File
Copy = National Parole Board   Copy = Offender
Copy = Offender PS File (if file exists)

Date and Time Locked 2008/05/12 13:39

TIME IS BASED ON A 24-HOUR CLOCK PERIOD.

3 HEARING/AUDIENCE

N.B. It is essential to deal with remanded cases as quickly as possible. N.B. Il est essentiel de s'occuper des renvois dès que possible.	Time/Heure 1407	Date d/j m/m y/a 04 05 99	Remanded/Renvoi ☐ Yes/Oui ☒ No/Non
Refusal witnessed (signature)/Témoin du refus (signature)		Title/Titre	

Statement of misconduct in part 1 read to offender and he/she	Yes Oui	No Non	La déclaration d'inconduite dans la première partie a été lue au (à la) contrevenant(e) et il (elle)
+ was advised of right to present arguments and explanations to dispute the allegations	☑	☐	+ a été avisé(e) de son droit de présenter des arguments et des explications pou contester les allégations
+ was advised of right to question the person(s) making the allegation	☑	☐	+ a été avisé(e) de son droit d'interroger la (les) personne(s) faisant l'allégation
+ was advised of right to call witnesses	☑	☐	+ a été avisé(e) de son droit d'appeler des témoins
+ admits misconduct as written	☐	☐	+ reconnaît l'inconduite telle que rédigée
+ denies misconduct as written	☑	☐	+ nie l'inconduite telle que rédigée
+ refuses to admit or deny	☐	☐	+ refuse de reconnaître ou de nier

Summary of Offender's version of incident/Compte rendu de la version de l'incident donné par le (la) contrevenant(e)

INMATE THOMAS, SHANE - 679946509 PLEADS NOT GUILTY
THE INMATE STATES THAT IT WAS THE OFFICER THAT
WAS CAUSING ALL THE PROBLEM.

Note: Inmate Requests Assistance/Representative/Remarque: Le (la) detenu(e) requiert de l'assistance/représentant(e) ☐ Yes/Oui ☒ No/Non | Assistance Provided/Assistance donnée ☐ Yes/Oui ☐ No/Non | If no, provide reason(s) Si non, donnez les raiso

Reasons/Raisons

Signature of witnesses testifying at hearing Signature des témoins qui ont témoigné à l'audience 1	2	3
4	5	6
Signatures of witnesses called by offender Signature des témoins appelés par le (la) contrevenant(e) 1	2	3
Additional comments attached Commentaires supplémentaires ci-inclus ☒ Yes/Oui ☐ No/Non		Superintendent's Signature Signature du (de la) surintendant(e) R. M. McArthur

4 DISPOSITION/DÉCISION

☐ Not guilty of Misconduct Non coupable d'inconduite	☒ Guilty of Misconduct Coupable d'inconduite	Regulation/section/sub-section Règlement/article/paragraphe 278 (32) (

Penalty imposed/Peine infligée

3 DAYS L.O.A.P.

Comments/Commentaires

0847 /

☐ Reporting Officer present Agent(e) auteur(e) du rapport présent(e)	☒ Reporting Officer advised Agent(e) auteur(e) du rapport avisé(e)	Additional comments attached Commentaires supplémentaires ci-inclus ☒ Yes Oui

Signature of Superintendent Signature du (de la) surintendant(e) R. M. McArthur	Signature of Senior Officer present Signature de l'Agent(e) principal(e) présent(e)	Date d/j m/m 04 05

Information is being collected under the authority of the Ministry of Correctional Services Act for the purposes of administering Court Orders and/or other lawful dispositions. Yo Offender information is subject to the "Maintenance and Use of Records" provisions of the Young Offenders Act. Les renseignements sont recueillis en vertu de la Loi sur le min des Services correctionnels dans le but d'assurer l'application des ordonnances de tribunal ou de toute autre disposition légitime. Les renseignements sur les jeunes contreve sont régis par les dispositions de la Loi sur les jeunes contrevenants concernant la conservation et l'utilisation des dossiers.

Ministry of the Solicitor General and Correctional Services | Ministère du Solliciteur général et des Services correctio[nnels]

ONOMS

Misconduct Report
Rapport d'inconduite

This report must be forwarded to the Superintendent for his attention and subsequently included in the offender's file./Ce rapport doit être porté à l'attention du (de la) surintendant(e) et inséré dans le dossier du (de la) contrevenant(e).

[Na]me / Nom	Given/Middle / Prénoms	Institution/File No. / Établissement/Nº de dossier	Misconduct date / Date de l'inconduite d/j m/m y/a
Thomas	Shane	M.T. W.D.C. 679 946 509	11 07 99
[DE]SCRIPTION / DÉTAIL		Regulation/section/sub-section/Règlement/article/paragraphe: Reg. 778/90 Sec 29. Sub sec. (4)(B)	

[A]n inmate commits a misconduct if the inmate commits [or] threatens to commit an assault upon another person;

Sir: On Monday 12th July 1999, I was assigned duties on [...], from 0645 hours to 1500 hours shift. Approximately 2000 hours, [...] 11th July 1999 (Sunday) - Inmate Thomas, Shane #679 946 509 did [com]mit an assault on inmate [redacted] on [...]-washroom. Inmate Thomas, Shane informed of misconduct for [a]ssault and removed from unit 1AR and escorted to Male [S]egregation - approximately 0750 hours - 12 July 1999.

Additional comments attached / Commentaires supplémentaires ci-inclus ☐ Yes / Oui ☐ No / Non

[Sig]nature of witnesses to misconduct / [Sig]nature des témoins de l'inconduite	2	3
[...] Thomas, Shane #679 946 509		
	Reporting officer's signature/title / Signature/titre de l'agent(e) auteur(e) du rapport: C/O2 Mackenzie Haines [signature]	Date d/j m/m y/a: 12 07 99

[ ] INVESTIGATION / ENQUÊTE

[P]ersons interviewed/including witnesses / [P]ersonnes interrogées/témoins y compris	2	3
	5	6

[...] Thomas, S. interviewed today. Item #1 read to him. No witnesses or documents offered [...] at adjudication. Denies assault. Claims horseplaying. Intends to deny misconduct. Recommend stringent [...] penalty.

26

Additional comments attached / Commentaires supplémentaires ci-inclus ☐ Yes / Oui ☐ No / Non

Referred to:
- ☑ Superintendent for action
- ☑ Superintendent for information
- ☑ Reporting officer advised

Offender status following investigation/awaiting hearing
- ☑ Was advised of allegation made against him/her
- ☑ Advised of right to interview with Superintendent
- ☑ Placed in segregation
- ☐ Not segregated
- ☐ Intends to admit to misconduct (Complete No. 4 on reverse)
- ☑ Intends to deny misconduct (Complete Nos. 3 & 4 on reverse)
- ☐ Further investigation recommended
- ☐ No further action recommended

Renvoyer:
- ☐ Au (à la) surintendant(e) pour action
- ☐ Au (à la) surintendant(e) à titre d'information
- ☐ À l'agent(e) auteur(e) du rapport avisé(e)

Statut du (de la) contrevenant(e) suite à l'enquête/dans l'attente de l'audience
- ☐ A été avisé(e) de l'allégation faite contre lui (elle)
- ☐ A été avisé(e) de son droit d'avoir une entrevue avec le (la) surintendant(e)
- ☐ Mis(e) en isolement
- ☐ Pas en isolement
- ☐ A l'intention de reconnaître sa mauvaise conduite (Remplir nº 4 au verso)
- ☐ A l'intention de nier sa mauvaise conduite (Remplir les nºs 3 et 4 au verso)
- ☐ Enquête supplémentaire recommandée
- ☐ Pas d'autre action recommandée

Witnesses who may be required at hearing / Témoins susceptibles d'être appelés à l'audience		
	Investigating officer's signature / Signature de l'agent(e) chargé(e) de l'enquête: [signature] Cardoza	Date d/j m/m y/a: 12 07 99

[...]5-003 (71-9913) 09/93

Original - Offender file / Dossier du (de la) contrevenant(e)
Copy / Double - as applicable / selon le cas - Accounts office / Bureau de la comptabilité - Classification Dept. / Service des classifications

3 HEARING/AUDIENCE

N.B. It is essential to deal with remanded cases as quickly as possible. *N.B. Il est essentiel de s'occuper des renvois dès que possible.*	Time/Heure 1330	Date d/j m/m y/a 12 07 99	Remanded/Renvoi ☐ Yes/Oui ☒ No/Non
Refusal witnessed (signature)/Témoin du refus (signature) M. Richard		Title/Titre OM 6	

Statement of misconduct in part 1 read to offender and he/she	Yes Oui	No Non	*La déclaration d'inconduite dans la première partie a été lue au (à la) contrevenant(e) et il (elle)*
+ was advised of right to present arguments and explanations to dispute the allegations	☒	☐	*+ a été avisé(e) de son droit de présenter des arguments et des explications pour contester les allégations*
+ was advised of right to question the person(s) making the allegation	☒	☐	*+ a été avisé(e) de son droit d'interroger la (les) personne(s) faisant l'allégation*
+ was advised of right to call witnesses	☒	☐	*+ a été avisé(e) de son droit d'appeler des témoins*
+ admits misconduct as written	☐	☐	*+ reconnaît l'inconduite telle que rédigée*
+ denies misconduct as written	☒	☐	*+ nie l'inconduite telle que rédigée*
+ refuses to admit or deny	☐	☐	*+ refuse de reconnaître ou de nier*

Summary of Offender's version of Incident/Compte rendu de la version de l'incident donné par le (la) contrevenant(e)

CLAIMS HORSE PLAYING

VIDEO TAPE SHOWS HIS INVOLVEMENT IN CHOKING I/M [redacted]

Note: Inmate Requests Assistance/Representative/Remarque: Le (la) detenu(e) requiert de l'assistance/représentant(e) ☐ Yes/Oui ☒ No/Non — Assistance Provided/Assistance donnée ☐ Yes/Oui ☒ No/Non — If no, provide reason(s) Si non, donnez les raisons

Reasons/Raisons

Signature of witnesses testifying at hearing Signature des témoins qui ont témoigné à l'audience 1	2	3
4	5	6
Signatures of witnesses called by offender Signature des témoins appelés par le (la) contrevenant(e) 1	2	3

26

Additional comments attached Commentaires supplémentaires ci-inclus	☐ Yes/Oui ☒ No/Non	Superintendent's Signature Signature du (de la) surintendant(e)

4 DISPOSITION/DÉCISION

☐ Not guilty of Misconduct Non coupable d'inconduite	☒ Guilty of Misconduct Coupable d'inconduite	Regulation/section/sub-section Règlement/article/paragraphe

Penalty Imposed/Peine Infligée

778-32-1-1

29. DAYS C.C. LOAP. 32-2-1

DEF

Ontario Ministry of the Solicitor General and Correctional Services / Ministère du Solliciteur général et des Services correctionnels

Misconduct Report
Rapport d'inconduite

This report must be forwarded to the Superintendent for his/her attention and subsequently included in the offender's file./Ce rapport doit être porté à l'attention du (de la) surintendant(e) et inséré dans le dossier du (de la) contrevenant(e).

Name	Client Identification No./N° matricule	Misconduct Date/ Date de l'inconduite
THOMAS, SHANE	0799946509	17 Aug 99

DESCRIPTION/DÉTAIL — Regulation/section/sub-section/Règlement/article/paragraphe: M.C.S. ACT REG. 778 29 (1) (b)

Inmate commits a misconduct if the inmate: commits or threatens to commit assault upon another person. On Tues 17 Aug 1999 2115 hrs I/M's Thomas, Shane and [redacted] were involved in a physical altercation which needed a code 1 called to separate them. Both inmates were taken to health care and then into segregation.

Occurrence Report(s) / Rapport(s) d'événement(s)	☑ Yes / Oui ☐ No / Non	Written Statement / Déclaration écrite	☑ Yes / Oui ☐ No / Non	Additional documents attached / Document supplémentaires ci-inclus	☑ Yes / Oui ☐ No / Non

Signature of witnesses to misconduct / Signature des témoins de l'inconduite: 1. [signature] 2. 3.

Reporting officer's signature/title / Signature/titre de l'agent(e) auteur(e) du rapport: [signature] — Date: 17 Aug 99

INVESTIGATION/ENQUÊTE

Persons interviewed/including witnesses / Personnes interrogées/témoins y compris: 1. [redacted] 2. 3. 4. 5. 6.

On Tuesday August 17th 1999 I had occasion to investigate this misconduct. Inmate THOMAS admits to hitting inmate [redacted] (16 Aug 99) and to following him on the unit this evening. THOMAS states he believed inmate [redacted] and friends (he did not know who or how many) were going to "Rush" him. Further THOMAS states that he thought [redacted] wanted to finish retaliate for yesterday. FYI

Referred to:
- ☐ Superintendent for action
- ☑ Superintendent for information
- ☑ Reporting officer advised

Renvoyer:
- ☐ Au (à la) surintendant(e) pour action
- ☐ Au (à la) surintendant(e) à titre d'information

Statut du (de la) détenu(e) suite à l'enquête/dans l'attente ...
- ☐ Avisé(e) et reçu avis écrit de l'allégation faite contre lui(elle)
... une entrevue avec le (la) surintendant(e)

26

Ministry of the Solicitor General and Correctional Services

Ministère du Solliciteur général et des Services correctionnels

Misconduct Report
Rapport d'inconduite

This report must be forwarded to the Superintendent for his attention and subsequently included in the offender's file./Ce rapport doit être porté à l'attention du (de la) surintendant(e) et inséré dans le dossier du (de la) contrevenant(e).

Surname / Nom	Given/Middle/Prénoms	Institution/File No./Établissement/Nº de dossier	Misconduct date/Date de l'inconduite
THOMAS	SHANE	# 679 946 509 Metro Toronto West Detention Centre	29 08 99

1 DESCRIPTION/DÉTAIL

Regulation/section/sub-section/Règlement/article/paragraphe: 778/90 29(1)(b)

Any inmate commits a misconduct if the inmate commits or threatens to commit an assault upon another person;

Sir:

On Sunday August 29, 1999, at about 11:00 hrs, at Metro Toronto West Detention Centre, unit 2 B right, inmate THOMAS, Shane # 679-946-509 assaulted inmate [redacted] by slapping inmate [redacted] causing some injuries, contrary to Regulation 778/90 Section 29, subsection (1)(b) of the Ministry of Correctional Service Act.

Additional comments attached/Commentaires supplémentaires ci-inclus ☒ Yes/Oui ☐ No/Non

Signature of witnesses to misconduct / Signature des témoins de l'inconduite	2	3
1 Not witnessed	—	—
4 —	Reporting officer's signature/title / Signature/titre de l'agent(e) auteur(e) du rapport: JChandra CO2 J. CHANDRA	Date d/j m/m y/a: 29 08 99

2 INVESTIGATION/ENQUÊTE

Persons interviewed/including witnesses / Personnes interrogées/témoins y compris	2	3
1 THOMAS SHANE # 679 946 509	—	—
4 ~~Thomas, Shane #67~~	5 —	6 —

26

I/m Thomas, Shane # 679 946 509 admitted slapping inmate [redacted]. Inmate Thomas Shane # 679 946 509 ~~pto~~ removed to segregation.

I/M was interviewed by me. + The information was given to the documen officer by me. I/M THOMAS slapped the other I/m as he viewed the other [redacted] — so he claims. I/M interviewed stated that he has been threatened and assaulted several times in the past two days by the two I/m identified.

Additional comments attached/Commentaires supplémentaires ci-inclus ☒ Yes/Oui ☐ No/Non

I/M Thomas has no witness + does not require the documenting officer present at the adjudication

Referred to: ☒ Superintendent for action ☐ Superintendent for information

Renvoyer: ☐ Au (à la) surintendant(e) pour action ☐ Au (à la) surintendant(e) à titre d'information

3 HEARING/AUDIENCE

N.B. It is essen[illegible] deal with remanded cases as quickly as possible. N.B. Il est essen[illegible] de s'occuper des renvois dès que possible.	Time/Heure: 1740	Date d/j m/m y/a: 30 08 99	Remanded/Renvoi: ☑ Yes/Oui ☐ No/Non
Refusal witnessed (signature)/Témoin du refus (signature)		Title/Titre: O.M.16.	

Statement of misconduct in part I read to offender and he/she / La déclaration d'inconduite dans la première partie a été lue au (à la) contrevenant(e) et il (elle)

	Yes Oui	No Non	
was advised of right to present arguments and explanations to dispute the allegations	☑	☐	a été avisé(e) de son droit de présenter des arguments et des explications pour contester les allégations
was advised of right to question the person(s) making the allegation	☑	☐	a été avisé(e) de son droit d'interroger la (les) personne(s) faisant l'allégation
was advised of right to call witnesses	☑	☐	a été avisé(e) de son droit d'appeler des témoins
admits misconduct as written	☑	☐	reconnaît l'inconduite telle que rédigée
denies misconduct as written	☐	☐	nie l'inconduite telle que rédigée
refuses to admit or deny	☐	☐	refuse de reconnaître ou de nier

Summary of Offender's version of incident/Compte rendu de la version de l'incident donné par le (la) contrevenant(e)

Y/m Thomas pleads guilty and says that he only slapped the other inmate once.

Note: Inmate Requests Assistance/Representative/Remarque: Le (la) detenu(e) requiert de l'assistance/représentant(e) ☐ Yes/Oui ☑ No/Non | Assistance Provided/Assistance donnée ☐ Yes/Oui ☑ No/Non | If no, provide reason(s) Si non, donnez les raisons

Reasons/Raisons

Signature of witnesses testifying at hearing Signature des témoins qui ont témoigné à l'audience 1	2	3
4	5	6
Signatures of witnesses called by offender Signature des témoins appelés par le (la) contrevenant(e) 1	2	3
Additional comments attached Commentaires supplémentaires ci-inclus	☐ Yes/Oui ☐ No/Non	Superintendent's Signature Signature du (de la) surintendant(e)

4 DISPOSITION/DÉCISION

☐ Not guilty of Misconduct Non coupable d'inconduite	☑ Guilty of Misconduct Coupable d'inconduite	Regulation/section/sub-section Règlement/article/paragraphe 778(32)(1)(1)

Penalty imposed/Peine infligée

Guilty 30 days LOAP inlet.

8636. B230

Correctional Service Canada / Service correctionnel Canada

PROTECTED / PROTÉGÉE A ☐ B ☐ C ☐ ONCE COMPLETED / UNE FOIS REMPLIE

PERSONAL INFORMATION BANK - FICHIER DE RENSEIGNEMENTS PERSONNELS

INMATE OFFENCE REPORT AND NOTIFICATION OF CHARGE / RAPPORT DE L'INFRACTION D'UN DÉTENU ET AVIS DE L'ACCUSATION

NOTE: Reference document CD 580. / NOTA: Document de référence DC 580.

PUT AWAY ON FILE / CLASSER AU DOSSIER — See reverse / Voir au verso

Institution - Établissement	MILLHAVEN
Resp. Centre Code - Code du centre de resp.	
Location of offence - Lieu de l'infraction	'A'-UNIT CORRIDOR
Date and time of offence / Date et l'heure de l'infraction (Y-A M D-J, Time - Heure)	00/03/03 1700
FPS number / Numéro SED	464271D
Family name / Nom de famille	THOMAS
Given name(s) / Prénom(s)	
Date of birth / Date de naissance	

DESCRIPTION OF OFFENCE (including names of witnesses, unusual behaviour of offender, etc.)
DESCRIPTION DE L'INFRACTION (y compris le nom des témoins, comportement inhabituel du délinquant, etc.)

ON THE ABOVE APPROXIMATE DATE AND TIME, THIS WRITER DID OBSERVE 'A'-UNIT FEEDING. I/M THOMAS (FPS#464271D) DID RECEIVE A MEAL FROM THE 'A' SERVERY LINE, I/M THOMAS STOOD AT THE DOOR OF THE FOOD STEWARD'S OFFICE AND BRIEFLY SPOKE WITH MS. BARTROW. I/M THOMAS APPEARED UPSET AS HE LEFT THE OFFICE. THE INMATE TOOK A FEW STEPS FORWARD TOWARD THE CONDIMENT BINS AND THREW HIS FOOD TRAY SPILLING HIS MEAL ONTO THE FLOOR.

Date report written / Date de la rédaction du rapport (Y-A M D-J)	00/03/03
Name of witnessing officer - Nom de l'agent témoin	MICHAEL DAFOE
Signature	Michael Dafoe
Physical evidence - Preuve(s)	☐ Yes / Oui ☒ No / Non
If yes, provide a brief description - Dans l'affirmative, fournir une brève description	
Disposition	
Supervisor or officer in charge of the institution advised / Avis donné au surveillant ou à l'agent responsable de l'établ.	☐ Yes / Oui
Disposition of inmate - Mesure prise à l'égard du détenu	☐ Admin. seg. / Isolement préventif ☐ Confined to cell / Retenu dans sa cellule ☑ Normal association / Intégration normale
Other witnessing officer - Autre agent témoin	[signature]

DECISION TAKEN - DÉCISION PRISE

I have reviewed this report and determine that a charge is warranted under section 40 of the Corrections and Conditional Release Act.
J'ai lu ce rapport et décidé qu'une accusation est justifiée en vertu de l'article 40 de la Loi sur le système correctionnel et la mise en liberté sous condition.

Yes / Oui — No / Non	☑ Yes / Oui ☐ No / Non
Signature	[signature]
Position Title - Titre du poste	CCO
Date charge laid / Date l'accusation imposée (Y-A M D-J)	00 03 06
Offence category - Catégorie de l'infraction	☑ Minor / Mineure ☐ Serious / Grave
Referred to - Renvoyé au	☑ Minor offence court / Tribunal des infractions mineures ☐ Serious offence court / Tribunal des infractions graves
For hearing a charge under Section 40 of the Corrections & Conditional Release Act. / Pour l'audition du chef d'accusation en vertu de l'article 40 de la Loi sur le système correctionnel et la mise en liberté sous condition. (Specify - Préciser) (See reverse side for offences - Voir la liste d'infractions au verso)	C
Proposed date of hearing / Date prévue de l'audition (Hour - Heure, Y-A M D-J)	1300 00 03 13
Title - Titre	CCO
Signature	[signature]
Delivered to inmate / Transmis au détenu (Hour - Heure, Y-A M D-J)	2040 00/03/06
Title - Titre	A/Con
Signature	[signature]

I have been advised of my right to retain and instruct counsel. / J'ai été informé de mon droit d'avoir recours aux services d'un avocat.

Y-A M D-J ☐ Inmate refused to sign / Détenu a refusé de signer

Inmate - Signature - Détenu | Date | Time - Heure | Witnessing CSC official - Signature - Agent responsable témoin

HEARING OF CHARGE - AUDITION DU CHEF D'ACCUSATION

Plea - Plaidoyer	☐ Guilty / Coupable ☑ Not guilty / Non coupable ☐ Refused to plea / Refus de plaider
Remanded to - Audition ajourné à (Hour - Heure, Y-A M D-J)	

Reason - Motif

[illegible] ... his diet

4A41 OMS

Correctional Service Canada | Service correctionnel Canada

PROTECTED / PROTÉGÉE A ☐ B ☐ C ☐ ONCE COMPLETED / UNE FOIS REMPLIE

PERSONAL INFORMATION BANK - FICHIER DE RENSEIGNEMENTS PERSONNELS

INMATE OFFENCE REPORT AND NOTIFICATION OF CHARGE

RAPPORT DE L'INFRACTION D'UN DÉTENU ET AVIS DE L'ACCUSATION

NOTE: Reference document CD 580. / NOTA: Document de référence DC 580.

PUT AWAY ON FILE / CLASSER AU DOSSIER — See reverse / Voir au verso

Institution - Établissement	Collins Bay
Resp. Centre Code - Code du centre de resp.	440
Location of offence - Lieu de l'infraction	Hospital Barrier
Date and time of offence / Date et l'heure de l'infraction (Y-A M D-J)	00·10·12
Time - Heure	08:10
FPS number / Numéro SED	464271 D
Family name / Nom de famille	Thomas
Given name(s) / Prénom(s)	
Date of birth / Date de naissance	

DESCRIPTION OF OFFENCE (including names of witnesses, unusual behaviour of offender, etc.)
DESCRIPTION DE L'INFRACTION (y compris le nom des témoins, comportement inhabituel du délinquant, etc.)

On the above date + time I/m Thomas was asked to return to his block to change his shirt. I/m Thomas replied "Fuck off I don't have time for you."

Date report written / Date de la rédaction du rapport (Y-A M D-J)	00·10·12
Name of witnessing officer - Nom de l'agent témoin	J. Vezina CX2
Signature	J. Vezina
Physical evidence - Preuve(s)	☐ Yes/Oui ☒ No/Non
If yes, provide a brief description - Dans l'affirmative, fournir une brève description	
Disposition	
Supervisor or officer in charge of the institution advised / Avis donné au surveillant ou à l'agent responsable de l'établ.	☒ Yes/Oui
Disposition of inmate - Mesure prise à l'égard du détenu	☐ Admin. seg. / Isolement préventif ☐ Confined to cell / Retenu dans sa cellule ☒ Normal association / Intégration normale
Other witnessing officer - Autre agent témoin	

DECISION TAKEN - DÉCISION PRISE

I have reviewed this report and determine that a charge is warranted under section 40 of the Corrections and Conditional Release Act.
J'ai lu ce rapport et décidé qu'une accusation est justifiée en vertu de l'article 40 de la Loi sur le système correctionnel et la mise en liberté sous condition.

	☒ Yes/Oui ☐ No/Non
Signature	Glenn Chambers
Position Title - Titre du poste	A/UM
Date charge laid / Date l'accusation imposée (Y-A M D-J)	00 10 13
Offence category - Catégorie de l'infraction	☒ Minor/Mineure ☐ Serious/Grave
Referred to - Renvoyé au	☒ Minor offence court / Tribunal des infractions mineures ☐ Serious offence court / Tribunal des infractions graves
For hearing a charge under Section 40 of the Corrections & Conditional Release Act. / Pour l'audition du chef d'accusation en vertu de l'article 40 de la Loi sur le système correctionnel et la mise en liberté sous condition. (Specify - Préciser) (See reverse side for offences - Voir la liste d'infractions au verso)	40(f)

at CBI not before

	Hour - Heure	Y-A	M	D-J	Title - Titre	Signature
Proposed date of hearing / Date prévue de l'audition	0900	00	10	17	A/UM	[signature]
Delivered to inmate / Transmis au détenu	0745	00	10	15	CX 2	[signature]

I have been advised of my right to retain and instruct counsel. / J'ai été informé de mon droit d'avoir recours aux services d'un avocat.

☒ Inmate refused to sign / Détenu a refusé de signer

Inmate - Signature - Détenu	Date (Y-A M D-J)	Time - Heure	Witnessing CSC official - Signature - Agent responsable témoin
	00 10 15	07:45	[signature]

HEARING OF CHARGE - AUDITION DU CHEF D'ACCUSATION

Plea - Plaidoyer	☐ Guilty/Coupable ☒ Not guilty/Non coupable ☐ Refused to plea/Refus de plaider
Remanded to - Audition ajourné à	Hour - Heure / Y-A / M / D-J

Reason - Motif

REMANDED FOR OFFICER'S APPEARANCE

y to Chip O'Connor
9 Mar 01
DA

Correctional Service Canada — Service correctionnel Canada

~~15396~~ 15330 QMS K117

PROTECTED / PROTÉGÉE A [ ] B [ ] C [X] ONCE COMPLETED / UNE FOIS REMPLIE

PERSONAL INFORMATION BANK - FICHIER DE RENSEIGNEMENTS PERSONNELS

INMATE OFFENCE REPORT AND NOTIFICATION OF CHARGE
RAPPORT DE L'INFRACTION D'UN DÉTENU ET AVIS DE L'ACCUSATION

NOTE: Reference document CD 580.
NOTA: Document de référence DC 580.

PUT AWAY ON FILE / CLASSER AU DOSSIER — See reverse / Voir au verso

Institution - Établissement	Millhaven Inst.
Resp. Centre Code - Code du centre de resp.	42110
Location of offence - Lieu de l'infraction	1K
Date and time of offence / Date et l'heure de l'infraction (Y-A M D-J)	01 01 30
Time - Heure	17:34
FPS number / Numéro SED	464 271D
Family name / Nom de famille	Thomas
Given name(s) / Prénom(s)	
Date of birth / Date de naissance	

DESCRIPTION OF OFFENCE (including names of witnesses, unusual behaviour of offender, etc.)
DESCRIPTION DE L'INFRACTION (y compris le nom des témoins, comportement inhabituel du délinquant, etc.)

At the above date and time while working in J-Ctrl inmate Thomas refused to lock-up. When asked to lock-up a second time ~~he~~ he replied "shut the fuck up bitch!"

Date report written / Date de la rédaction du rapport (Y-A M D-J)	01 01 30
Name of witnessing officer - Nom de l'agent témoin	A. Stewart
Signature	A. Stewart
Physical evidence - Preuve(s)	Yes / Oui [ ] No / Non [X]
If yes, provide a brief description - Dans l'affirmative, fournir une brève description	
Disposition	
Supervisor or officer in charge of the institution advised / Avis donné au surveillant ou à l'agent responsable de l'étab.	Yes / Oui [X]
Disposition of inmate - Mesure prise à l'égard du détenu	Admin. seg. / Isolement préventif [ ] Confined to cell / Retenu dans sa cellule [ ] Normal association / Intégration normale [X]
Other witnessing officer - Autre agent témoin	[signature]

DECISION TAKEN - DÉCISION PRISE

I have reviewed this report and determine that a charge is warranted under section 40 of the Corrections and Conditional Release Act.
J'ai lu ce rapport et décidé qu'une accusation est justifiée en vertu de l'article 40 de la Loi sur le système correctionnel et la mise en liberté sous condition

Yes / Oui [X] No / Non [ ] Signature [signature]
Position Title - Titre du poste: CCO
Date charge laid / Date l'accusation imposée (Y-A M D-J): 01 01 31

Offence category - Catégorie de l'infraction: Minor / Mineure [ ] Serious / Grave [X]
Referred to - Renvoyé au: Minor offence court / Tribunal des infractions mineures [ ] Serious offence court / Tribunal des infractions graves [X]
For hearing a charge under Section 40 of the Corrections & Conditional Release Act. / Pour l'audition du chef d'accusation en vertu de l'article 40 de la Loi sur le système correctionnel et la mise en liberté sous condition (Specify - Préciser) (See reverse side for offences - Voir la liste d'infractions au verso): F

	Hour - Heure	Y-A M D-J	Title - Titre	Signature
Proposed date of hearing / Date prévue de l'audition	1300	01 02 06	CCO	[signature]
Delivered to inmate / Transmis au détenu	1700	01 01 31	Cx 2	C. [signature]

I have been advised of my right to retain and instruct counsel.
J'ai été informé de mon droit d'avoir recours aux services d'un avocat.

[X] Inmate refused to sign / Détenu a refusé de signer

Inmate - Signature - Détenu: ______ Date (Y-A M D-J): ______ Time - Heure: 1700 Witnessing CSC official - Signature - Agent responsable témoin: C. [signature]

HEARING OF CHARGE - AUDITION DU CHEF D'ACCUSATION

Plea - Plaidoyer: Guilty / Coupable [ ] Not guilty / Non coupable [X] Refused to plea / Refus de plaider [ ]
Remanded to - Audition ajourné à: Hour - Heure / Y-A M D-J

Reason - Motif: FEB 27/01 TBST | March 20/01 prmpt for plea | April 27/01 prmpt to

9 Mar 01

15 5?1

Correctional Service Canada | Service correctionnel Canada

PROTECTED A ☐ B ☐ C ☒ ONCE COMPLETED / UNE FOIS REMPLIE

PERSONAL INFORMATION BANK - FICHIER DE RENSEIGNEMENTS PERSONNELS

INMATE OFFENCE REPORT AND NOTIFICATION OF CHARGE

NOTE: Reference document CD 580.

RAPPORT DE L'INFRACTION D'UN DÉTENU ET AVIS DE L'ACCUSATION

NOTA: Document de référence DC 580.

PUT AWAY ON FILE / CLASSER AU DOSSIER — See reverse / Voir au verso

Institution - Établissement	MI
Resp. Centre Code - Code du centre de resp.	42180
Location of offence - Lieu de l'infraction	IK K117
Date and time of offence / Date et l'heure de l'infraction (Y-A M D-J, Time - Heure)	01 01 30 — 1750 hr
FPS number / Numéro SED	4642710
Family name / Nom de famille	THOMAS
Given name(s) / Prénom(s)	
Date of birth / Date de naissance	

DESCRIPTION OF OFFENCE (including names of witnesses, unusual behaviour of offender, etc.)
DESCRIPTION DE L'INFRACTION (y compris le nom des témoins, comportement inhabituel du délinquant, etc.)

At approximately 1750 hrs, during a routine search, I found a "homemade shiv" approximately 10" long shaped like an icepick [redacted] inmate Thomas
Inmate Thomas is the only occupant of cell K117.

M Bouchard

421-2001-028

Date report written / Date de la rédaction du rapport (Y-A M D-J)	01 01 30
Name of witnessing officer - Nom de l'agent témoin	CO II M Bouchard
Signature	M Bouchard
Physical evidence - Pièce(s)	☒ Yes / Oui ☐ No / Non
If yes, provide a brief description - Dans l'affirmative, fournir une brève description	AS DESCRIBED ABOVE
Disposition	CONTRABAND LOCKER #1
Supervisor or officer in charge of the institution advised / Avis donné au surveillant ou à l'agent responsable de l'établ.	☒ Yes / Oui
Disposition of inmate - Mesure prise à l'égard du détenu	☐ Admin. seg. / Isolement préventif ☐ Confined to cell / Retenu dans sa cellule ☒ Normal association / Intégration normale
Other witnessing officer - Autre agent témoin	G Daniels

DECISION TAKEN - DÉCISION PRISE

I have reviewed this report and determine that a charge is warranted under section 40 of the Corrections and Conditional Release Act.
J'ai lu ce rapport et décidé qu'une accusation est justifiée en vertu de l'article 40 de la Loi sur le système correctionnel et la mise en liberté sous condition.

☒ Yes / Oui ☐ No / Non	Signature: [signature]
Position Title - Titre du poste	CCO
Date charge laid / Date l'accusation imposée (Y-A M D-J)	01 01 31
Offence category - Catégorie de l'infraction	☐ Minor / Mineure ☒ Serious / Grave
Referred to - Renvoyé au	☐ Minor offence court / Tribunal des infractions mineures ☒ Serious offence court / Tribunal des infractions graves
For hearing a charge under Section 40 of the Corrections & Conditional Release Act. / Pour l'audition du chef d'accusation en vertu de l'article 40 de la Loi sur le système correctionnel et la mise en liberté sous condition (Specify - Préciser) (See reverse side for offences - Voir le liste d'infractions au verso)	(i) 22(1)(e)
Proposed date of hearing / Date prévue de l'audition (Hour - Heure, Y-A M D-J)	1300 — 01 02 06
Title - Titre	CCO
Delivered to inmate / Transmis au détenu (Hour - Heure, Y-A M D-J)	1700 — 01 01 31
Title - Titre	Cx2
Signature	C Cyr

I have been advised of my right to retain and instruct counsel.
J'ai été informé de mon droit d'avoir recours aux services d'un avocat.

Y-A M D-J

☒ Inmate refused to sign / Détenu a refusé de signer

Inmate - Signature - Détenu	Date	Time - Heure	Witnessing CSC official - Signature - Agent responsable témoin
		1700	C Cyr

HEARING OF CHARGE - AUDITION DU CHEF D'ACCUSATION

Plea - Plaidoyer	☒ Guilty / Coupable ☐ Not guilty / Non coupable ☐ Refused to plea / Refus de plaider
Remanded to - Audition ajourné à	Hour - Heure / Y-A M D-J

Reason - Motif

FEB 27/01 TBNT. | March 20/01 prempt for plea
Mar 13/01 ... to set trial date | April 24/01 prempt. to ...

Correctional Service Canada / Service correctionnel Canada — 15674 ams — K117

PROTECTED / PROTÉGÉE A ☐ B ☐ C ☐ ONCE COMPLETED / UNE FOIS REMPLIE

PERSONAL INFORMATION BANK - FICHIER DE RENSEIGNEMENTS PERSONNELS

INMATE OFFENCE REPORT AND NOTIFICATION OF CHARGE

RAPPORT DE L'INFRACTION D'UN DÉTENU ET AVIS DE L'ACCUSATION

NOTE: Reference document CD 580. / NOTA: Document de référence DC 580.

PUT AWAY ON FILE / CLASSER AU DOSSIER — See reverse / Voir au verso

FPS number / Numéro SED: 464271D

Family name / Nom de famille: Thomas

Given name(s) / Prénom(s):

Date of birth / Date de naissance:

Institution - Établissement: Millhaven

Resp. Centre/Code - Code du centre de resp.:

Location of offence - Lieu de l'infraction:

Date and time of offence / Date et l'heure de l'infraction: 01 02 14 — Time - Heure: 1244

DESCRIPTION OF OFFENCE (including names of witnesses, unusual behaviour of offender, etc.)
DESCRIPTION DE L'INFRACTION (y compris le nom des témoins, comportement inhabituel du délinquant, etc.)

On the above time and date this inmate did have two other inmate in his cell.

[redacted]

26

Date report written / Date de la rédaction du rapport	Name of witnessing officer - Nom de l'agent témoin	Signature
01 02 14	P EDWARDS	P Edwards

Physical evidence - Preuve(s): ☐ Yes / Oui ☑ No / Non — If yes, provide a brief description - Dans l'affirmative, fournir une brève description. — Disposition

Supervisor or officer in charge of the institution advised / Avis donné au surveillant ou à l'agent responsable de l'établ.: ☑ Yes / Oui

Disposition of inmate - Mesure prise à l'égard du détenu: ☐ Admin. seg. / Isolement préventif ☐ Confined to cell / Retenu dans sa cellule ☑ Normal association / Intégration normale

Other witnessing officer - Autre agent témoin: P. Lorenz

DECISION TAKEN - DÉCISION PRISE

I have reviewed this report and determine that a charge is warranted under section 40 of the Corrections and Conditional Release Act.
J'ai lu ce rapport et décidé qu'une accusation est justifiée en vertu de l'article 40 de la Loi sur le système correctionnel et la mise en liberté sous condition.

☑ Yes / Oui ☐ No / Non — Signature: [signature] — Position Title - Titre du poste: CCO — Date charge laid / Date l'accusation imposée: 01 02 16

Offence category - Catégorie de l'infraction: ☑ Minor / Mineure ☐ Serious / Grave

Referred to - Renvoyé au: ☑ Minor offence court / Tribunal des infractions mineures ☐ Serious offence court / Tribunal des infractions graves

For hearing a charge under Section 40 of the Corrections & Conditional Release Act. / Pour l'audition du chef d'accusation en vertu de l'article 40 de la Loi sur le système correctionnel et la mise en liberté sous condition. (Specify - Préciser) (See reverse side for offences - Voir le liste d'infractions au verso)

	Hour - Heure	Y-A M D-J	Title - Titre	Signature
Proposed date of hearing / Date prévue de l'audition	1000	01 02 23	C CO	[signature]
Delivered to inmate / Transmis au détenu	1432	01 02 19	A/CX2	P Edwards

I have been advised of my right to retain and instruct counsel. / J'ai été informé de mon droit d'avoir recours aux services d'un avocat.

☐ Inmate refused to sign / Détenu a refusé de signer

Inmate - Signature - Détenu — Date — Time - Heure — Witnessing CSC official's Signature - Agent responsable témoin

HEARING OF CHARGE - AUDITION DU CHEF D'ACCUSATION

Plea - Plaidoyer: ☐ Guilty / Coupable ☐ Not guilty / Non coupable ☐ Refused to plea / Refus de plaider

Remanded to - Audition ajourné à: Hour - Heure, Y-A, M, D-J

Reason - Motif: This charge is not a charge. Cannot charge inmate for being in his cell.

Third party representation requested by inmate / Représentation par un tiers requise par le détenu: ☐ Yes / Oui ☐ No / Non

Representation - Représentation: ☐ Accepted / Acceptée ☐ Refused / Refusé

Name of representative - Nom du représentant:

Witness - Témoin — Witness - Témoin — Finding - Conclusion: ☐ Guilty / Coupable ☐ Not guilty / Non coupable

SANCTION AWARDED - SANCTION IMPOSÉE

Sentence suspended / Peine suspendue: ☐ Yes / Oui ☐ No / Non

☐ Warning or reprimand / Avertissement ou réprimande ☐ Loss of privileges / Perte de privilèges ☐ Order for restitution / Ordre de restitution ☐ Fine / Amende ☐ Extra duties / Travaux supplémentaires ☐ Disciplinary segregation / Isolement disciplinaire

Particulars of sentence - Détails sur la peine:

Names of Disciplinary Board Members - Nom des membres du Comité de discipline: [signature]

Date of hearing - Date de l'audition: 01 03 05 — Name of presiding officer - Nom du président: — Signature of presiding officer - Signature du président: [signature] 53

CSC/SCC 222 (R-96-08)
7530-21-036-4518

DISTRIBUTION — SEE INSTRUCTIONS ON REVERSE - VOIR LES INSTRUCTIONS AU VERSO

16392 am KH

Correctional Service Canada / Service correctionnel Canada

PROTECTED / PROTÉGÉE A ☐ B ☐ C ☐ ONCE COMPLETED / UNE FOIS REMPLIE

PERSONAL INFORMATION BANK - FICHIER DE RENSEIGNEMENTS PERSONNELS

INMATE OFFENCE REPORT AND NOTIFICATION OF CHARGE / **RAPPORT DE L'INFRACTION D'UN DÉTENU ET AVIS DE L'ACCUSATION**

NOTE: Reference document CD 580. / NOTA: Document de référence DC 580.

PUT AWAY ON FILE / CLASSER AU DOSSIER — See reverse / Voir au verso

Institution - Établissement	Millhaven
Resp. Centre Code - Code du centre de resp.	
Location of offence - Lieu de l'infraction	2L Landing J-Unit
Date and time of offence / Date et l'heure de l'infraction (Y-A M D-J; Time - Heure)	01-03-21 08:00
FPS number / Numéro SED	464271D
Family name / Nom de famille	Thomas
Given name(s) / Prénom(s)	
Date of birth / Date de naissance	

DESCRIPTION OF OFFENCE (including names of witnesses, unusual behaviour of offender, etc.)
DESCRIPTION DE L'INFRACTION (y compris le nom des témoins, comportement inhabituel du délinquant, etc.)

On the above stated date and time the above mentioned I/M refused a direct order to return to his range. The direct order was given by the reporting officer.

Date report written / Date de la rédaction du rapport (Y-A M D-J)	01-03-21
Name of witnessing officer - Nom de l'agent témoin	G Daniels
Signature	[signature]
Physical evidence - Preuve(s): Yes/Oui ☐ No/Non ☑	
If yes, provide a brief description - Dans l'affirmative, fournir une brève description	
Disposition	
Supervisor or officer in charge of the institution advised / Avis donné au surveillant ou à l'agent responsable de l'établ.: Yes/Oui ☑	
Disposition of inmate - Mesure prise à l'égard du détenu: Admin. seg. / Isolement préventif ☐; Confined to cell / Retenu dans sa cellule ☐; Normal association / Intégration normale ☑	
Other witnessing officer - Autre agent témoin	K Driscoll

DECISION TAKEN - DÉCISION PRISE

I have reviewed this report and determine that a charge is warranted under section 40 of the Corrections and Conditional Release Act.
J'ai lu ce rapport et décidé qu'une accusation est justifiée en vertu de l'article 40 de la Loi sur le système correctionnel et la mise en liberté sous condition.

Yes/Oui ☑ No/Non ☐	
Signature	[signature]
Position Title - Titre du poste	CCO
Date charge laid / Date l'accusation imposée (Y-A M D-J)	01 03 22
Offence category - Catégorie de l'infraction: Minor/Mineure ☑ Serious/Grave ☐	
Referred to - Renvoyé au: Minor offence court / Tribunal des infractions mineures ☑; Serious offence court / Tribunal des infractions graves ☐	
For hearing a charge under Section 40 of the Corrections & Conditional Release Act. / Pour l'audition du chef d'accusation en vertu de l'article 40 de la Loi sur le système correctionnel et la mise en liberté sous condition. (Specify - Préciser) (See reverse side for offences - Voir la liste d'infractions au verso)	A
Proposed date of hearing / Date prévue de l'audition (Hour - Heure; Y-A M D-J)	1000 01 03 29
Title - Titre	CCO
Signature	[signature]
Delivered to inmate / Transmis au détenu (Hour - Heure; Y-A M D-J)	1130 01 03 23
Title - Titre	CO2
Signature	[signature]

I have been advised of my right to retain and instruct counsel. / J'ai été informé de mon droit d'avoir recours aux services d'un avocat.

Y-A M D-J ☐ Inmate refused to sign / Détenu a refusé de signer

Inmate - Signature - Détenu | Date | Time - Heure | Witnessing CSC official - Signature - Agent responsable témoin

HEARING OF CHARGE - AUDITION DU CHEF D'ACCUSATION

Plea - Plaidoyer: Guilty / Coupable ☐; Not guilty / Non coupable ☒; Refused to plea / Refus de plaider ☐

Remanded to - Audition ajourné à: Hour - Heure | Y-A | M | D-J

Reason - Motif

CORRECTED C. O'CONNOR 23 May 01 DA

Correctional Service Canada / Service correctionnel Canada

116206 K-117 OMS

PROTECTED / PROTÉGÉE A ☐ B ☐ C ☒ ☐ ONCE COMPLETED / UNE FOIS REMPLIE

PERSONAL INFORMATION BANK - FICHIER DE RENSEIGNEMENTS PERSONNELS

INMATE OFFENCE REPORT AND NOTIFICATION OF CHARGE / RAPPORT DE L'INFRACTION D'UN DÉTENU ET AVIS DE L'ACCUSATION

NOTE: Reference document CD 580. / NOTA: Document de référence DC 580.

PUT AWAY ON FILE / CLASSER AU DOSSIER — See reverse / Voir au verso

Institution - Établissement	Millhaven
Resp. Centre Code - Code du centre de resp.	42100
Location of offence - Lieu de l'infraction	1K Barrier "J" Living Unit
Date and time of offence - Date et l'heure de l'infraction (Y-A M D-J; Time - Heure)	01 04 04; 7:45
FPS number - Numéro SED	464271D.
Family name - Nom de famille	Thomas
Given name(s) - Prénom(s)	
Date of birth - Date de naissance	

DESCRIPTION OF OFFENCE (including names of witnesses, unusual behaviour of offender, etc.)
DESCRIPTION DE L'INFRACTION (y compris le nom des témoins, comportement inhabituel du délinquant, etc.)

On the above date and approximate time upon returning from the institutional hospital inmate Thomas physically opened the barrier on 1K, while the barrier was trying to open on its own accord. Previous to this he approach the "J" Control window infront of 1K and punched it.

Date report written - Date de la rédaction du rapport (Y-A M D-J)	01 04 04
Name of witnessing officer - Nom de l'agent témoin	Paul Mekis CX-01
Signature	Paul Mekis
Physical evidence - Preuve(s)	☐ Yes / Oui ☒ No / Non
If yes, provide a brief description - Dans l'affirmative, fournir une brève description	
Disposition	
Supervisor or officer in charge of the institution advised - Avis donné au surveillant ou à l'agent responsable de l'établ.	☒ Yes / Oui
Disposition of inmate - Mesure prise à l'égard du détenu	☐ Admin. seg. / Isolement préventif ☐ Confined to cell / Retenu dans sa cellule ☐ Normal association / Intégration normale
Other witnessing officer - Autre agent témoin	Robert Robinson CX-01

DECISION TAKEN - DÉCISION PRISE

I have reviewed this report and determine that a charge is warranted under section 40 of the Corrections and Conditional Release Act.
J'ai lu ce rapport et décidé qu'une accusation est justifiée en vertu de l'article 40 de la Loi sur le système correctionnel et la mise en liberté sous condition

Yes / Oui ☐ No / Non ☐	
Signature	[signature]
Position Title - Titre du poste	CCO
Date charge laid - Date l'accusation imposée (Y-A M D-J)	01 04 06
Offence category - Catégorie de l'infraction	☐ Minor / Mineure ☑ Serious / Grave
Referred to - Renvoyé au	☐ Minor offence court / Tribunal des infractions mineures ☑ Serious offence court / Tribunal des infractions graves
For hearing a charge under Section 40 of the Corrections & Conditional Release Act. / Pour l'audition du chef d'accusation en vertu de l'article 40 de la Loi sur le système correctionnel et la mise en liberté sous condition. (Specify - Préciser) (See reverse side for offences - Voir la liste d'infractions au verso)	m i i
Proposed date of hearing - Date prévue de l'audition (Hour - Heure; Y-A M D-J)	1300; 01 04 17
Title - Titre	CCO
Signature	E77
Delivered to inmate - Transmis au détenu (Hour - Heure; Y-A M D-J)	1645; 01 04 09
Title - Titre	A/CX2
Signature	P Edwards

I have been advised of my right to retain and instruct counsel. / J'ai été informé de mon droit d'avoir recours aux services d'un avocat.

☑ Inmate refused to sign / Détenu a refusé de signer

Inmate - Signature - Détenu	Date (Y-A M D-J)	Time - Heure	Witnessing CSC official - Signature - Agent responsable témoin
	010409	1645	P Edwards

HEARING OF CHARGE - AUDITION DU CHEF D'ACCUSATION

Plea - Plaidoyer: ☒ Guilty / Coupable ☐ Not guilty / Non coupable ☐ Refused to plea / Refus de plaider

Remanded to - Audition ajourné à: Hour - Heure / Y-A M D-J

Reason - Motif

OMS 16740 K117

Correctional Service Canada — Service correctionnel Canada

PROTECTED / PROTÉGÉE A ☐ B ☐ C ☐ ONCE COMPLETED / UNE FOIS REMPLIE

PERSONAL INFORMATION BANK - FICHIER DE RENSEIGNEMENTS PERSONNELS

INMATE OFFENCE REPORT AND NOTIFICATION OF CHARGE

RAPPORT DE L'INFRACTION D'UN DÉTENU ET AVIS DE L'ACCUSATION

NOTE: Reference document CD 580. — NOTA: Document de référence DC 580.

PUT AWAY ON FILE / CLASSER AU DOSSIER — See reverse / Voir au verso

Institution - Établissement	MILLHAVEN
Resp. Centre Code - Code du centre de resp.	
Location of offence - Lieu de l'infraction	J-UNIT
Date and time of offence / Date et l'heure de l'infraction (Y-A M D-J; Time - Heure)	01 04 08 08:00
FPS number / Numéro SED	464271D
Family name / Nom de famille	THOMAS
Given name(s) / Prénom(s)	
Date of birth / Date de naissance	

DESCRIPTION OF OFFENCE (including names of witnesses, unusual behaviour of offender, etc.)
DESCRIPTION DE L'INFRACTION (y compris le nom des témoins, comportement inhabituel du délinquant, etc.)

At the above date and approx. time, inmate Thomas came up to the control and yelled "FUCK YOU, YOU FUCKING GOOF!"

Date report written / Date de la rédaction du rapport (Y-A M D-J)	01 04 08
Name of witnessing officer - Nom de l'agent témoin	M. MONTGOMERY
Signature	[signature]
Physical evidence - Preuve(s)	☐ Yes / Oui ☑ No / Non
If yes, provide a brief description - Dans l'affirmative, fournir une brève description	
Disposition	
Supervisor or officer in charge of the institution advised / Avis donné au surveillant ou à l'agent responsable de l'établ.	☑ Yes / Oui
Disposition of inmate - Mesure prise à l'égard du détenu	☐ Admin. seg. / Isolement préventif ☐ Confined to cell / Retenu dans sa cellule ☑ Normal association / Intégration normale
Other witnessing officer - Autre agent témoin	S. LLOYD

DECISION TAKEN - DÉCISION PRISE

I have reviewed this report and determine that a charge is warranted under section 40 of the Corrections and Conditional Release Act.
J'ai lu ce rapport et décidé qu'une accusation est justifiée en vertu de l'article 40 de la Loi sur le système correctionnel et la mise en liberté sous condition

☑ Yes / Oui ☐ No / Non — Signature [signature] — Position Title - Titre du poste: CCO — Date charge laid / Date l'accusation imposée (Y-A M D-J): 01 04 09

Offence category - Catégorie de l'infraction: ☑ Minor / Mineure ☐ Serious / Grave

Referred to - Renvoyé au: ☑ Minor offence court / Tribunal des infractions mineures ☐ Serious offence court / Tribunal des infractions graves

For hearing a charge under Section 40 of the Corrections & Conditional Release Act. Pour l'audition du chef d'accusation en vertu de l'article 40 de la Loi sur le système correctionnel et la mise en liberté sous condition. (Specify - Préciser) (See reverse side for offences - Voir la liste d'infractions au verso): F

	Hour - Heure	Y-A M D-J	Title - Titre	Signature
Proposed date of hearing / Date prévue de l'audition	1000	01 04 16	CCO	[signature]
Delivered to inmate / Transmis au détenu	1200	01 04 10	CX	[signature]

I have been advised of my right to retain and instruct counsel. — J'ai été informé de mon droit d'avoir recours aux services d'un avocat.

Y-A M D-J ☐ Inmate refused to sign / Détenu a refusé de signer

Inmate - Signature - Détenu — Date — Time - Heure — Witnessing CSC official - Signature - Agent responsable témoin

HEARING OF CHARGE - AUDITION DU CHEF D'ACCUSATION

Plea - Plaidoyer: ☐ Guilty / Coupable ☐ Not guilty / Non coupable ☐ Refused to plea / Refus de plaider

Remanded to - Audition ajourné à: Hour - Heure, Y-A M D-J

Reason - Motif

16822 OMS — K119

Correctional Service Canada / Service correctionnel Canada

PROTECTED / PROTÉGÉE A ☐ B ☐ C ☐ ONCE COMPLETED / UNE FOIS REMPLIE

PERSONAL INFORMATION BANK - FICHIER DE RENSEIGNEMENTS PERSONNELS

INMATE OFFENCE REPORT AND NOTIFICATION OF CHARGE

RAPPORT DE L'INFRACTION D'UN DÉTENU ET AVIS DE L'ACCUSATION

NOTE: Reference document CD 580. / NOTA: Document de référence DC 580.

PUT AWAY ON FILE / CLASSER AU DOSSIER — See reverse / Voir au verso

Institution - Établissement	MI
Resp. Centre Code - Code du centre de resp.	
Location of offence - Lieu de l'infraction	1K Unit
Date and time of offence / Date et l'heure de l'infraction (Y-A M D-J / Time - Heure)	01 04 10 / 2140
FPS number / Numéro SED	THOMAS
Family name / Nom de famille	4642710
Given name(s) / Prénom(s)	
Date of birth / Date de naissance	

DESCRIPTION OF OFFENCE (including names of witnesses, unusual behaviour of offender, etc.)
DESCRIPTION DE L'INFRACTION (y compris le nom des témoins, comportement inhabituel du délinquant, etc.)

At the above date this inmate did delay the Unit Routine by not locking up 5 min. after the 5 min warning was given. This made the unit staff aprox 10 min late in getting to N area to bring back yard. This made 1K stores aprox. 12 min late.

Date report written / Date de la rédaction du rapport (Y-A M D-J)	01 04 10
Name of witnessing officer - Nom de l'agent témoin	CX2 LAIRD
Signature	[signature]
Physical evidence - Preuve(s)	☐ Yes/Oui ☒ No/Non
If yes, provide a brief description - Dans l'affirmative, fournir une brève description	
Disposition	
Supervisor or officer in charge of the institution advised / Avis donné au surveillant ou à l'agent responsable de l'établ.	☒ Yes/Oui
Disposition of inmate - Mesure prise à l'égard du détenu	☐ Admin. seg. / Isolement préventif ☐ Confined to cell / Retenu dans sa cellule ☒ Normal association / Intégration normale
Other witnessing officer - Autre agent témoin	A Murdoch

DECISION TAKEN - DÉCISION PRISE

I have reviewed this report and determine that a charge is warranted under section 40 of the Corrections and Conditional Release Act.
J'ai lu ce rapport et décidé qu'une accusation est justifiée en vertu de l'article 40 de la Loi sur le système correctionnel et la mise en liberté sous condition

Yes/Oui ☒ No/Non ☐	Signature: R Deslauriers
Position Title - Titre du poste	IPSO
Date charge laid / Date l'accusation imposée (Y-A M D-J)	01 04 11
Offence category - Catégorie de l'infraction	☒ Minor/Mineure ☐ Serious/Grave
Referred to - Renvoyé au	☒ Minor offence court / Tribunal des infractions mineures ☐ Serious offence court / Tribunal des infractions graves
For hearing a charge under Section 40 of the Corrections & Conditional Release Act. / Pour l'audition du chef d'accusation en vertu de l'article 40 de la Loi sur le système correctionnel et la mise en liberté sous condition. (Specify - Préciser) (See reverse side for offences - Voir la liste d'infractions au verso)	"R"

	Hour - Heure	Y-A M D-J	Title - Titre	Signature
Proposed date of hearing / Date prévue de l'audition	1000	01 04 24	IPSO	R Deslauriers
Delivered to inmate / Transmis au détenu	1500	01 04 11	CO2	[signature]

I have been advised of my right to retain and instruct counsel. / J'ai été informé de mon droit d'avoir recours aux services d'un avocat.

Y-A M D-J ☐ Inmate refused to sign / Détenu a refusé de signer

Inmate - Signature - Détenu | Date | Time - Heure | Witnessing CSC official - Signature - Agent responsable témoin

HEARING OF CHARGE - AUDITION DU CHEF D'ACCUSATION

Plea - Plaidoyer	☐ Guilty/Coupable ☒ Not guilty/Non coupable ☐ Refused to plea/Refus de plaider
Remanded to - Audition ajourné à	Hour - Heure / Y-A M D-J
Reason - Motif	

OMS 16971 K117

Correctional Service Canada / Service correctionnel Canada

PROTECTED / PROTÉGÉE A ☐ B ☐ C ☐ ONCE COMPLETED / UNE FOIS REMPLIE

PERSONAL INFORMATION BANK - FICHIER DE RENSEIGNEMENTS PERSONNELS

INMATE OFFENCE REPORT AND NOTIFICATION OF CHARGE

RAPPORT DE L'INFRACTION D'UN DÉTENU ET AVIS DE L'ACCUSATION

NOTE: Reference document CD 580. / NOTA: Document de référence DC 580.

PUT AWAY ON FILE / CLASSER AU DOSSIER — See reverse / Voir au verso

Institution - Établissement	MILLHAVEN
Resp. Centre Code - Code du centre de resp.	
FPS number / Numéro SED	464271D
Family name / Nom de famille	THOMAS
Given name(s) / Prénom(s)	
Location of offence - Lieu de l'infraction	J-UNIT 2L RANGE
Date and time of offence / Date et l'heure de l'infraction (Y-A M D-J)	01 04 19
Time - Heure	19:35
Date of birth / Date de naissance	

DESCRIPTION OF OFFENCE (including names of witnesses, unusual behaviour of offender, etc.)
DESCRIPTION DE L'INFRACTION (y compris le nom des témoins, comportement inhabituel du délinquant, etc.)

At the above date and approx. time, while returning from recreation inmate Thomas went onto 2L range and stayed there for approx 5 minutes. Inmate Thomas lives on 1K range.

Date report written / Date de la rédaction du rapport (Y-A M D-J)	01 04 19
Name of witnessing officer - Nom de l'agent témoin	M. MONTGOMERY
Signature	[signature]
Physical evidence - Preuve(s)	☐ Yes/Oui ☑ No/Non
If yes, provide a brief description - Dans l'affirmative, fournir une brève description	
Disposition	
Supervisor or officer in charge of the institution advised - Avis donné au surveillant ou à l'agent responsable de l'établ.	☑ Yes/Oui
Disposition of inmate - Mesure prise à l'égard du détenu	☐ Admin. seg. / Isolement préventif ☐ Confined to cell / Retenu dans sa cellule ☑ Normal association / Intégration normale
Other witnessing officer - Autre agent témoin	R. HALEY

DECISION TAKEN - DÉCISION PRISE

I have reviewed this report and determine that a charge is warranted under section 40 of the Corrections and Conditional Release Act.
J'ai lu ce rapport et décidé qu'une accusation est justifiée en vertu de l'article 40 de la Loi sur le système correctionnel et la mise en liberté sous condition

☑ Yes/Oui ☐ No/Non Signature [signature]

Position Title - Titre du poste: CCO

Date charge laid / Date l'accusation imposée (Y-A M D-J): 01 04 20

Offence category - Catégorie de l'infraction: ☐ Minor / Mineure ☐ Serious / Grave

Referred to - Renvoyé au: ☑ Minor offence court / Tribunal des infractions mineures ☐ Serious offence court / Tribunal des infractions graves

For hearing a charge under Section 40 of the Corrections & Conditional Release Act. / Pour l'audition du chef d'accusation en vertu de l'article 40 de la Loi sur le système correctionnel et la mise en liberté sous condition. (Specify - Préciser) (See reverse side for offences - Voir la liste d'infractions au verso): R

	Hour - Heure	Y-A M D-J	Title - Titre	Signature
Proposed date of hearing / Date prévue de l'audition	1000	01 04 27	CCO	[signature]
Delivered to inmate / Transmis au détenu	1100	01 04 23	A/CX2	P Edwards

I have been advised of my right to retain and instruct counsel. / J'ai été informé de mon droit d'avoir recours aux services d'un avocat.

Y-A M D-J ☐ Inmate refused to sign / Détenu a refusé de signer

Inmate - Signature - Détenu   Date   Time - Heure   Witnessing CSC official - Signature - Agent responsable témoin

HEARING OF CHARGE - AUDITION DU CHEF D'ACCUSATION

Plea - Plaidoyer: ☐ Guilty / Coupable ☒ Not guilty / Non coupable ☐ Refused to plea / Refus de plaider

Remanded to - Audition ajourné à: Hour - Heure   Y-A M D-J

Reason - Motif

179/75 Keep OMS

Correctional Service Canada / Service correctionnel Canada

PROTECTED / PROTÉGÉE A ☐ B ☐ C ☒ ONCE COMPLETED / UNE FOIS REMPLIE

PERSONAL INFORMATION BANK - FICHIER DE RENSEIGNEMENTS PERSONNELS

INMATE OFFENCE REPORT AND NOTIFICATION OF CHARGE

RAPPORT DE L'INFRACTION D'UN DÉTENU ET AVIS DE L'ACCUSATION

NOTE: Reference document CD 580. / NOTA: Document de référence DC 580.

PUT AWAY ON FILE / CLASSER AU DOSSIER — See reverse / Voir au verso

Institution - Établissement	MILLHAVEN
Resp. Centre Code - Code du centre de resp.	42100
Location of offence - Lieu de l'infraction	J-UNIT
Date and time of offence - Date et l'heure de l'infraction (Y-A M D-J / Time - Heure)	01 06 10 / 1605
FPS number - Numéro SED	464271D
Family name - Nom de famille	THOMAS
Given name(s) - Prénom(s)	
Date of birth - Date de naissance	

DESCRIPTION OF OFFENCE (including names of witnesses, unusual behaviour of offender, etc.)
DESCRIPTION DE L'INFRACTION (y compris le nom des témoins, comportement inhabituel du délinquant, etc.)

INMATE THOMAS FPS# 464271D REFUSED A DIRECT ORDER TO RETURN TO HIS CELL FOR COUNT.

Date report written - Date de la rédaction du rapport (Y-A M D-J)	01 06 10
Name of witnessing officer - Nom de l'agent témoin	BRAD SULLIVAN CX1
Signature	B. Sullivan
Physical evidence - Preuve(s)	☐ Yes/Oui ☒ No/Non
If yes, provide a brief description - Dans l'affirmative, fournir une brève description	
Disposition	
Supervisor or officer in charge of the institution advised / Avis donné au surveillant ou à l'agent responsable de l'établ.	☒ Yes/Oui
Disposition of inmate - Mesure prise à l'égard du détenu	☐ Admin. seg. / Isolement préventif ☐ Confined to cell / Retenu dans sa cellule ☐ Normal association / Intégration normale
Other witnessing officer - Autre agent témoin	D Hunt CX1

DECISION TAKEN - DÉCISION PRISE

I have reviewed this report and determine that a charge is warranted under section 40 of the Corrections and Conditional Release Act.
J'ai lu ce rapport et décidé qu'une accusation est justifiée en vertu de l'article 40 de la Loi sur le système correctionnel et la mise en liberté sous condition

☒ Yes/Oui ☐ No/Non — Signature [signature] — Position Title - Titre du poste: CCO — Date charge laid / Date l'accusation imposée (Y-A M D-J): 01 06 11

Offence category - Catégorie de l'infraction: ☐ Minor/Mineure ☐ Serious/Grave

Referred to - Renvoyé au: ☒ Minor offence court / Tribunal des infractions mineures ☐ Serious offence court / Tribunal des infractions graves

For hearing a charge under Section 40 of the Corrections & Conditional Release Act. / Pour l'audition du chef d'accusation en vertu de l'article 40 de la Loi sur le système correctionnel et la mise en liberté sous condition. (Specify - Préciser) (See reverse side for offences - Voir la liste d'infractions au verso): A

	Hour - Heure	Y-A M D-J	Title - Titre	Signature
Proposed date of hearing - Date prévue de l'audition	1000	01 06 18	CCO	[signature]
Delivered to inmate - Transmis au détenu	1000	01 06 12	Cx	[signature]

I have been advised of my right to retain and instruct counsel. / J'ai été informé de mon droit d'avoir recours aux services d'un avocat.

Y-A M D-J ☐ Inmate refused to sign / Détenu a refusé de signer

Inmate - Signature - Détenu | Date | Time - Heure | Witnessing CSC official - Signature - Agent responsable témoin

HEARING OF CHARGE - AUDITION DU CHEF D'ACCUSATION

Plea - Plaidoyer: ☐ Guilty/Coupable ☐ Not guilty/Non coupable ☐ Refused to plea/Refus de plaider

Remanded to - Audition ajourné à: Hour - Heure | Y-A | M | D-J

Reason - Motif

Copy faxed to C Urmina, 21 June 01

DA. 17994

Correctional Service Canada / Service correctionnel Canada

PROTECTED / PROTÉGÉE A ☐ B ☐ C ☑ ONCE COMPLETED / UNE FOIS REMPLIE

PERSONAL INFORMATION BANK - FICHIER DE RENSEIGNEMENTS PERSONNELS

INMATE OFFENCE REPORT AND NOTIFICATION OF CHARGE

RAPPORT DE L'INFRACTION D'UN DÉTENU ET AVIS DE L'ACCUSATION

NOTE: Reference document CD 580. / NOTA: Document de référence DC 580.

PUT AWAY ON FILE / CLASSER AU DOSSIER — See reverse / Voir au verso

Institution - Établissement: Millhaven

Resp. Centre Code - Code du centre de resp.: 42100

FPS number / Numéro SED: 464271 D.

Family name / Nom de famille: Thomas

Given name(s) / Prénom(s):

Location of offence - Lieu de l'infraction: K117.

Date and time of offence / Date et l'heure de l'infraction: Y-A 2001 M 06 D-J 13 Time - Heure 0950

Date of birth / Date:

DESCRIPTION OF OFFENCE (including names of witnesses, unusual behaviour of offender, etc.) / DESCRIPTION DE L'INFRACTION (y compris le nom des témoins, comportement inhabituel du délinquant, etc.)

On above date at approx 0950 a search of K117 was conducted. A brew approx. gallons was removed from under the shelf. A piece of sandpaper found behind the Television and a homemade plastic weapon approx 9" long found under a towel on the desk

SUBSTANCE TESTING

The substance was tested in accordance with established and approved procedures.

Tested positive for: Alcohol

Received from: S Fredenburgh

Received by: K. Swedarin

Date: 2001 06 13 Time: 1030

Tested by: K. Swedarin

Date: 01/06/13 Time: 1205

Date report written / Date de la rédaction du rapport: 2001/06/13

Name of witnessing officer - Nom de l'agent témoin: S Fredenburgh.

Signature:

Physical evidence - Preuve(s): ☑ Yes / Oui ☐ No / Non

If yes, provide a brief description - Dans l'affirmative, fournir une brève description: Brew approx 6gallons Weapon Sandpaper

Disposition: 1850 office 2001-139.

Supervisor or officer in charge of the institution advised / Avis donné au surveillant ou à l'agent responsable de l'établ.: ☐ Yes / Oui

Disposition of inmate - Mesure prise à l'égard du détenu: ☐ Admin. seg. / Isolement préventif ☐ Confined to cell / Retenu dans sa cellule ☐ Normal association / Intégration normale

Other witnessing officer - Autre agent témoin:

DECISION TAKEN - DÉCISION PRISE

I have reviewed this report and determine that a charge is warranted under section 40 of the Corrections and Conditional Release Act.
J'ai lu ce rapport et décidé qu'une accusation est justifiée en vertu de l'article 40 de la Loi sur le système correctionnel et la mise en liberté sous condition

☑ Yes / Oui ☐ No / Non Signature: Position Title - Titre du poste: CCO

Date charge laid / Date l'accusation imposée: Y-A 01 M 06 D-J 14

Offence category - Catégorie de l'infraction: ☐ Minor / Mineure ☑ Serious / Grave

Referred to - Renvoyé au: ☐ Minor offence court / Tribunal des infractions mineures ☑ Serious offence court / Tribunal des infractions graves

For hearing a charge under Section 40 of the Corrections & Conditional Release Act. / Pour l'audition du chef d'accusation en vertu de l'article 40 de la Loi sur le système correctionnel et la mise en liberté sous condition. (Specify - Préciser) (See reverse side for offences - Voir la liste d'infractions au verso): (i)

Proposed date of hearing / Date prévue de l'audition: Hour - Heure 1300 Y-A 01 M 06 D-J 26 Title - Titre: CCO Signature:

Delivered to inmate / Transmis au détenu: Hour - Heure 1550 Y-A 01 M 06 D-J 14 Title - Titre: COI Signature: Barbosa

I have been advised of my right to retain and instruct counsel. / J'ai été informé de mon droit d'avoir recours aux services d'un avocat.

☒ Inmate refused to sign / Détenu a refusé de signer

Inmate - Signature - Détenu | Date: 01 06 14 | Time - Heure: 1550 | Witnessing CSC official - Signature - Agent responsable témoin: Barbosa

HEARING OF CHARGE - AUDITION DU CHEF D'ACCUSATION

Plea - Plaidoyer: ☑ Guilty / Coupable ☐ Not guilty / Non coupable ☐ Refused to plea / Refus de plaider

Remanded to - Audition ajourné à: Hour - Heure Y-A M D-J

Reason - Motif: July 24/01 | Sept 25/01 set date / Oct 9/01 ... set date

K 117 PROTECTED / PROTÉGÉE A ☐ B ☐ C ☒ ONCE COMPLETED / UNE FOIS REMPLIE

Correctional Service Canada / Service correctionnel Canada

PERSONAL INFORMATION BANK - FICHIER DE RENSEIGNEMENTS PERSONNELS

INMATE OFFENCE REPORT AND NOTIFICATION OF CHARGE
RAPPORT DE L'INFRACTION D'UN DÉTENU ET AVIS DE L'ACCUSATION

NOTE: Reference document CD 580. / NOTA: Document de référence DC 580.

PUT AWAY ON FILE / CLASSER AU DOSSIER — See reverse / Voir au verso

Institution - Établissement	Millhaven
Resp. Centre Code - Code du centre de resp.	42100
Location of offence - Lieu de l'infraction	1K range.
Date and time of offence / Date et l'heure de l'infraction (Y-A M D-J, Time - Heure)	2001/06/13 1105
FPS number / Numéro SED	464271D.
Family name / Nom de famille	Thomas.
Given name(s) / Prénom(s)	
Date of birth / Date de naissance	

DESCRIPTION OF OFFENCE (including names of witnesses, unusual behaviour of offender, etc.)
DESCRIPTION DE L'INFRACTION (y compris le nom des témoins, comportement inhabituel du délinquant, etc.)

On above date at approx 1105 this officer ordered I/m Thomas to lockup. He stated that he was not going to and he wanted to go to the committee room. I explained to him that the committee room was closed and he could go in the PM. He ~~again~~ stated he wanted to go "Now". The Keeper was notified and Thomas eventually locked up. This delayed ~~count~~ routine by approx 10 minutes.

Date report written / Date de la rédaction du rapport	2001/06/13
Name of witnessing officer - Nom de l'agent témoin	S. Fredenburgh
Signature	[signature]
Physical evidence - Preuve(s)	No / Non ☒
If yes, provide a brief description - Dans l'affirmative, fournir une brève description	
Supervisor or officer in charge of the institution advised / Avis donné au surveillant ou à l'agent responsable de l'établ.	Yes / Oui ☒
Disposition of inmate - Mesure prise à l'égard du détenu	Normal association / Intégration normale ☒
Other witnessing officer - Autre agent témoin	CS R Haley / B Schure

DECISION TAKEN - DÉCISION PRISE

I have reviewed this report and determine that a charge is warranted under section 40 of the Corrections and Conditional Release Act.
J'ai lu ce rapport et décidé qu'une accusation est justifiée en vertu de l'article 40 de la Loi sur le système correctionnel et la mise en liberté sous condition

Yes / Oui ☒ No / Non ☐	Signature: [signature]
Position Title - Titre du poste	CCO
Date charge laid / Date l'accusation imposée (Y-A M D-J)	01 06 14
Offence category - Catégorie de l'infraction	Minor / Mineure ☒ Serious / Grave ☐
Referred to - Renvoyé au	Minor offence court / Tribunal des infractions mineures ☒; Serious offence court / Tribunal des infractions graves ☐
For hearing a charge under Section 40 of the Corrections & Conditional Release Act. / Pour l'audition du chef d'accusation en vertu de l'article 40 de la Loi sur le système correctionnel et la mise en liberté sous condition. (Specify - Préciser) (See reverse side for offences - Voir la liste d'infractions au verso)	R
Proposed date of hearing / Date prévue de l'audition	Hour - Heure 1000; Y-A M D-J 01 06 21; Title - Titre CCO; Signature [signature]
Delivered to inmate / Transmis au détenu	Hour - Heure 1940; Y-A M D-J 2001/06 15; Title - Titre CO II; Signature [signature]

I have been advised of my right to retain and instruct counsel. / J'ai été informé de mon droit d'avoir recours aux services d'un avocat.

Y-A M D-J ☐ Inmate refused to sign / Détenu a refusé de signer

Inmate - Signature - Détenu | Date | Time - Heure | Witnessing CSC official - Signature - Agent responsable témoin

HEARING OF CHARGE - AUDITION DU CHEF D'ACCUSATION

Plea - Plaidoyer: ☐ Guilty / Coupable ☐ Not guilty / Non coupable ☐ Refused to plea / Refus de plaider

Remanded to - Audition ajourné à: Hour - Heure | Y-A | M | D-J

Reason - Motif

CC 1805 0945 Q

Correctional Service Canada — Service correctionnel Canada

PROTECTED / PROTÉGÉE A ☐ B ☒ C ☐ ONCE COMPLETED / UNE FOIS REMPLIE

PERSONAL INFORMATION BANK - FICHIER DE RENSEIGNEMENTS PERSONNELS

INMATE OFFENCE REPORT AND NOTIFICATION OF CHARGE — **RAPPORT DE L'INFRACTION D'UN DÉTENU ET AVIS DE L'ACCUSATION**

NOTE: Reference document CD 580. — NOTA: Document de référence DC 580.

PUT AWAY ON FILE / CLASSER AU DOSSIER — See reverse / Voir au verso

Institution - Établissement	MILLHAVEN INST.
Resp. Centre Code - Code du centre de resp.	4200
FPS number / Numéro SED	464271D.
Family name / Nom de famille	THOMAS
Given name(s) / Prénom(s)	
Date of birth / Date de naissance	
Location of offence - Lieu de l'infraction	N AREA / HOSPITAL CORRIDOOR
Date and time of offence / Date et l'heure de l'infraction (Y-A M D-J, Time - Heure)	01 06 17 1250

DESCRIPTION OF OFFENCE (including names of witnesses, unusual behaviour of offender, etc.)
DESCRIPTION DE L'INFRACTION (y compris le nom des témoins, comportement inhabituel du délinquant, etc.)

On the above date and time while going to yard for a barbeque, I/m THOMAS FPS #464271D passed through the N AREA barrier to go to the yard but waited for [redacted] threw the contraband to I/m THOMAS who then dumped it in the A UNIT coister. It was later discovered to be and empty plastic bag of brew like smell. RH

Date report written / Date de la rédaction du rapport (Y-A M D-J)	01 06 17
Name of witnessing officer - Nom de l'agent témoin	R. HALEY · CoI
Signature	[signature]
Physical evidence - Preuve(s)	Yes/Oui ☐ No/Non ☐
If yes, provide a brief description - Dans l'affirmative, fournir une brève description	
Disposition	
Supervisor or officer in charge of the institution advised / Avis donné au surveillant ou à l'agent responsable de l'établ.	Yes/Oui ☐
Disposition of inmate - Mesure prise à l'égard du détenu	Admin. seg. / Isolement préventif ☐ Confined to cell / Retenu dans sa cellule ☐ Normal association / Intégration normale ☐
Other witnessing officer - Autre agent témoin	B. LAIRD CoII

DECISION TAKEN - DÉCISION PRISE

I have reviewed this report and determine that a charge is warranted under section 40 of the Corrections and Conditional Release Act.
J'ai lu ce rapport et décidé qu'une accusation est justifiée en vertu de l'article 40 de la Loi sur le système correctionnel et la mise en liberté sous condition.

Yes/Oui ☒ No/Non ☐ Signature	[signature]
Position Title - Titre du poste	CCO
Date charge laid / Date l'accusation imposée (Y-A M D-J)	01 06 18
Offence category - Catégorie de l'infraction	Minor/Mineure ☒ Serious/Grave ☐
Referred to - Renvoyé au	Minor offence court / Tribunal des infractions mineures ☒ Serious offence court / Tribunal des infractions graves ☐
For hearing a charge under Section 40 of the Corrections & Conditional Release Act. / Pour l'audition du chef d'accusation en vertu de l'article 40 de la Loi sur le système correctionnel et la mise en liberté sous condition. (Specify - Préciser) (See reverse side for offences - Voir la liste d'infractions au verso)	A

	Hour - Heure	Y-A M D-J	Title - Titre	Signature
Proposed date of hearing / Date prévue de l'audition	1000	01 06 25	CCO	[signature]
Delivered to inmate / Transmis au détenu	1300	01 06 19	Co. II	Edwards

I have been advised of my right to retain and instruct counsel. — J'ai été informé de mon droit d'avoir recours aux services d'un avocat.

Y-A M D-J ☐ Inmate refused to sign / Détenu a refusé de signer

Inmate - Signature - Détenu | Date | Time - Heure | Witnessing CSC official - Signature - Agent responsable témoin

HEARING OF CHARGE - AUDITION DU CHEF D'ACCUSATION

Plea - Plaidoyer: Guilty/Coupable ☐ Not guilty/Non coupable ☐ Refused to plea/Refus de plaider ☐

Remanded to - Audition ajourné à: Hour - Heure | Y-A | M

26

Copy [illegible] 30 July 01 DA 18086 (MD) OMD

Correctional Service Canada | Service correctionnel Canada

PROTECTED / PROTÉGÉE A ☐ B ☐ C ☒ ☐ ONCE COMPLETED / UNE FOIS REMPLIE

PERSONAL INFORMATION BANK - FICHIER DE RENSEIGNEMENTS PERSONNELS

INMATE OFFENCE REPORT AND NOTIFICATION OF CHARGE / **RAPPORT DE L'INFRACTION D'UN DÉTENU ET AVIS DE L'ACCUSATION**

NOTE: Reference document CD 580. / NOTA: Document de référence DC 580.

PUT AWAY ON FILE / CLASSER AU DOSSIER — See reverse / Voir au verso

Institution - Établissement	Millhaven Inst
Resp. Centre Code - Code du centre de resp.	42180
Location of offence - Lieu de l'infraction	171K
Date and time of offence / Date et l'heure de l'infraction (Y-A M D-J, Time - Heure)	01 06 18 1420
FPS number / Numéro SED	464271D
Family name / Nom de famille	Thomas
Given name(s) / Prénom(s)	
Date of birth / Date de naissance	

DESCRIPTION OF OFFENCE (including names of witnesses, unusual behaviour of offender, etc.)
DESCRIPTION DE L'INFRACTION (y compris le nom des témoins, comportement inhabituel du délinquant, etc.)

At approximately 1420 hours while removing the cell effects from the above inmates cell a steel weapon approx length 8 inches was found

[redacted]

421-2001-141

Date report written / Date de la rédaction du rapport (Y-A M D-J)	01 06 18
Name of witnessing officer - Nom de l'agent témoin	BCT Jones
Signature	B Jones
Physical evidence - Preuve(s)	☒ Yes / Oui ☐ No / Non
If yes, provide a brief description - Dans l'affirmative, fournir une brève description	8" Steel shank (approx length)
Disposition	IPSO
Supervisor or officer in charge of the institution advised / Avis donné au surveillant ou à l'agent responsable de l'établ.	☒ Yes / Oui
Disposition of inmate - Mesure prise à l'égard du détenu	☐ Admin. seg. / Isolement préventif ☐ Confined to cell / Retenu dans sa cellule ☐ Normal association / Intégration normale
Other witnessing officer - Autre agent témoin	P. Edwards

DECISION TAKEN - DÉCISION PRISE

I have reviewed this report and determine that a charge is warranted under section 40 of the Corrections and Conditional Release Act.
J'ai lu ce rapport et décidé qu'une accusation est justifiée en vertu de l'article 40 de la Loi sur le système correctionnel et la mise en liberté sous condition

☒ Yes / Oui ☐ No / Non — Signature	[signature]
Position Title - Titre du poste	CCO
Date charge laid / Date l'accusation imposée (Y-A M D-J)	01 06 19
Offence category - Catégorie de l'infraction	☐ Minor / Mineure ☒ Serious / Grave
Referred to - Renvoyé au	☐ Minor offence court / Tribunal des infractions mineures ☒ Serious offence court / Tribunal des infractions graves
For hearing a charge under Section 40 of the Corrections & Conditional Release Act. / Pour l'audition du chef d'accusation en vertu de l'article 40 de la Loi sur le système correctionnel et la mise en liberté sous condition (Specify - Préciser) (See reverse side for offences - Voir la liste d'infractions au verso)	(i) 22(1)(c)
Proposed date of hearing / Date prévue de l'audition (Hour - Heure, Y-A M D-J)	1300 01 06 26
Title - Titre	CCO
Signature	[signature]
Delivered to inmate / Transmis au détenu (Hour - Heure, Y-A M D-J)	09^15 01 06 21
Title - Titre	CX 1
Signature	[signature]

I have been advised of my right to retain and instruct counsel. / J'ai été informé de mon droit d'avoir recours aux services d'un avocat.

☒ Inmate refused to sign / Détenu a refusé de signer

Inmate - Signature - Détenu	Date (Y-A M D-J)	Time - Heure	Witnessing CSC official - Signature - Agent responsable témoin
	01 06 21	09^15	[signature]

HEARING OF CHARGE - AUDITION DU CHEF D'ACCUSATION

Plea - Plaidoyer: ☒ Guilty / Coupable ☐ Not guilty / Non coupable ☐ Refused to plea / Refus de plaider

Remanded to - Audition ajourné à: Hour - Heure | Y-A | M | D-J

—Jan 8/02 indicated G/P

Reason - Motif

July 27/01 [illegible] | Sept 25/01 set date | Oct 9/01 bumped set date

Copy faxed to Mr. O'Connor, 30 [illegible]

18284

Correctional Service Canada / Service correctionnel Canada

PROTECTED / PROTÉGÉE A ☐ B ☒ C ☐ ONCE COMPLETED / UNE FOIS REMPLIE

K208

PERSONAL INFORMATION BANK - FICHIER DE RENSEIGNEMENTS PERSONNELS

INMATE OFFENCE REPORT AND NOTIFICATION OF CHARGE

RAPPORT DE L'INFRACTION D'UN DÉTENU ET AVIS DE L'ACCUSATION

NOTE: Reference document CD 580. / NOTA: Document de référence DC 580.

PUT AWAY ON FILE / CLASSER AU DOSSIER — See reverse / Voir au verso

Institution - Établissement	M I
Resp. Centre Code - Code du centre de resp.	42100
Location of offence - Lieu de l'infraction	2K
Date and time of offence / Date et l'heure de l'infraction (Y-A M D-J / Time - Heure)	01 06 26 / 2200
FPS number / Numéro SED	464271D
Family name / Nom de famille	Thomas
Given name(s) / Prénom(s)	
Date of birth / Date de naissance	

DESCRIPTION OF OFFENCE (including names of witnesses, unusual behaviour of offender, etc.)
DESCRIPTION DE L'INFRACTION (y compris le nom des témoins, comportement inhabituel du délinquant, etc.)

on the above date and approx. time this I/m disobeyed a direct order to return to his cell and lock-up

Date report written / Date de la rédaction du rapport (Y-A M D-J)	01 06 26
Name of witnessing officer - Nom de l'agent témoin	R. Finucan
Signature	[signature]
Physical evidence - Preuve(s)	Yes/Oui ☐ No/Non ☒
If yes, provide a brief description - Dans l'affirmative, fournir une brève description	
Disposition	
Supervisor or officer in charge of the institution advised / Avis donné au surveillant ou à l'agent responsable de l'établ.	Yes/Oui ☒
Disposition of inmate - Mesure prise à l'égard du détenu	Admin. seg. / Isolement préventif ☐ Confined to cell / Retenu dans sa cellule ☐ Normal association / Intégration normale ☒
Other witnessing officer - Autre agent témoin	[signature]

DECISION TAKEN - DÉCISION PRISE

I have reviewed this report and determine that a charge is warranted under section 40 of the Corrections and Conditional Release Act.
J'ai lu ce rapport et décidé qu'une accusation est justifiée en vertu de l'article 40 de la Loi sur le système correctionnel et la mise en liberté sous condition.

Yes/Oui ☒ No/Non ☐	Signature: [signature]
Position Title - Titre du poste	CCO
Date charge laid / Date l'accusation imposée (Y-A M D-J)	01 06 27
Offence category - Catégorie de l'infraction	Minor/Mineure ☐ Serious/Grave ☒
Referred to - Renvoyé au	Minor offence court / Tribunal des infractions mineures ☐ Serious offence court / Tribunal des infractions graves ☒
For hearing a charge under Section 40 of the Corrections & Conditional Release Act. / Pour l'audition du chef d'accusation en vertu de l'article 40 de la Loi sur le système correctionnel et la mise en liberté sous condition. (Specify - Préciser) (See reverse side for offences - Voir la liste d'infractions au verso)	A
Proposed date of hearing / Date prévue de l'audition (Hour - Heure / Y-A M D-J)	1300 / 01 07 10
Title - Titre	CCO
Signature	[signature]
Delivered to inmate / Transmis au détenu (Hour - Heure / Y-A M D-J)	1337 / 01 06 29
Title - Titre	
Signature	

I have been advised of my right to retain and instruct counsel. / J'ai été informé de mon droit d'avoir recours aux services d'un avocat.

☒ Inmate refused to sign / Détenu a refusé de signer

Inmate - Signature - Détenu	Date	Time - Heure	Witnessing CSC official - Signature - Agent responsable témoin
[signature]	01 06 29	1338	[signature]

HEARING OF CHARGE - AUDITION DU CHEF D'ACCUSATION

Plea - Plaidoyer	Guilty/Coupable ☒ Not guilty/Non coupable ☐ Refused to plea/Refus de plaider ☐
Remanded to - Audition ajourné à (Hour - Heure / Y-A M D-J)	
Reason - Motif	[illegible] 24/01 [illegible] | Cont 25/01 set date [illegible]

Correctional Service Canada / Service correctionnel Canada

PROTÉGÉE

PERSONAL INFORMATION BANK - FICHIER DE RENSEIGNEMENTS PERSONNELS

INMATE OFFENCE REPORT AND NOTIFICATION OF CHARGE — RAPPORT DE L'INFRACTION D'UN DÉTENU ET AVIS DE L'ACCUSATION

NOTE: Reference document CD 580. — NOTA: Document de référence DC 580.

PUT AWAY ON FILE / CLASSER AU DOSSIER — See reverse / Voir au verso

Institution - Établissement	MILLHAVEN
Resp. Centre Code - Code du centre de resp.	421D
FPS number / Numéro SED	464271D
Family name / Nom de famille	THOMAS
Location of offence - Lieu de l'infraction	MSU - 2K RANGE
Given name(s) / Prénom(s)	
Date and time of offence / Date et l'heure de l'infraction (Y-A M D-J, Time - Heure)	01 06 27, 22:45
Date of birth / Date de naissance	

DESCRIPTION OF OFFENCE (including names of witnesses, unusual behaviour of offender, etc.)
DESCRIPTION DE L'INFRACTION (y compris le nom des témoins, comportement inhabituel du délinquant, etc.)

At the above time and date Mr Thomas refused to return to his cell for the instructional count. He was given several direct orders by c/s Dorling and still refused.
As a result Mr Thomas was escorted to LCA by several officers.

Date report written / Date de la rédaction du rapport	Name of witnessing officer - Nom de l'agent témoin	Signature
01 06 27	CO 4 McMILLAN	[signature]

Physical evidence - Preuve(s): ☐ Yes / Oui ☑ No / Non — If yes, provide a brief description - Dans l'affirmative, fournir une brève description — Disposition

Supervisor or officer in charge of the institution advised / Avis donné au surveillant ou à l'agent responsable de l'établ.: ☑ Yes / Oui

Disposition of inmate - Mesure prise à l'égard du détenu: ☑ Admin. seg. / Isolement préventif ☐ Confined to cell / Retenu dans sa cellule ☐ Normal association / Intégration normale

Other witnessing officer - Autre agent témoin: Fredenburg [signature]

DECISION TAKEN - DÉCISION PRISE

I have reviewed this report and determine that a charge is warranted under section 40 of the Corrections and Conditional Release Act.
J'ai lu ce rapport et décidé qu'une accusation est justifiée en vertu de l'article 40 de la Loi sur le système correctionnel et la mise en liberté sous condition.

☑ Yes / Oui ☐ No / Non — Signature [signature] — Position Title - Titre du poste: CCO — Date charge laid / Date l'accusation imposée: 01 06 28

Offence category - Catégorie de l'infraction: ☐ Minor / Mineure ☑ Serious / Grave

Referred to - Renvoyé au: ☐ Minor offence court / Tribunal des infractions mineures ☑ Serious offence court / Tribunal des infractions graves

For hearing a charge under Section 40 of the Corrections & Conditional Release Act. (Specify - Préciser) (See reverse side for offences - Voir la liste d'infractions au verso): A

	Hour - Heure	Y-A M D-J	Title - Titre	Signature
Proposed date of hearing / Date prévue de l'audition	1300	01 07 10	CCO	[signature]
Delivered to inmate / Transmis au détenu	12[illegible]	[illegible]	CX2	[signature]

I have been advised of my right to retain and instruct counsel. — J'ai été informé de mon droit d'avoir recours aux services d'un avocat.

☑ Inmate refused to sign / Détenu a refusé de signer

REFUSED TO SIGN — [illegible] — [illegible] — [signature]

Inmate - Signature - Détenu — Date — Time - Heure — Witnessing CSC official - Signature - Agent responsable témoin

HEARING OF CHARGE - AUDITION DU CHEF D'ACCUSATION

Plea - Plaidoyer: ☑ Guilty / Coupable ☐ Not guilty / Non coupable ☐ Refused to plea / Refus de plaider

Remanded to - Audition ajournée à: Hour - Heure, Y-A M D-J — 1000 13/01 trial

Reason - Motif: July 27/01 Trial; Aug 21/01 set date; Sept 25/01 set date; Oct 9/01 [illegible] set date

Third party representation requested by inmate / Représentation par un tiers requise par le détenu — Representation - Représentation — Name of representative - Nom du représentant

Copy faxed to ... 30 gu ... D11 18254

K208

Correctional Service Canada | Service correctionnel Canada

PROTECTED / PROTÉGÉE A ☐ B ☐ C ☒ ONCE COMPLETED / UNE FOIS REMPLIE

PERSONAL INFORMATION BANK - FICHIER DE RENSEIGNEMENTS PERSONNELS

INMATE OFFENCE REPORT AND NOTIFICATION OF CHARGE

RAPPORT DE L'INFRACTION D'UN DÉTENU ET AVIS DE L'ACCUSATION

NOTE: Reference document CD 580. NOTA: Document de référence DC 580.

PUT AWAY ON FILE / CLASSER AU DOSSIER — See reverse / Voir au verso

FPS number / Numéro SED: #464Z710

Family name / Nom de famille: THOMAS

Given name(s) / Prénom(s):

Date of birth / Date de naissance:

Institution - Établissement: MILLHAVEN

Resp. Centre Code - Code du centre de resp.: 4210

Location of offence - Lieu de l'infraction: RANGE 2L CELL 208

Date and time of offence / Date et l'heure de l'infraction: Y-A M D-J 2001 06 27 — Time - Heure 00:01

DESCRIPTION OF OFFENCE (including names of witnesses, unusual behaviour of offender, etc.)
DESCRIPTION DE L'INFRACTION (y compris le nom des témoins, comportement inhabituel du délinquant, etc.)

- ON THE ABOVE NOTED DATE, TIME AND PLACE I/m THOMAS COVERED HIS CELL WINDOW. I/m REFUSED DIRECTION FROM THIS OFFICER TO REMOVE WINDOW COVER. THESE ACTIONS DELAYED AND INTERFERE WITH THE 00:01 COUNT.

Date report written / Date de la rédaction du rapport: Y-A M D-J 2001-06-27

Name of witnessing officer - Nom de l'agent témoin: EDWARD HICKS CX I

Signature: [signature]

Physical evidence - Preuve(s): ☐ Yes / Oui ☒ No / Non

If yes, provide a brief description - Dans l'affirmative, fournir une brève description:

Disposition:

Supervisor or officer in charge of the institution advised / Avis donné au surveillant ou à l'agent responsable de l'établ.: ☒ Yes / Oui A/S CROSBIE

Disposition of inmate - Mesure prise à l'égard du détenu: ☐ Admin. seg. / Isolement préventif ☐ Confined to cell / Retenu dans sa cellule ☒ Normal association / Intégration normale

Other witnessing officer - Autre agent témoin: S. KINDERCUK

DECISION TAKEN - DÉCISION PRISE

I have reviewed this report and determine that a charge is warranted under section 40 of the Corrections and Conditional Release Act.
J'ai lu ce rapport et décidé qu'une accusation est justifiée en vertu de l'article 40 de la Loi sur le système correctionnel et la mise en liberté sous condition.

☒ Yes / Oui ☐ No / Non — Signature: [signature] — Position Title - Titre du poste: CCO — Date charge laid / Date l'accusation imposée: Y-A M D-J 01 06 27

Offence category - Catégorie de l'infraction: ☐ Minor / Mineure ☒ Serious / Grave

Referred to - Renvoyé au: ☐ Minor offence court / Tribunal des infractions mineures ☒ Serious offence court / Tribunal des infractions graves

For hearing a charge under Section 40 of the Corrections & Conditional Release Act.
Pour l'audition du chef d'accusation en vertu de l'article 40 de la Loi sur le système correctionnel et la mise en liberté sous condition.
(Specify - Préciser) (See reverse side for offences - Voir la liste d'infractions au verso)
M ii

Proposed date of hearing / Date prévue de l'audition: Hour - Heure 1300 — Y-A M D-J 01 07 10 — Title - Titre: CCO — Signature: [signature]

Delivered to inmate / Transmis au détenu: Hour - Heure 1338 — Y-A M D-J 01 06 29 — Title - Titre: — Signature:

I have been advised of my right to retain and instruct counsel. J'ai été informé de mon droit d'avoir recours aux services d'un avocat.

☒ Inmate refused to sign / Détenu a refusé de signer

Inmate - Signature - Détenu: — Date (Y-A M D-J): 01 06 29 — Time - Heure: 1338 — Witnessing CSC official - Signature - Agent responsable témoin: [signature]

HEARING OF CHARGE - AUDITION DU CHEF D'ACCUSATION

Plea - Plaidoyer: ☒ Guilty / Coupable ☐ Not guilty / Non coupable ☐ Refused to plea / Refus de plaider

Remanded to - Audition ajourné à: Hour - Heure, Y-A M D-J

Reason - Motif: [illegible handwriting]

18479

Correctional Service Canada / Service correctionnel Canada

PROTECTED / PROTÉGÉE A ☐ B ☐ C ☐ ONCE COMPLETED / UNE FOIS REMPLIE

PERSONAL INFORMATION BANK - FICHIER DE RENSEIGNEMENTS PERSONNELS

INMATE OFFENCE REPORT AND NOTIFICATION OF CHARGE / **RAPPORT DE L'INFRACTION D'UN DÉTENU ET AVIS DE L'ACCUSATION**

NOTE: Reference document CD 580. / NOTA: Document de référence DC 580.

PUT AWAY ON FILE / CLASSER AU DOSSIER — See reverse / Voir au verso

Institution - Établissement	MILLHAVEN
Resp. Centre Code - Code du centre de resp.	
Location of offence - Lieu de l'infraction	2K J. UNIT
Date and time of offence / Date et l'heure de l'infraction (Y-A M D-J)	01.07.06
Time - Heure	1530
FPS number / Numéro SED	464271D
Family name / Nom de famille	THOMAS
Given name(s) / Prénom(s)	
Date of birth / Date de naissance	

DESCRIPTION OF OFFENCE (including names of witnesses, unusual behaviour of offender, etc.)
DESCRIPTION DE L'INFRACTION (y compris le nom des témoins, comportement inhabituel du délinquant, etc.)

At 1530 hrs, 6 Jul 01, while attempting to lock up I/m THOMAS, FPS 464271D, he refused to do so. Writer gave I/m THOMAS a direct order. ~~he did not comply~~ to lock up, however he failed to do so.

Date report written / Date de la rédaction du rapport (Y-A M D-J)	01.07.06
Name of witnessing officer - Nom de l'agent témoin	S. Stewart
Signature	[signature]
Physical evidence - Preuve(s)	☐ Yes / Oui ☒ No / Non
If yes, provide a brief description - Dans l'affirmative, fournir une brève description	
Disposition	
Supervisor or officer in charge of the institution advised / Avis donné au surveillant ou à l'agent responsable de l'établ.	☐ Yes / Oui
Disposition of inmate - Mesure prise à l'égard du détenu	☐ Admin. seg. / Isolement préventif ☐ Confined to cell / Retenu dans sa cellule ☒ Normal association / Intégration normale
Other witnessing officer - Autre agent témoin	B. Pond

DECISION TAKEN - DÉCISION PRISE

I have reviewed this report and determine that a charge is warranted under section 40 of the Corrections and Conditional Release Act.
J'ai lu ce rapport et décidé qu'une accusation est justifiée en vertu de l'article 40 de la Loi sur le système correctionnel et la mise en liberté sous condition

☒ Yes / Oui ☐ No / Non	Signature: [signature]
Position Title - Titre du poste	A/CCO
Date charge laid / Date l'accusation imposée (Y-A M D-J)	01 07 09
Offence category - Catégorie de l'infraction	☒ Minor / Mineure ☐ Serious / Grave
Referred to - Renvoyé au	☒ Minor offence court / Tribunal des infractions mineures ☐ Serious offence court / Tribunal des infractions graves
For hearing a charge under Section 40 of the Corrections & Conditional Release Act. / Pour l'audition du chef d'accusation en vertu de l'article 40 de la Loi sur le système correctionnel et la mise en liberté sous condition. (Specify - Préciser) (See reverse side for offences - Voir la liste d'infractions au verso)	40 (a)

	Hour - Heure	Y-A M D-J	Title - Titre	Signature
Proposed date of hearing / Date prévue de l'audition	1330	01 07 16	A/CCO	[signature]
Delivered to inmate / Transmis au détenu	1521	01 07 09	CO1	[signature]

I have been advised of my right to retain and instruct counsel. / J'ai été informé de mon droit d'avoir recours aux services d'un avocat.

☒ Inmate refused to sign / Détenu a refusé de signer

Inmate - Signature - Détenu	Date (Y-A M D-J)	Time - Heure	Witnessing CSC official - Signature - Agent responsable témoin
[signature]	01 07 09	1521	[signature]

HEARING OF CHARGE - AUDITION DU CHEF D'ACCUSATION

Plea - Plaidoyer	☐ Guilty / Coupable ☐ Not guilty / Non coupable ☐ Refused to plea / Refus de plaider
Remanded to - Audition ajourné à	Hour - Heure: Y-A M D-J
Reason - Motif	

Copy faxed to M. McConner 30 July 01 / 8488 DA

OMS

Correctional Service Canada — Service correctionnel Canada

PROTECTED / PROTÉGÉE A ☐ B ☐ C ☒ ONCE COMPLETED / UNE FOIS REMPLIE

PERSONAL INFORMATION BANK - FICHIER DE RENSEIGNEMENTS PERSONNELS

INMATE OFFENCE REPORT AND NOTIFICATION OF CHARGE — **RAPPORT DE L'INFRACTION D'UN DÉTENU ET AVIS DE L'ACCUSATION**

NOTE: Reference document CD 580. — NOTA: Document de référence DC 580.

PUT AWAY ON FILE / CLASSER AU DOSSIER — See reverse / Voir au verso

Institution - Établissement	Millhaven
Resp. Centre Code - Code du centre de resp.	42100
Location of offence - Lieu de l'infraction	2K range.
Date and time of offence / Date et l'heure de l'infraction (Y-A M D-J, Time - Heure)	
FPS number / Numéro SED	464271-D.
Family name / Nom de famille	Thomas.
Given name(s) / Prénom(s)	
Date of birth / Date de naissance	

DESCRIPTION OF OFFENCE (including names of witnesses, unusual behaviour of offender, etc.)
DESCRIPTION DE L'INFRACTION (y compris le nom des témoins, comportement inhabituel du délinquant, etc.)

At 1540 hrs I gave a direct order to I/m Thomas to return to his cell as range activities time was complete as per routine + mayor Inst. Count was to begin. Thomas told me "Fuck off Fredrick" I then repeated direct order and Thomas only laughed + remained on the range. The offender was on 2K-Range. when the above incident happened.

Date report written / Date de la rédaction du rapport (Y-A M D-J)	Name of witnessing officer - Nom de l'agent témoin	Signature
01 07 07	B. Fredrick	[signature]

Physical evidence - Preuve(s): ☐ Yes / Oui ☐ No / Non — If yes, provide a brief description - Dans l'affirmative, fournir une brève description — Disposition

Supervisor or officer in charge of the institution advised / Avis donné au surveillant ou à l'agent responsable de l'établ.: ☒ Yes / Oui

Disposition of inmate - Mesure prise à l'égard du détenu: ☒ Admin. seg. / Isolement préventif ☐ Confined to cell / Retenu dans sa cellule ☐ Normal association / Intégration normale

Other witnessing officer - Autre agent témoin: [signature] Fredenburgh

DECISION TAKEN - DÉCISION PRISE

I have reviewed this report and determine that a charge is warranted under section 40 of the Corrections and Conditional Release Act.
J'ai lu ce rapport et décidé qu'une accusation est justifiée en vertu de l'article 40 de la Loi sur le système correctionnel et la mise en liberté sous condition

☒ Yes / Oui ☐ No / Non — Signature: M Cassidy — Position Title - Titre du poste: A/CCO — Date charge laid / Date d'accusation imposée (Y-A M D-J): 01 07 10

Offence category - Catégorie de l'infraction: ☐ Minor / Mineure ☒ Serious / Grave

Referred to - Renvoyé au: ☐ Minor offence court / Tribunal des infractions mineures ☒ Serious offence court / Tribunal des infractions graves

For hearing a charge under Section 40 of the Corrections & Conditional Release Act. / Pour l'audition du chef d'accusation en vertu de l'article 40 de la Loi sur le système correctionnel et la mise en liberté sous condition. (Specify - Préciser) (See reverse side for offences - Voir la liste d'infractions au verso): 40 (f)

	Hour - Heure	Y-A	M	D-J	Title - Titre	Signature
Proposed date of hearing / Date prévue de l'audition	1330	01	07	17	A/CCO	M Cassidy
Delivered to inmate / Transmis au détenu	1140	01	07	10	CX-01	R Gallimore

I have been advised of my right to retain and instruct counsel. — J'ai été informé de mon droit d'avoir recours aux services d'un avocat.

☒ Inmate refused to sign / Détenu a refusé de signer

x Refused — Inmate - Signature - Détenu — Date (Y-A M D-J): 01 07 10 — Time - Heure: 1140 — Witnessing CSC official - Signature - Agent responsable témoin: R Gallimore

HEARING OF CHARGE - AUDITION DU CHEF D'ACCUSATION

Plea - Plaidoyer: ☐ Guilty / Coupable ☐ Not guilty / Non coupable ☐ Refused to plea / Refus de plaider

Remanded to - Audition ajourné à: Hour - Heure, Y-A M D-J

[illegible] sept 25/01 [illegible]

E(Ilen 18606 PA159

Correctional Service Canada — Service correctionnel Canada

PROTECTED / PROTÉGÉE A ☐ B ☐ C ☐ ONCE COMPLETED / UNE FOIS REMPLIE

PERSONAL INFORMATION BANK - FICHIER DE RENSEIGNEMENTS PERSONNELS

INMATE OFFENCE REPORT AND NOTIFICATION OF CHARGE — **RAPPORT DE L'INFRACTION D'UN DÉTENU ET AVIS DE L'ACCUSATION**

NOTE: Reference document CD 580. — NOTA: Document de référence DC 580.

PUT AWAY ON FILE / CLASSER AU DOSSIER — See reverse / Voir au verso

Institution - Établissement	MI
Resp. Centre Code - Code du centre de resp.	42100
Location of offence - Lieu de l'infraction	K208
Date and time of offence / Date et l'heure de l'infraction (Y-A M D-J)	01 07 11
Time - Heure	1000
FPS number / Numéro SED	464271D
Family name / Nom de famille	Thomas
Given name(s) / Prénom(s)	
Date of birth / Date de naissance	

DESCRIPTION OF OFFENCE (including names of witnesses, unusual behaviour of offender, etc.)
DESCRIPTION DE L'INFRACTION (y compris le nom des témoins, comportement inhabituel du délinquant, etc.)

During the removal of i/m Thomas's personal effects from cell K208 two broken Food trays were removed from thecell

Date report written / Date de la rédaction du rapport (Y-A M D-J)	01 07 11
Name of witnessing officer - Nom de l'agent témoin	coll Vella
Signature	[signature]
Physical evidence - Preuve(s)	☑ Yes / Oui ☐ No / Non
If yes, provide a brief description - Dans l'affirmative, fournir une brève description	Broken Trays
Disposition	IPSO
Supervisor or officer in charge of the institution advised / Avis donné au surveillant ou à l'agent responsable de l'étab.	☑ Yes / Oui
Disposition of inmate - Mesure prise à l'égard du détenu	☑ Admin. seg. / Isolement préventif ☐ Confined to cell / Retenu dans sa cellule ☐ Normal association / Intégration normale
Other witnessing officer - Autre agent témoin	coll Korosi

DECISION TAKEN - DÉCISION PRISE

I have reviewed this report and determine that a charge is warranted under section 40 of the Corrections and Conditional Release Act.
J'ai lu ce rapport et décidé qu'une accusation est justifiée en vertu de l'article 40 de la Loi sur le système correctionnel et la mise en liberté sous condition

☑ Yes / Oui ☐ No / Non — Signature	R.G. Deslauriers
Position Title - Titre du poste	IPSO
Date charge laid / Date l'accusation imposée (Y-A M D-J)	01 07 12
Offence category - Catégorie de l'infraction	☑ Minor / Mineure ☐ Serious / Grave
Referred to - Renvoyé au	☑ Minor offence court / Tribunal des infractions mineures ☐ Serious offence court / Tribunal des infractions graves
For hearing a charge under Section 40 of the Corrections & Conditional Release Act. / Pour l'audition du chef d'accusation en vertu de l'article 40 de la Loi sur le système correctionnel et la mise en liberté sous condition. (Specify - Préciser) (See reverse side for offences - Voir la liste d'infractions au verso)	"C"
Proposed date of hearing / Date prévue de l'audition — Hour - Heure	1000
Y-A M D-J	01 07 24
Title - Titre	IPSO
Signature	R.G. Deslauriers
Delivered to inmate / Transmis au détenu — Hour - Heure	0909
Y-A M D-J	01 07 13
Title - Titre	CO1
Signature	[signature]

I have been advised of my right to retain and instruct counsel. — J'ai été informé de mon droit d'avoir recours aux services d'un avocat.

☑ Inmate refused to sign / Détenu a refusé de signer

Inmate - Signature - Détenu	Date (Y-A M D-J)	Time - Heure	Witnessing CSC official - Signature - Agent responsable témoin
	010713	0907	[signature]

HEARING OF CHARGE - AUDITION DU CHEF D'ACCUSATION

Plea - Plaidoyer	Remanded to - Audition ajourné à
☐ Guilty / Coupable ☐ Not guilty / Non coupable ☐ Refused to plea / Refus de plaider	Hour - Heure / Y-A M D-J

Reason - Motif

DA 18697 ECAI2

Correctional Service Canada / Service correctionnel Canada

PROTECTED / PROTÉGÉE A ☐ B ☒ C ☐ ONCE COMPLETED / UNE FOIS REMPLIE

PERSONAL INFORMATION BANK - FICHIER DE RENSEIGNEMENTS PERSONNELS

INMATE OFFENCE REPORT AND NOTIFICATION OF CHARGE / **RAPPORT DE L'INFRACTION D'UN DÉTENU ET AVIS DE L'ACCUSATION**

NOTE: Reference document CD 580. / NOTA: Document de référence DC 580.

PUT AWAY ON FILE / CLASSER AU DOSSIER — See reverse / Voir au verso

Institution - Établissement: MILLHAVEN
Resp. Centre Code - Code du centre de resp.: 421D

FPS number / Numéro SED: 464271D
Family name / Nom de famille: THOMAS
Given name(s) / Prénom(s):
Date of birth / Date de naissance:

Location of offence - Lieu de l'infraction: SEGREGATION

Date and time of offence / Date et l'heure de l'infraction: 2001/07/16 09:30

DESCRIPTION OF OFFENCE (including names of witnesses, unusual behaviour of offender, etc.)
DESCRIPTION DE L'INFRACTION (y compris le nom des témoins, comportement inhabituel du délinquant, etc.)

On the above noted date and time, while searching the personal effects of inmate THOMAS [illegible] prior to returning them to his possession, this officer found two (2) home-made weapons. The first weapon was knife-like in appearance, approx. 19cm long [redacted] The second weapon was also knife-like, [redacted] approx. 22cm long and partially sharpened. [redacted]

Date report written / Date de la rédaction du rapport: 2001/07/16
Name of witnessing officer - Nom de l'agent témoin: JOHN PELKEY
Signature: [signature]

Physical evidence - Preuve(s): ☒ Yes / Oui ☐ No / Non
If yes, provide a brief description - Dans l'affirmative, fournir une brève description: 2 Knife-Like Home-made weapons
Disposition: 2001-186+187 C.S-DOERING

Supervisor or officer in charge of the institution advised / Avis donné au surveillant ou à l'agent responsable de l'établ.: ☒ Yes / Oui

Disposition of inmate - Mesure prise à l'égard du détenu: ☐ Admin. seg. / Isolement préventif ☐ Confined to cell / Retenu dans sa cellule ☐ Normal association / Intégration normale

Other witnessing officer - Autre agent témoin: FRED GILCHRIST

DECISION TAKEN - DÉCISION PRISE

I have reviewed this report and determine that a charge is warranted under section 40 of the Corrections and Conditional Release Act.
J'ai lu ce rapport et décidé qu'une accusation est justifiée en vertu de l'article 40 de la Loi sur le système correctionnel et la mise en liberté sous condition

☑ Yes / Oui ☐ No / Non — Signature: [signature] — Position Title - Titre du poste: CCO

Date charge laid / Date l'accusation imposée: 01 07 17

Offence category - Catégorie de l'infraction: ☐ Minor / Mineure ☑ Serious / Grave

Referred to - Renvoyé au: ☐ Minor offence court / Tribunal des infractions mineures ☑ Serious offence court / Tribunal des infractions graves

For hearing a charge under Section 40 of the Corrections & Conditional Release Act. / Pour l'audition du chef d'accusation en vertu de l'article 40 de la Loi sur le système correctionnel et la mise en liberté sous condition. (Specify - Préciser) (See reverse side for offences - Voir la liste d'infractions au verso): (i)

	Hour - Heure	Y-A M D-J	Title - Titre	Signature
Proposed date of hearing / Date prévue de l'audition	1300	01 07 24	C CO	[signature]
Delivered to inmate / Transmis au détenu	1920	01 07 17	CX2	K Kane

I have been advised of my right to retain and instruct counsel. / J'ai été informé de mon droit d'avoir recours aux services d'un avocat.

☒ Inmate refused to sign / Détenu a refusé de signer

Inmate - Signature - Détenu	Date	Time - Heure	Witnessing CSC official - Signature - agent témoin
	01 07 17	1920	[signature] [redacted]

HEARING OF CHARGE - AUDITION DU CHEF D'ACCUSATION

Plea - Plaidoyer: ☑ Guilty / Coupable ☐ Not guilty / Non coupable ☐ Refused to plea / Refus de plaider

Remanded to - Audition ajourné à: Hour - Heure / Y-A M D-J

Aug 21/01, TBA (pending L.A.) || Oct 9/01, [illegible]

DIY 9083

OMS

Correctional Service Canada — Service correctionnel Canada

PROTÉGÉ / PROTÉGÉE A ☐ B ☒ C ☐ ONCE COMPLETED / UNE FOIS REMPLIE

PERSONAL INFORMATION BANK - FICHIER DE RENSEIGNEMENTS PERSONNELS

INMATE OFFENCE REPORT AND NOTIFICATION OF CHARGE — **RAPPORT DE L'INFRACTION D'UN DÉTENU ET AVIS DE L'ACCUSATION**

NOTE: Reference document CD 580. — NOTA: Document de référence DC 580.

PUT AWAY ON FILE / CLASSER AU DOSSIER — See reverse / Voir au verso

Institution - Établissement	MILLHAVEN INST.
Resp. Centre Code - Code du centre de resp.	4216
Location of offence - Lieu de l'infraction	SEGREGATION
Date and time of offence / Date et l'heure de l'infraction (Y-A M D-J; Time - Heure)	01 07 30; 13:20
FPS number / Numéro SED	464271D
Family name / Nom de famille	THOMAS (ECA#12)
Given name(s) / Prénom(s)	
Date of birth / Date de naissance	

DESCRIPTION OF OFFENCE (including names of witnesses, unusual behaviour of offender, etc.)
DESCRIPTION DE L'INFRACTION (y compris le nom des témoins, comportement inhabituel du délinquant, etc.)

On the above date and approximate time, while collecting trays after lunch feeding, I/m THOMAS did try to pass a bag of orange liquid to I/m [redacted] through the food slot. There was approximately 2 litres of liquid in the bag, which tested positive for alcohol.

SUBSTANCE TESTING

The substance was tested in accordance with the established and approved procedures.

Tested positive for: Homemade Alcohol
Received From: CX1 Gallimore
Received by: CS Crosbie
Date: July 30/01 Time: 13 25
Tested by: C/S Crosbie
Date: July 30/01 Time: 13 26

Date report written / Date de la rédaction du rapport (Y-A M D-J)	01 07 30
Name of witnessing officer - Nom de l'agent témoin	GALLIMORE CX 01
Signature	[signature]
Physical evidence - Preuve(s)	☒ Yes / Oui ☐ No / Non
If yes, provide a brief description - Dans l'affirmative, fournir une brève description	
Disposition	421-2001-202
Supervisor or officer in charge of the institution advised / Avis donné au surveillant ou à l'agent responsable de l'établ.	☒ Yes / Oui
Disposition of inmate - Mesure prise à l'égard du détenu	☒ Admin. seg. / Isolement préventif ☐ Confined to cell / Retenu dans sa cellule ☐ Normal association / Intégration normale
Other witnessing officer - Autre agent témoin	CX-01 J. PELKEY

DECISION TAKEN - DÉCISION PRISE

I have reviewed this report and determine that a charge is warranted under section 40 of the Corrections and Conditional Release Act.
J'ai lu ce rapport et décidé qu'une accusation est justifiée en vertu de l'article 40 de la Loi sur le système correctionnel et la mise en liberté sous condition

☐ Yes / Oui ☐ No / Non — Signature	[signature]
Position Title - Titre du poste	C.S.O
Date charge laid / Date l'accusation imposée (Y-A M D-J)	01 08 02
Offence category - Catégorie de l'infraction	☐ Minor / Mineure ☒ Serious / Grave
Referred to - Renvoyé au	☐ Minor offence court / Tribunal des infractions mineures ☒ Serious offence court / Tribunal des infractions graves
For hearing a charge under Section 40 of the Corrections & Conditional Release Act. / Pour l'audition du chef d'accusation en vertu de l'article 40 de la Loi sur le système correctionnel et la mise en liberté sous condition. (Specify - Préciser) (See reverse side for offences - Voir la liste d'infractions au verso)	(i) 26
Proposed date of hearing / Date prévue de l'audition (Hour - Heure; Y-A M D-J)	1200; 01 08 07
Title - Titre	CCO
Delivered to inmate / Transmis au détenu (Hour - Heure; Y-A M D-J; Title - Titre; Signature)	

I have been advised of my right to retain and instruct counsel. — J'ai été informé de mon droit d'avoir recours aux services d'un avocat.

☒ Inmate refused to sign / Détenu a refusé de signer

Inmate - Signature - Détenu	Date (Y-A M D-J)	Time - Heure	Witnessing CSC official - Signature - Agent responsable témoin
	01 07 31	11:45	[signature]

HEARING OF CHARGE - AUDITION DU CHEF D'ACCUSATION

Plea - Plaidoyer: ☐ Guilty / Coupable ☒ Not guilty / Non coupable ☐ Refused to plea / Refus de plaider

Remanded to - Audition ajourné à: Hour - Heure; Y-A M D-J

Reason - Motif: AUG 21/01 PdC. Oct 9/01 next set date

Correctional Service Canada

INMATE OFFENCE REPORT AND NOTIFICATION OF CHARGE

NOTE: Reference document CD 580.

SUBSTANCE TEST: The substance was tested in accordance with the established and approved procedures.
Tested positive for: ALCOHOL
Received From: JOHN PELKEY
Received by: C.S. CROSBIE
Date: 2001/08/06 Time: 10:16
Tested by: J. CROSBIE
Date: 2001/08/07 Time: 13:52

19143

B ☒ C ☐ ONCE COMPLETED / UNE FOIS REMPLIE

FICHIER DE RENSEIGNEMENTS PERSONNELS — See reverse / Voir au verso

42710

THOMAS

Institution - Établissement: MILLHAVEN

Location of offence - Lieu de l'infraction: ECA CELL #12 42100

Given name(s) / Prénom(s):

Date and time of offence / Date et l'heure de l'infraction: 2001 08 06 — Time - Heure: 10:06

Date of birth / Date de naissance:

DESCRIPTION OF OFFENCE (including names of witnesses, unusual behaviour of offender, etc.)
DESCRIPTION DE L'INFRACTION (y compris le nom des témoins, comportement inhabituel du délinquant, etc.)

On the above date at approximately 10:06 hrs. this officer found a clear plastic bottle approximately one liter in size containing an orange liquid which had a smell consistent with that of alcohol. Upon testing said liquid proved to be alcohol. See test documentation. OSOR + POST SEARCH Attached.

Date report written / Date de la rédaction du rapport: 2001/08/06
Name of witnessing officer - Nom de l'agent témoin: JOHN PELKEY
Signature:

Physical evidence - Preuve(s): ☒ Yes/Oui ☐ No/Non
If yes, provide a brief description - Dans l'affirmative, fournir une brève description: Sample Taken for Testing
Disposition: 421-2001-210 Sample Retained, balance destroyed

Supervisor or officer in charge of the institution advised / Avis donné au surveillant ou à l'agent responsable de l'établ.: ☐ Yes/Oui
Disposition of inmate - Mesure prise à l'égard du détenu: ☒ Admin. seg. / Isolement préventif ☐ Confined to cell / Retenu dans sa cellule ☐ Normal association / Intégration normale
Other witnessing officer - Autre agent témoin: T.A. BONNIER

DECISION TAKEN - DÉCISION PRISE

I have reviewed this report and determine that a charge is warranted under section 40 of the Corrections and Conditional Release Act.
J'ai lu ce rapport et décidé qu'une accusation est justifiée en vertu de l'article 40 de la Loi sur le système correctionnel et la mise en liberté sous condition

☒ Yes/Oui ☐ No/Non Signature: [signature]
Position Title - Titre du poste: A/CCo
Date charge laid / Date l'accusation imposée: 01 08 07

Offence category - Catégorie de l'infraction: ☐ Minor/Mineure ☒ Serious/Grave
Referred to - Renvoyé au: ☐ Minor offence court / Tribunal des infractions mineures ☒ Serious offence court / Tribunal des infractions graves
For hearing a charge under Section 40 of the Corrections & Conditional Release Act. Pour l'audition du chef d'accusation en vertu de l'article 40 de la Loi sur le système correctionnel et la mise en liberté sous condition. (Specify - Préciser) (See reverse side for offences - Voir la liste d'infractions au verso): 40 (i)

Proposed date of hearing / Date prévue de l'audition: Hour - Heure 1330; Y-A 01 M 08 D-J 14; Title - Titre: A/CCo; Signature: [signature]

Delivered to inmate / Transmis au détenu: Hour - Heure 21:15; 01 08 09; Title - Titre: CX 1; Signature: Denison

I have been advised of my right to retain and instruct counsel. / J'ai été informé de mon droit d'avoir recours aux services d'un avocat.

Y-A M D-J ☐ Inmate refused to sign / Détenu a refusé de signer

Inmate - Signature - Détenu | Date | Time - Heure | Witnessing CSC official - Signature - Agent responsable témoin

HEARING OF CHARGE - AUDITION DU CHEF D'ACCUSATION

Plea - Plaidoyer: ☒ Guilty/Coupable ☐ Not guilty/Non coupable ☐ Refused to plea/Refus de plaider
Remanded to - Audition ajourné à: Hour - Heure / Y-A / M / D-J

Reason - Motif: [illegible]

Faxed to Mr. O'Connor as OCC DA

19387

Correctional Service Canada / Service correctionnel Canada

PROTECTED / PROTÉGÉE A ☐ B ☐ C ☒ ONCE COMPLETED / UNE FOIS REMPLIE

PERSONAL INFORMATION BANK - FICHIER DE RENSEIGNEMENTS PERSONNELS

INMATE OFFENCE REPORT AND NOTIFICATION OF CHARGE / **RAPPORT DE L'INFRACTION D'UN DÉTENU ET AVIS DE L'ACCUSATION**

NOTE: Reference document CD 580. / NOTA: Document de référence DC 580.

PUT AWAY ON FILE / CLASSER AU DOSSIER — See reverse / Voir au verso

Institution - Établissement	MILLHAVEN
Resp. Centre Code - Code du centre de resp.	42112
Location of offence - Lieu de l'infraction	V+C
Date and time of offence / Date et l'heure de l'infraction (Y-A M D-J, Time - Heure)	01 08 18 1450
FPS number / Numéro SED	464271D
Family name / Nom de famille	THOMAS
Given name(s) / Prénom(s)	SHANE
Date of birth / Date de naissance	

DESCRIPTION OF OFFENCE (including names of witnesses, unusual behaviour of offender, etc.)
DESCRIPTION DE L'INFRACTION (y compris le nom des témoins, comportement inhabituel du délinquant, etc.)

At approximately 1450 hrs while clearing the open visits I found a package of cigarettes and lighter on the above inmate. When informed that they were not going back with him he become very abusive to me verbally and extremely threatening. He had to be ordered out of V+C area several times. He was escorted by several officers to C.C.A.

Date report written / Date de la rédaction du rapport (Y-A M D-J)	01 08 18
Name of witnessing officer - Nom de l'agent témoin	R. E. GOODWIN
Signature	R.E. Good...
Physical evidence - Preuve(s)	☒ Yes / Oui ☐ No / Non
If yes, provide a brief description - Dans l'affirmative, fournir une brève description	ONE DISPOSABLE LIGHTER; 18 EXPORT A CIGARETTES
Disposition	CONFISCATED AND TURNED IN AS EVIDENCE
Supervisor or officer in charge of the institution advised / Avis donné au surveillant ou à l'agent responsable de l'établ.	☐ Yes / Oui
Disposition of inmate - Mesure prise à l'égard du détenu	☐ Admin. seg. / Isolement préventif ☐ Confined to cell / Retenu dans sa cellule ☐ Normal association / Intégration normale
Other witnessing officer - Autre agent témoin	OTIS SACREY

DECISION TAKEN - DÉCISION PRISE

I have reviewed this report and determine that a charge is warranted under section 40 of the Corrections and Conditional Release Act.
J'ai lu ce rapport et décidé qu'une accusation est justifiée en vertu de l'article 40 de la Loi sur le système correctionnel et la mise en liberté sous condition

☒ Yes / Oui ☐ No / Non	Signature: [signature]
Position Title - Titre du poste	CCO
Date charge laid / Date l'accusation imposée (Y-A M D-J)	01 08 20
Offence category - Catégorie de l'infraction	☐ Minor / Mineure ☒ Serious / Grave
Referred to - Renvoyé au	☐ Minor offence court / Tribunal des infractions mineures ☒ Serious offence court / Tribunal des infractions graves
For hearing a charge under Section 40 of the Corrections & Conditional Release Act. / Pour l'audition du chef d'accusation en vertu de l'article 40 de la Loi sur le système correctionnel et la mise en liberté sous condition. (Specify - Préciser) (See reverse side for offences - Voir la liste d'infractions au verso)	F
Proposed date of hearing / Date prévue de l'audition (Hour - Heure, Y-A M D-J)	1300 01 08 28
Title - Titre	CCO
Delivered to inmate / Transmis au détenu (Hour - Heure, Y-A M D-J)	2215 01 08 20
Title - Titre	CS

I have been advised of my right to retain and instruct counsel. / J'ai été informé de mon droit d'avoir recours aux services d'un avocat.

☒ Inmate refused to sign / Détenu a refusé de signer

Inmate - Signature - Détenu	Date (Y-A M D-J)	Time - Heure	Witnessing CSC official - Signature - Agent responsable témoin
	01 08 20	2215	[signature]

HEARING OF CHARGE - AUDITION DU CHEF D'ACCUSATION

Plea - Plaidoyer: ☒ Guilty / Coupable ☐ Not guilty / Non coupable ☐ Refused to plea / Refus de plaider

Remanded to - Audition ajourné à: Hour - Heure, Y-A M D-J

Reason - Motif: Sept 25/01 (T30?) ... NOV 13/01 ...

Correctional Service Canada — Service correctionnel Canada

PROTECTED / PROTÉGÉE A ☐ B ☒ C ☐ ONCE COMPLETED / UNE FOIS REMPLIE

PERSONAL INFORMATION BANK - FICHIER DE RENSEIGNEMENTS PERSONNELS

INMATE OFFENCE REPORT AND NOTIFICATION OF CHARGE — **RAPPORT DE L'INFRACTION D'UN DÉTENU ET AVIS DE L'ACCUSATION**

NOTE: Reference document CD 580. — NOTA: Document de référence DC 580.

PUT AWAY ON FILE / CLASSER AU DOSSIER — See reverse / Voir au verso

Institution - Établissement: MI — Resp. Centre Code - Code du centre de resp.: 421D

FPS number / Numéro SED: 464271D

Family name / Nom de famille: THOMAS

Given name(s) / Prénom(s):

Location of offence - Lieu de l'infraction: S. Central Area

Date and time of offence / Date et l'heure de l'infraction: Y-A M D-J 01-09-04 Time - Heure 1800

Date of birth / Date de naissance:

DESCRIPTION OF OFFENCE (including names of witnesses, unusual behaviour of offender, etc.)
DESCRIPTION DE L'INFRACTION (y compris le nom des témoins, comportement inhabituel du délinquant, etc.)

On the above date + approx. time this Officer intercepted an object thrown by I/M THOMAS from S. central barrier to the yard barrier. Object wrapped in a sock was an approx. 8" homemade ICE Pick.

421-2001-270

Date report written / Date de la rédaction du rapport: 01-09-04 — Name of witnessing officer - Nom de l'agent témoin: L.C. LEMAIRE — Signature: L.C. Lemaire CXI

Physical evidence - Preuve(s): ☒ Yes / Oui ☐ No / Non — If yes, provide a brief description - Dans l'affirmative, fournir une brève description: Approx. 8" homemade ICE Pick — Disposition: IPSC Locker #2

Supervisor or officer in charge of the institution advised / Avis donné au surveillant ou à l'agent responsable de l'établ.: ☒ Yes / Oui

Disposition of inmate - Mesure prise à l'égard du détenu: ☒ Admin. seg. / Isolement préventif ☐ Confined to cell / Retenu dans sa cellule ☐ Normal association / Intégration normale

Other witnessing officer - Autre agent témoin: A. Wilson

DECISION TAKEN - DÉCISION PRISE

I have reviewed this report and determine that a charge is warranted under section 40 of the Corrections and Conditional Release Act. / J'ai lu ce rapport et décidé qu'une accusation est justifiée en vertu de l'article 40 de la Loi sur le système correctionnel et la mise en liberté sous condition.

☒ Yes / Oui ☐ No / Non — Signature: [signature] — Position Title - Titre du poste: CCO — Date charge laid / Date l'accusation imposée: 01 09 05

Offence category - Catégorie de l'infraction: ☐ Minor / Mineure ☒ Serious / Grave

Referred to - Renvoyé au: ☐ Minor offence court / Tribunal des infractions mineures ☒ Serious offence court / Tribunal des infractions graves

For hearing a charge under Section 40 of the Corrections & Conditional Release Act. / Pour l'audition du chef d'accusation en vertu de l'article 40 de la Loi sur le système correctionnel et la mise en liberté sous condition. (Specify - Préciser) (See reverse side for offences - Voir la liste d'infractions au verso): (i)

	Hour - Heure	Y-A	M	D-J	Title - Titre	Signature
Proposed date of hearing / Date prévue de l'audition	1300	01	09	12	CCO	[signature]
Delivered to inmate / Transmis au détenu	1345	01	09	07	CX1	R. Marshall

I have been advised of my right to retain and instruct counsel. — J'ai été informé de mon droit d'avoir recours aux services d'un avocat.

☒ Inmate refused to sign / Détenu a refusé de signer

Inmate - Signature - Détenu	Date (Y-A M D-J)	Time - Heure	Witnessing CSC official - Signature - Agent responsable témoin
	01 09 07	1345	R. Marshall

HEARING OF CHARGE - AUDITION DU CHEF D'ACCUSATION

Plea - Plaidoyer: ☒ Guilty / Coupable ☐ Not guilty / Non coupable ☐ Refused to plea / Refus de plaider

Remanded to - Audition ajourné à: Hour - Heure / Y-A / M / D-J

Reason - Motif: Sept 25/01 TBA ... Oct 30/01, prompt set date ... Oct 11/01 set date ... Dec 11/01 ...

Third party representation requested by inmate / Représentation par un tiers requise par le détenu — Representation - Représentation — Name of representative - Nom du représentant

Correctional Service Canada — Service correctionnel Canada

200218

PROTECTED / PROTÉGÉE A ☐ B ☒ C ☐ ONCE COMPLETED / UNE FOIS REMPLIE

PERSONAL INFORMATION BANK - FICHIER DE RENSEIGNEMENTS PERSONNELS

INMATE OFFENCE REPORT AND NOTIFICATION OF CHARGE — **RAPPORT DE L'INFRACTION D'UN DÉTENU ET AVIS DE L'ACCUSATION**

NOTE: Reference document CD 580. — NOTA: Document de référence DC 580.

PUT AWAY ON FILE / CLASSER AU DOSSIER — See reverse / Voir au verso

Institution - Établissement	MILLHAVEN
Resp. Centre Code - Code du centre de resp.	92100
Location of offence - Lieu de l'infraction	J-UNIT 2K.
Date and time of offence / Date et l'heure de l'infraction (Y-A M D-J; Time - Heure)	01 09 17 — 1345
FPS number / Numéro SED	464271D
Family name / Nom de famille	THOMAS
Given name(s) / Prénom(s)	
Date of birth / Date de naissance	

DESCRIPTION OF OFFENCE (including names of witnesses, unusual behaviour of offender, etc.)
DESCRIPTION DE L'INFRACTION (y compris le nom des témoins, comportement inhabituel du délinquant, etc.)

UPON HIS RETURN FROM AN INTERVIEW AT "N" AREA THOMAS WENT TO HIS RANGE, TOOK SOMETHING UNKNOWN FROM ANOTHER OFFENDER AND LEFT THE RANGE. I GAVE HIM CLEAR DIRECTION TO RETURN TO HIS RANGE AND WAS IGNORED.

Date report written / Date de la rédaction du rapport (Y-A M D-J)	01 09 17
Name of witnessing officer - Nom de l'agent témoin	BRAD SULLIVAN CX1
Signature	B. Sullivan
Physical evidence - Preuve(s)	☐ Yes / Oui ☑ No / Non
If yes, provide a brief description - Dans l'affirmative, fournir une brève description	
Disposition	
Supervisor or officer in charge of the institution advised / Avis donné au surveillant ou à l'agent responsable de l'établ.	☑ Yes / Oui
Disposition of inmate - Mesure prise à l'égard du détenu	☐ Admin. seg. / Isolement préventif ☐ Confined to cell / Retenu dans sa cellule ☑ Normal association / Intégration normale
Other witnessing officer - Autre agent témoin	G. Daniels

DECISION TAKEN - DÉCISION PRISE

I have reviewed this report and determine that a charge is warranted under section 40 of the Corrections and Conditional Release Act.
J'ai lu ce rapport et décidé qu'une accusation est justifiée en vertu de l'article 40 de la Loi sur le système correctionnel et la mise en liberté sous condition

☑ Yes / Oui ☐ No / Non — Signature	[signature]
Position Title - Titre du poste	CCO
Date charge laid / Date l'accusation imposée (Y-A M D-J)	01 09 18
Offence category - Catégorie de l'infraction	☑ Minor / Mineure ☐ Serious / Grave
Referred to - Renvoyé au	☑ Minor offence court / Tribunal des infractions mineures ☐ Serious offence court / Tribunal des infractions graves
For hearing a charge under Section 40 of the Corrections & Conditional Release Act. / Pour l'audition du chef d'accusation en vertu de l'article 40 de la Loi sur le système correctionnel et la mise en liberté sous condition. (Specify - Préciser) (See reverse side for offences - Voir la liste d'infractions au verso)	R

	Hour - Heure	Y-A M D-J	Title - Titre	Signature
Proposed date of hearing / Date prévue de l'audition	1000	01 09 20	CCO	[signature]
Delivered to inmate / Transmis au détenu	1200	01 09 19	CX	C. Campbell

I have been advised of my right to retain and instruct counsel. — J'ai été informé de mon droit d'avoir recours aux services d'un avocat.

Y-A M D-J ☐ Inmate refused to sign / Détenu a refusé de signer

Inmate - Signature - Détenu — Date — Time - Heure — Witnessing CSC official - Signature - Agent responsable témoin

HEARING OF CHARGE - AUDITION DU CHEF D'ACCUSATION

Plea - Plaidoyer: ☐ Guilty / Coupable ☐ Not guilty / Non coupable ☐ Refused to plea / Refus de plaider

Remanded to - Audition ajourné à: Hour - Heure — Y-A M D-J

Reason - Motif

Name of representative - Nom du représentant

25 Oct 01 DA 20516 K221

Correctional Service Canada — Service correctionnel Canada

PROTECTED / PROTÉGÉE A ☐ B ☒ C ☐ ONCE COMPLETED / UNE FOIS REMPLIE

PERSONAL INFORMATION BANK - FICHIER DE RENSEIGNEMENTS PERSONNELS

INMATE OFFENCE REPORT AND NOTIFICATION OF CHARGE — **RAPPORT DE L'INFRACTION D'UN DÉTENU ET AVIS DE L'ACCUSATION**

NOTE: Reference document CD 580. — NOTA: Document de référence DC 580.

PUT AWAY ON FILE / CLASSER AU DOSSIER — See reverse / Voir au verso

Institution - Établissement	MILLHAVEN
Resp. Centre Code - Code du centre de resp.	42180
Location of offence - Lieu de l'infraction	J-UNIT K227
Date and time of offence / Date et l'heure de l'infraction (Y-A M D-J, Time - Heure)	01 10 03 17:10
FPS number / Numéro SED	464271D
Family name / Nom de famille	THOMAS
Given name(s) / Prénom(s)	
Date of birth / Date de naissance	

DESCRIPTION OF OFFENCE (including names of witnesses, unusual behaviour of offender, etc.)
DESCRIPTION DE L'INFRACTION (y compris le nom des témoins, comportement inhabituel du délinquant, etc.)

At the above date and approx. time a piece of plexiglass approx. 3 inches wide and 9 inches long with a point at one end, was found hidden [redacted] in cell K227. Inmate Thomas's cell

421-2001-289

Date report written / Date de la rédaction du rapport (Y-A M D-J)	Name of witnessing officer - Nom de l'agent témoin	Signature
01 10 03	M. MONTGOMERY	[signature]

Physical evidence - Preuve(s)	If yes, provide a brief description - Dans l'affirmative, fournir une brève description	Disposition
☒ Yes / Oui ☐ No / Non	3"x9" plexiglass	IPSO LOCKER

Supervisor or officer in charge of the institution advised / Avis donné au surveillant ou à l'agent responsable de l'établ.	Disposition of inmate - Mesure prise à l'égard du détenu	Other witnessing officer - Autre agent témoin
☒ Yes / Oui	☐ Admin. seg. / Isolement préventif ☐ Confined to cell / Retenu dans sa cellule ☒ Normal association / Intégration normale	L. McMillan

DECISION TAKEN - DÉCISION PRISE

I have reviewed this report and determine that a charge is warranted under section 40 of the Corrections and Conditional Release Act.
J'ai lu ce rapport et décidé qu'une accusation est justifiée en vertu de l'article 40 de la Loi sur le système correctionnel et la mise en liberté sous condition

	Signature	Position Title - Titre du poste	Date charge laid / Date l'accusation imposée (Y-A M D-J)
☒ Yes / Oui ☐ No / Non	[signature]	A/CCO	01 10 04

Offence category - Catégorie de l'infraction	Referred to - Renvoyé au	For hearing a charge Under Section 40 of the Corrections & Conditional Release Act. / Pour l'audition du chef d'accusation en vertu de l'article 40 de la Loi sur le système correctionnel et la mise en liberté sous condition. (Specify - Préciser) (See reverse side for offences - Voir la liste d'infractions au verso)
☐ Minor / Mineure ☒ Serious / Grave	☐ Minor offence court / Tribunal des infractions mineures ☒ Serious offence court / Tribunal des infractions graves	i

	Hour - Heure	Y-A M D-J	Title - Titre	Signature
Proposed date of hearing / Date prévue de l'audition	1300	01 10 16	A/CCO	[signature]
Delivered to inmate / Transmis au détenu	21:00	01 10 05	CO II	[signature]

I have been advised of my right to retain and instruct counsel. — J'ai été informé de mon droit d'avoir recours aux services d'un avocat.

☒ Inmate refused to sign / Détenu a refusé de signer

Inmate - Signature - Détenu	Date (Y-A M D-J)	Time - Heure	Witnessing CSC official - Signature - Agent responsable témoin
	01 10 05	21:00	[signature]

HEARING OF CHARGE - AUDITION DU CHEF D'ACCUSATION

Plea - Plaidoyer	Remanded to - Audition ajourné à (Hour - Heure, Y-A M D-J)
☒ Guilty / Coupable ☐ Not guilty / Non coupable ☐ Refused to plea / Refus de plaider	

Reason - Motif [illegible]

22(1)(e)

20606 ...

Correctional Service Canada | Service correctionnel Canada

PROTECTED / PROTÉGÉE A ☐ B ☐ C ☐ ONCE COMPLETED / UNE FOIS REMPLIE

PERSONAL INFORMATION BANK - FICHIER DE RENSEIGNEMENTS PERSONNELS

INMATE OFFENCE REPORT AND NOTIFICATION OF CHARGE | RAPPORT DE L'INFRACTION D'UN DÉTENU ET AVIS DE L'ACCUSATION

NOTE: Reference document CD 580. | NOTA: Document de référence DC 580.

PUT AWAY ON FILE / CLASSER AU DOSSIER — See reverse / Voir au verso

Institution - Établissement	Millhaven
Resp. Centre Code - Code du centre de resp.	
Location of offence / Lieu de l'infraction	J-Unit
Date and time of offence / Date et l'heure de l'infraction (Y-A M D-J, Time - Heure)	01 10 09 18:25
FPS number / Numéro SED	464271D
Family name / Nom de famille	THOMAS
Given name(s) / Prénom(s)	
Date of birth / Date de naissance	

DESCRIPTION OF OFFENCE (including names of witnesses, unusual behaviour of offender, etc.)
DESCRIPTION DE L'INFRACTION (y compris le nom des témoins, comportement inhabituel du délinquant, etc.)

On the above date and time, J-Unit was returning from yard. Range Two K returned from yard at 18:15 hrs, followed by range 2M at 18:20 hrs. At 18:25 hours, inmate THOMAS returned to the unit from yard to proceed to his cell on range Two K.

Date report written / Date de la rédaction du rapport (Y-A M D-J)	01 10 09
Name of witnessing officer - Nom de l'agent témoin	J. Marcotte
Signature	[signature]
Physical evidence / Preuve(s)	☐ Yes/Oui ☒ No/Non
If yes, provide a brief description - Dans l'affirmative, fournir une brève description	N/A
Disposition	N/A
Supervisor or officer in charge of the institution advised / Avis donné au surveillant ou à l'agent responsable de l'établ.	☒ Yes/Oui
Disposition of inmate - Mesure prise à l'égard du détenu	☐ Admin. seg. / Isolement préventif ☐ Confined to cell / Retenu dans sa cellule ☒ Normal association / Intégration normale
Other witnessing officer - Autre agent témoin	T. WRIGHT

DECISION TAKEN - DÉCISION PRISE

I have reviewed this report and determine that a charge is warranted under section 40 of the Corrections and Conditional Release Act.
J'ai lu ce rapport et décidé qu'une accusation est justifiée en vertu de l'article 40 de la Loi sur le système correctionnel et la mise en liberté sous condition.

☒ Yes/Oui ☐ No/Non — Signature [signature] — Position Title - Titre du poste: A/CCO — Date charge laid / Date l'accusation imposée (Y-A M D-J): 01 10 10

Offence category / Catégorie de l'infraction: ☒ Minor/Mineure ☐ Serious/Grave

Referred to - Renvoyé au: ☒ Minor offence court / Tribunal des infractions mineures ☐ Serious offence court / Tribunal des infractions graves

For hearing a charge under Section 40 of the Corrections & Conditional Release Act. Pour l'audition du chef d'accusation en vertu de l'article 40 de la Loi sur le système correctionnel et la mise en liberté sous condition. (Specify - Préciser) (See reverse side for offences - Voir la liste d'infractions au verso): R

	Hour - Heure	Y-A	M	D-J	Title - Titre	Signature
Proposed date of hearing / Date prévue de l'audition	1300	01	10	15	A/CCO	[signature]
Delivered to inmate / Transmis au détenu	1000	01	10	11	CX2	[signature]

I have been advised of my right to retain and instruct counsel. | J'ai été informé de mon droit d'avoir recours aux services d'un avocat.

Y-A M D-J ☐ Inmate refused to sign / Détenu a refusé de signer

Inmate - Signature - Détenu | Date | Time - Heure | Witnessing CSC official - Signature - Agent responsable témoin

HEARING OF CHARGE - AUDITION DU CHEF D'ACCUSATION

Plea - Plaidoyer: ☐ Guilty/Coupable ☐ Not guilty/Non coupable ☐ Refused to plea/Refus de plaider

Remanded to - Audition ajourné à: Hour - Heure | Y-A | M | D-J

Reason - Motif

K227

Correctional Service Canada | Service correctionnel Canada

20631

PROTECTED / PROTÉGÉE A ☐ B ☐ C ☐ ONCE COMPLETED / UNE FOIS REMPLIE

PERSONAL INFORMATION BANK - FICHIER DE RENSEIGNEMENTS PERSONNELS

INMATE OFFENCE REPORT AND NOTIFICATION OF CHARGE | **RAPPORT DE L'INFRACTION D'UN DÉTENU ET AVIS DE L'ACCUSATION**

NOTE: Reference document CD 580. | NOTA: Document de référence DC 580.

PUT AWAY ON FILE / CLASSER AU DOSSIER — See reverse / Voir au verso

Institution - Établissement	Millhaven
Resp. Centre Code - Code du centre de resp.	
Location of offence - Lieu de l'infraction	J-Unit 2K range
Date and time of offence / Date et l'heure de l'infraction (Y-A M D-J, Time - Heure)	1 10 10, 1815
FPS number / Numéro SED	464271D
Family name / Nom de famille	Thomas
Given name(s) / Prénom(s)	
Date of birth / Date de naissance	

DESCRIPTION OF OFFENCE (including names of witnesses, unusual behaviour of offender, etc.)
DESCRIPTION DE L'INFRACTION (y compris le nom des témoins, comportement inhabituel du délinquant, etc.)

on the above date and time I/m thomas returned with the 2M range. He lives on the 2K range. This caused the routine movement to be delayed.

Date report written / Date de la rédaction du rapport (Y-A M D-J)	Name of witnessing officer - Nom de l'agent témoin	Signature
1 10 10	cx Matos	P. [signature]

Physical evidence - Preuve(s)	If yes, provide a brief description - Dans l'affirmative, fournir une brève description	Disposition
☐ Yes / Oui ☑ No / Non		

Supervisor or officer in charge of the institution advised / Avis donné au surveillant ou à l'agent responsable de l'établ.	Disposition of inmate - Mesure prise à l'égard du détenu	Other witnessing officer - Autre agent témoin
☑ Yes / Oui	☐ Admin. seg. / Isolement préventif ☐ Confined to cell / Retenu dans sa cellule ☐ Normal association / Intégration normale	B. Jones.

DECISION TAKEN - DÉCISION PRISE

I have reviewed this report and determine that a charge is warranted under section 40 of the Corrections and Conditional Release Act.
J'ai lu ce rapport et décidé qu'une accusation est justifiée en vertu de l'article 40 de la Loi sur le système correctionnel et la mise en liberté sous condition.

☑ Yes / Oui ☐ No / Non — Signature: [signature] — Position Title - Titre du poste: A/CCO — Date charge laid / Date l'accusation imposée (Y-A M D-J): 01 10 11

Offence category - Catégorie de l'infraction	Referred to - Renvoyé au	For hearing a charge under Section 40 of the Corrections & Conditional Release Act. / Pour l'audition du chef d'accusation en vertu de l'article 40 de la Loi sur le système correctionnel et la mise en liberté sous condition. (Specify - Préciser) (See reverse side for offences - Voir la liste d'infractions au verso)
☑ Minor / Mineure ☐ Serious / Grave	☑ Minor offence court / Tribunal des infractions mineures ☐ Serious offence court / Tribunal des infractions graves	R

	Hour - Heure	Y-A M D-J	Title - Titre	Signature
Proposed date of hearing / Date prévue de l'audition	1300	01 10 16	A/ICCO	[signature]
Delivered to inmate / Transmis au détenu	1000	01 10 12	CXI	[signature]

I have been advised of my right to retain and instruct counsel. | J'ai été informé de mon droit d'avoir recours aux services d'un avocat.

Y-A M D-J ☐ Inmate refused to sign / Détenu a refusé de signer

Inmate - Signature - Détenu | Date | Time - Heure | Witnessing CSC official - Signature - Agent responsable témoin

HEARING OF CHARGE - AUDITION DU CHEF D'ACCUSATION

Plea - Plaidoyer: ☐ Guilty / Coupable ☐ Not guilty / Non coupable ☐ Refused to plea / Refus de plaider

Remanded to - Audition ajourné à: Hour - Heure | Y-A | M | D-J

20782 2K227

Correctional Service Canada — Service correctionnel Canada

PROTECTED / PROTÉGÉE A ☐ B ☐ C ☐ ONCE COMPLETED / UNE FOIS REMPLIE

PERSONAL INFORMATION BANK - FICHIER DE RENSEIGNEMENTS PERSONNELS

INMATE OFFENCE REPORT AND NOTIFICATION OF CHARGE — **RAPPORT DE L'INFRACTION D'UN DÉTENU ET AVIS DE L'ACCUSATION**

NOTE: Reference document CD 580. — NOTA: Document de référence DC 580.

PUT AWAY ON FILE / CLASSER AU DOSSIER — See reverse / Voir au verso

Institution - Établissement: MI

Resp. Centre Code - Code du centre de resp.:

FPS number / Numéro SED: 464271D

Family name / Nom de famille: Thomas

Given name(s) / Prénom(s):

Location of offence - Lieu de l'infraction: J unit

Date and time of offence / Date et l'heure de l'infraction: Y-A M D-J 01 10 16 — Time - Heure 2016

Date of birth / Date de naissance:

DESCRIPTION OF OFFENCE (including names of witnesses, unusual behaviour of offender, etc.)
DESCRIPTION DE L'INFRACTION (y compris le nom des témoins, comportement inhabituel du délinquant, etc.)

The above I/m returned from yard and decided to go visit friends on the other ranges. The I/m was given a direct order to return to his range but refused.

Date report written / Date de la rédaction du rapport: Y-A M D-J 01 10 16

Name of witnessing officer - Nom de l'agent témoin: B Jones

Signature: B Jones

Physical evidence - Preuve(s): ☐ Yes / Oui ☒ No / Non — If yes, provide a brief description - Dans l'affirmative, fournir une brève description

Disposition:

Supervisor or officer in charge of the institution advised / Avis donné au surveillant ou à l'agent responsable de l'établ.: ☒ Yes / Oui

Disposition of inmate - Mesure prise à l'égard du détenu: ☐ Admin. seg. / Isolement préventif ☐ Confined to cell / Retenu dans sa cellule ☒ Normal association / Intégration normale

Other witnessing officer - Autre agent témoin: J Orser

DECISION TAKEN - DÉCISION PRISE

I have reviewed this report and determine that a charge is warranted under section 40 of the Corrections and Conditional Release Act.
J'ai lu ce rapport et décidé qu'une accusation est justifiée en vertu de l'article 40 de la Loi sur le système correctionnel et la mise en liberté sous condition.

☒ Yes / Oui ☐ No / Non — Signature: [signature]

Position Title - Titre du poste: CCO

Date charge laid / Date l'accusation imposée: Y-A M D-J 01 10 17

Offence category - Catégorie de l'infraction: ☒ Minor / Mineure ☐ Serious / Grave

Referred to - Renvoyé au: ☒ Minor offence court / Tribunal des infractions mineures ☐ Serious offence court / Tribunal des infractions graves

For hearing a charge under Section 40 of the Corrections & Conditional Release Act.
Pour l'audition du chef d'accusation en vertu de l'article 40 de la Loi sur le système correctionnel et la mise en liberté sous condition.
(Specify - Préciser) (See reverse side for offences - Voir la liste d'infractions au verso): A

Proposed date of hearing / Date prévue de l'audition: Hour - Heure 1000 — Y-A M D-J 01 10 24 — Title - Titre: CCO — Signature: [signature]

Delivered to inmate / Transmis au détenu: Hour - Heure 1100 — Y-A M D-J 01 10 18 — Title - Titre: CO2 — Signature: [signature]

I have been advised of my right to retain and instruct counsel. — J'ai été informé de mon droit d'avoir recours aux services d'un avocat.

Y-A M D-J

☐ Inmate refused to sign / Détenu a refusé de signer

Inmate - Signature - Détenu — Date — Time - Heure — Witnessing CSC official - Signature - Agent responsable témoin

HEARING OF CHARGE - AUDITION DU CHEF D'ACCUSATION

Plea - Plaidoyer: ☐ Guilty / Coupable ☐ Not guilty / Non coupable ☐ Refused to plea / Refus de plaider

Remanded to - Audition ajourné à: Hour - Heure — Y-A M D-J

Reason - Motif

2001-020-845 K227

Correctional Service Canada | Service correctionnel Canada

PROTECTED / PROTÉGÉE A ☐ B ☐ C ☐ ONCE COMPLETED / UNE FOIS REMPLIE

PERSONAL INFORMATION BANK - FICHIER DE RENSEIGNEMENTS PERSONNELS

INMATE OFFENCE REPORT AND NOTIFICATION OF CHARGE / **RAPPORT DE L'INFRACTION D'UN DÉTENU ET AVIS DE L'ACCUSATION**

NOTE: Reference document CD 580. / NOTA: Document de référence DC 580.

PUT AWAY ON FILE / CLASSER AU DOSSIER — See reverse / Voir au verso

Institution - Établissement	MILLHAVEN
Resp. Centre Code - Code du centre de resp.	
Location of offence - Lieu de l'infraction	J-UNIT
Date and time of offence / Date et l'heure de l'infraction (Y-A M D-J; Time - Heure)	01-10-21; 1827
FPS number / Numéro SED	464271D
Family name / Nom de famille	THOMAS
Given name(s) / Prénom(s)	
Date of birth / Date de naissance	

DESCRIPTION OF OFFENCE (including names of witnesses, unusual behaviour of offender, etc.)
DESCRIPTION DE L'INFRACTION (y compris le nom des témoins, comportement inhabituel du délinquant, etc.)

when returning from yard at 1827 hrs. I/M THOMAS returned with range 2M. I/M THOMAS lives on range 2K.

Date report written / Date de la rédaction du rapport (Y-A M D-J)	01-10-21
Name of witnessing officer - Nom de l'agent témoin	C. MATCHETT
Signature	C. Matchett
Physical evidence - Preuve(s): Yes/Oui, No/Non	No / Non ✓
If yes, provide a brief description - Dans l'affirmative, fournir une brève description	
Disposition	
Supervisor or officer in charge of the institution advised / Avis donné au surveillant ou à l'agent responsable de l'établ.	Yes / Oui ✓
Disposition of inmate - Mesure prise à l'égard du détenu: Admin. seg. / Isolement préventif; Confined to cell / Retenu dans sa cellule; Normal association / Intégration normale	Normal association / Intégration normale ✓
Other witnessing officer - Autre agent témoin	A Murdoch

DECISION TAKEN - DÉCISION PRISE

I have reviewed this report and determine that a charge is warranted under section 40 of the Corrections and Conditional Release Act.
J'ai lu ce rapport et décidé qu'une accusation est justifiée en vertu de l'article 40 de la Loi sur le système correctionnel et la mise en liberté sous condition

Yes / Oui; No / Non	Yes / Oui ✓
Signature	[signature]
Position Title - Titre du poste	CCO
Date charge laid / Date l'accusation imposée (Y-A M D-J)	01 10 22
Offence category - Catégorie de l'infraction: Minor / Mineure; Serious / Grave	Minor / Mineure ✓
Referred to - Renvoyé au: Minor offence court / Tribunal des infractions mineures; Serious offence court / Tribunal des infractions graves	Minor offence court / Tribunal des infractions mineures ✓
For hearing a charge under Section 40 of the Corrections & Conditional Release Act. / Pour l'audition du chef d'accusation en vertu de l'article 40 de la Loi sur le système correctionnel et la mise en liberté sous condition. (Specify - Préciser) (See reverse side for offences - Voir la liste d'infractions au verso)	R
Proposed date of hearing / Date prévue de l'audition (Hour - Heure; Y-A M D-J)	1000; 01 10 29
Title - Titre	CCO
Signature	[signature]
Delivered to inmate / Transmis au détenu (Hour - Heure; Y-A M D-J)	1000; 011023
Title - Titre	CO2
Signature	[signature]

I have been advised of my right to retain and instruct counsel. / J'ai été informé de mon droit d'avoir recours aux services d'un avocat.

Y-A M D-J

☐ Inmate refused to sign / Détenu a refusé de signer

Inmate - Signature - Détenu | Date | Time - Heure | Witnessing CSC official - Signature - Agent responsable témoin

HEARING OF CHARGE - AUDITION DU CHEF D'ACCUSATION

Plea - Plaidoyer	Remanded to - Audition ajourné à
Guilty / Coupable ✓; Not guilty / Non coupable ☐; Refused to plea / Refus de plaider ☐	Hour - Heure; Y-A M D-J

Reason - Motif

Correctional Service Canada / Service correctionnel Canada

20968 [handwritten]

PROTECTED / PROTÉGÉE A ☐ B ☐ C ☐ ONCE COMPLETED / UNE FOIS REMPLIE

PERSONAL INFORMATION BANK - FICHIER DE RENSEIGNEMENTS PERSONNELS

INMATE OFFENCE REPORT AND NOTIFICATION OF CHARGE / **RAPPORT DE L'INFRACTION D'UN DÉTENU ET AVIS DE L'ACCUSATION**

NOTE: Reference document CD 580. / NOTA: Document de référence DC 580.

PUT AWAY ON FILE / CLASSER AU DOSSIER — See reverse / Voir au verso

FPS number / Numéro SED	464271D
Family name / Nom de famille	THOMAS
Given name(s) / Prénom(s)	
Date of birth / Date de naissance	
Institution - Établissement	MILLHAVEN INST.
Resp. Centre Code - Code du centre de resp.	42100
Location of offence - Lieu de l'infraction	INSTITUTIONAL HOSPITAL VESTIBULE
Date and time of offence / Date et l'heure de l'infraction (Y-A M D-J, Time - Heure)	01 10 26 0810

DESCRIPTION OF OFFENCE (including names of witnesses, unusual behaviour of offender, etc.)
DESCRIPTION DE L'INFRACTION (y compris le nom des témoins, comportement inhabituel du délinquant, etc.)

At the above date and time, I/M THOMAS became verbally abusive and confrontational during a frisk search. THOMAS ignored repeated orders to place his hands on the wall, then refused an order to leave the hospital, attempting to step around the officer. THOMAS finally complied, but was very verbally abusive again while leaving.

Date report written / Date de la rédaction du rapport (Y-A M D-J)	Name of witnessing officer - Nom de l'agent témoin	Signature
01 10 26	CX-02 H. PAGE	[signature]

Physical evidence - Preuve(s): ☐ Yes / Oui ☒ No / Non — If yes, provide a brief description - Dans l'affirmative, fournir une brève description — Disposition

Supervisor or officer in charge of the institution advised / Avis donné au surveillant ou à l'agent responsable de l'établ.: ☒ Yes / Oui

Disposition of inmate - Mesure prise à l'égard du détenu: ☐ Admin. seg. / Isolement préventif ☐ Confined to cell / Retenu dans sa cellule ☒ Normal association / Intégration normale

Other witnessing officer - Autre agent témoin: CX-01 RAYNER

DECISION TAKEN - DÉCISION PRISE

I have reviewed this report and determine that a charge is warranted under section 40 of the Corrections and Conditional Release Act.
J'ai lu ce rapport et décidé qu'une accusation est justifiée en vertu de l'article 40 de la Loi sur le système correctionnel et la mise en liberté sous condition

☒ Yes / Oui ☐ No / Non — Signature: [signature] — Position Title - Titre du poste: CCO — Date charge laid / Date l'accusation imposée (Y-A M D-J): 01 10 29

Offence category - Catégorie de l'infraction: ☒ Minor / Mineure ☐ Serious / Grave

Referred to - Renvoyé au: ☒ Minor offence court / Tribunal des infractions mineures ☐ Serious offence court / Tribunal des infractions graves

For hearing a charge under Section 40 of the Corrections & Conditional Release Act. / Pour l'audition du chef d'accusation en vertu de l'article 40 de la Loi sur le système correctionnel et la mise en liberté sous condition. (Specify - Préciser) (See reverse side for offences - Voir la liste d'infractions au verso): F

	Hour - Heure	Y-A M D-J	Title - Titre	Signature
Proposed date of hearing / Date prévue de l'audition	1000	01 11 05	CCO	[signature]
Delivered to inmate / Transmis au détenu	0900	01 10 30	CX2	R. J[signature]

I have been advised of my right to retain and instruct counsel. / J'ai été informé de mon droit d'avoir recours aux services d'un avocat.

Y-A M D-J ☐ Inmate refused to sign / Détenu a refusé de signer

Inmate - Signature - Détenu | Date | Time - Heure | Witnessing CSC official - Signature - Agent responsable témoin

HEARING OF CHARGE - AUDITION DU CHEF D'ACCUSATION

Plea - Plaidoyer: ☒ Guilty / Coupable ☐ Not guilty / Non coupable ☐ Refused to plea / Refus de plaider

Remanded to - Audition ajourné à: Hour - Heure | Y-A | M | D-J

Reason - Motif

20969

Correctional Service Canada — Service correctionnel Canada

PROTECTED / PROTÉGÉE A ☐ B ☐ C ☐ ONCE COMPLETED / UNE FOIS REMPLIE

PERSONAL INFORMATION BANK - FICHIER DE RENSEIGNEMENTS PERSONNELS

INMATE OFFENCE REPORT AND NOTIFICATION OF CHARGE
RAPPORT DE L'INFRACTION D'UN DÉTENU ET AVIS DE L'ACCUSATION

NOTE: Reference document CD 580. / NOTA: Document de référence DC 580.

PUT AWAY ON FILE / CLASSER AU DOSSIER — See reverse / Voir au verso

Institution - Établissement	Millhaven
Resp. Centre Code - Code du centre de resp.	
Location of offence - Lieu de l'infraction	'J' Unit
Date and time of offence - Date et l'heure de l'infraction (Y-A M D-J / Time - Heure)	01 10 26 / 1955
FPS number - Numéro SED	464271D
Family name - Nom de famille	THOMAS
Given name(s) - Prénom(s)	
Date of birth - Date de naissance	

DESCRIPTION OF OFFENCE (including names of witnesses, unusual behaviour of offender, etc.)
DESCRIPTION DE L'INFRACTION (y compris le nom des témoins, comportement inhabituel du délinquant, etc.)

On the above date and approx. time I/M THOMAS FPS#464271[D] did return with the wrong range during 1930 HRS movement from recreation. I/M THOMAS resides on 2K range, However he returned with 1K range.

Date report written - Date de la rédaction du rapport (Y-A M D-J)	01 10 26
Name of witnessing officer - Nom de l'agent témoin	L. Ethier CX1
Signature	L. Ethier
Physical evidence - Preuve(s)	☐ Yes / Oui ☒ No / Non
If yes, provide a brief description - Dans l'affirmative, fournir une brève description	
Disposition	
Supervisor or officer in charge of the institution advised - Avis donné au surveillant ou à l'agent responsable de l'établ.	☒ Yes / Oui
Disposition of inmate - Mesure prise à l'égard du détenu	☐ Admin. seg. / Isolement préventif ☐ Confined to cell / Retenu dans sa cellule ☒ Normal association / Intégration normale
Other witnessing officer - Autre agent témoin	W. Wright

DECISION TAKEN - DÉCISION PRISE

I have reviewed this report and determine that a charge is warranted under section 40 of the Corrections and Conditional Release Act.
J'ai lu ce rapport et décidé qu'une accusation est justifiée en vertu de l'article 40 de la Loi sur le système correctionnel et la mise en liberté sous condition

Yes / Oui ☒ No / Non ☐ — Signature	[signature]
Position Title - Titre du poste	CCO
Date charge laid - Date l'accusation imposée (Y-A M D-J)	01 10 29
Offence category - Catégorie de l'infraction	☒ Minor / Mineure ☐ Serious / Grave
Referred to - Renvoyé au	☒ Minor offence court / Tribunal des infractions mineures ☐ Serious offence court / Tribunal des infractions graves
For hearing a charge under Section 40 of the Corrections & Conditional Release Act. / Pour l'audition du chef d'accusation en vertu de l'article 40 de la Loi sur le système correctionnel et la mise en liberté sous condition. (Specify - Préciser) (See reverse side for offences - Voir la liste d'infractions au verso)	R
Proposed date of hearing - Date prévue de l'audition (Hour - Heure / Y-A M D-J)	1000 / 01 11 05
Title - Titre	CCO
Signature	[signature]
Delivered to inmate - Transmis au détenu (Hour - Heure / Y-A M D-J)	0900 / 01 10 30
Title - Titre	CX2
Signature	R [signature]

I have been advised of my right to retain and instruct counsel. / J'ai été informé de mon droit d'avoir recours aux services d'un avocat.

Y-A M D-J ☐ Inmate refused to sign / Détenu a refusé de signer

Inmate - Signature - Détenu | Date | Time - Heure | Witnessing CSC official - Signature - Agent responsable témoin

HEARING OF CHARGE - AUDITION DU CHEF D'ACCUSATION

Plea - Plaidoyer: ☒ Guilty / Coupable ☐ Not guilty / Non coupable ☐ Refused to plea / Refus de plaider

Remanded to - Audition ajourné à: Hour - Heure | Y-A M D-J

Reason - Motif

21601 Oms R227

Correctional Service Canada / Service correctionnel Canada

PROTECTED / PROTÉGÉE A ☐ B ☐ C ☐ ONCE COMPLETED / UNE FOIS REMPLIE

PERSONAL INFORMATION BANK - FICHIER DE RENSEIGNEMENTS PERSONNELS

INMATE OFFENCE REPORT AND NOTIFICATION OF CHARGE

RAPPORT DE L'INFRACTION D'UN DÉTENU ET AVIS DE L'ACCUSATION

NOTE: Reference document CD 580. / NOTA: Document de référence DC 580.

PUT AWAY ON FILE / CLASSER AU DOSSIER — See reverse / Voir au verso

Institution - Établissement: Millhaven

Resp. Centre Code - Code du centre de resp.:

FPS number / Numéro SED: 464271D

Family name / Nom de famille: Thomas

Location of offence - Lieu de l'infraction: J Unit

Given name(s) / Prénom(s):

Date and time of offence / Date et l'heure de l'infraction: Y-A M D-J 01-11-24; Time - Heure 13:40

Date of birth / Date de naissance:

DESCRIPTION OF OFFENCE (including names of witnesses, unusual behaviour of offender, etc.)
DESCRIPTION DE L'INFRACTION (y compris le nom des témoins, comportement inhabituel du délinquant, etc.)

On the above stated date and time the above I/M refused a direct order to lock up. The above I/M did not lock up until he was escorted by the floor staff to his cell.

Date report written / Date de la rédaction du rapport: Y-A M D-J 01-11-24

Name of witnessing officer - Nom de l'agent témoin: G Daniels

Signature: G Daniels

Physical evidence - Preuve(s): ☐ Yes / Oui ☒ No / Non

If yes, provide a brief description - Dans l'affirmative, fournir une brève description:

Disposition:

Supervisor or officer in charge of the institution advised / Avis donné au surveillant ou à l'agent responsable de l'établ.: ☒ Yes / Oui

Disposition of inmate - Mesure prise à l'égard du détenu: ☐ Admin. seg. / Isolement préventif ☐ Confined to cell / Retenu dans sa cellule ☒ Normal association / Intégration normale

Other witnessing officer - Autre agent témoin:

DECISION TAKEN - DÉCISION PRISE

I have reviewed this report and determine that a charge is warranted under section 40 of the Corrections and Conditional Release Act.
J'ai lu ce rapport et décidé qu'une accusation est justifiée en vertu de l'article 40 de la Loi sur le système correctionnel et la mise en liberté sous condition.

☒ Yes / Oui ☐ No / Non Signature: [signature]

Position Title - Titre du poste: CCO

Date charge laid / Date l'accusation imposée: Y-A M D-J 01 11 26

Offence category - Catégorie de l'infraction: ☒ Minor / Mineure ☐ Serious / Grave

Referred to - Renvoyé au: ☒ Minor offence court / Tribunal des infractions mineures ☐ Serious offence court / Tribunal des infractions graves

For hearing a charge under Section 40 of the Corrections & Conditional Release Act.
Pour l'audition du chef d'accusation en vertu de l'article 40 de la Loi sur le système correctionnel et la mise en liberté sous condition.
(Specify - Préciser) (See reverse side for offences - Voir la liste d'infractions au verso): A

	Hour - Heure	Y-A M D-J	Title - Titre	Signature
Proposed date of hearing / Date prévue de l'audition	1600	01 12 04	CCO	[signature]
Delivered to inmate / Transmis au détenu	1000	01 11 27	CX2	[signature]

I have been advised of my right to retain and instruct counsel.
J'ai été informé de mon droit d'avoir recours aux services d'un avocat.

Y-A M D-J

☐ Inmate refused to sign / Détenu a refusé de signer

Inmate - Signature - Détenu | Date | Time - Heure | Witnessing CSC official - Signature - Agent responsable témoin

HEARING OF CHARGE - AUDITION DU CHEF D'ACCUSATION

Plea - Plaidoyer: ☐ Guilty / Coupable ☒ Not guilty / Non coupable ☐ Refused to plea / Refus de plaider

Remanded to - Audition ajourné à: Hour - Heure | Y-A | M | D-J

Reason - Motif:

Correctional Service Canada | Service correctionnel Canada

21797

PROTECTED / PROTÉGÉE A ☐ B ☐ C ☒ ONCE COMPLETED / UNE FOIS REMPLIE

PERSONAL INFORMATION BANK - FICHIER DE RENSEIGNEMENTS PERSONNELS

INMATE OFFENCE REPORT AND NOTIFICATION OF CHARGE

RAPPORT DE L'INFRACTION D'UN DÉTENU ET AVIS DE L'ACCUSATION

NOTE: Reference document CD 580.

NOTA: Document de référence DC 580.

PUT AWAY ON FILE / CLASSER AU DOSSIER — See reverse / Voir au verso

Institution - Établissement	Millhaven
Resp. Centre Code - Code du centre de resp.	42100
Location of offence - Lieu de l'infraction	2L landings
Date and time of offence / Date et l'heure de l'infraction (Y-A, M, D-J, Time - Heure)	
FPS number / Numéro SED	464271 D
Family name / Nom de famille	Thomas
Given name(s) / Prénom(s)	
Date of birth / Date de naissance	

DESCRIPTION OF OFFENCE (including names of witnesses, unusual behaviour of offender, etc.)
DESCRIPTION DE L'INFRACTION (y compris le nom des témoins, comportement inhabituel du délinquant, etc.)

On the above date and time, I saw I/m Thomas 464271 D throw what appeared to be a homemade weapon into the 2L kitchen area. It landed beside the fridge.

421-2001-360.

Date report written / Date de la rédaction du rapport (Y-A M D-J)	01 11 30
Name of witnessing officer - Nom de l'agent témoin	Chris Bucholtz CX 1
Signature	[signature]
Physical evidence - Preuve(s)	☒ Yes / Oui ☐ No / Non
If yes, provide a brief description - Dans l'affirmative, fournir une brève description	home made weapon approx 7-8 inches
Disposition	1980
Supervisor or officer in charge of the institution advised / Avis donné au surveillant ou à l'agent responsable de l'établ.	☒ Yes / Oui
Disposition of inmate - Mesure prise à l'égard du détenu	☒ Admin. seg. / Isolement préventif ☐ Confined to cell / Retenu dans sa cellule ☐ Normal association / Intégration normale
Other witnessing officer - Autre agent témoin	[signature]

DECISION TAKEN - DÉCISION PRISE

I have reviewed this report and determine that a charge is warranted under section 40 of the Corrections and Conditional Release Act.
J'ai lu ce rapport et décidé qu'une accusation est justifiée en vertu de l'article 40 de la Loi sur le système correctionnel et la mise en liberté sous condition

☑ Yes / Oui ☐ No / Non — Signature: [signature] — Position Title - Titre du poste: S/O — Date charge laid / Date l'accusation imposée (Y-A M D-J): 01 12 03

Offence category - Catégorie de l'infraction: ☐ Minor / Mineure ☑ Serious / Grave

Referred to - Renvoyé au: ☐ Minor offence court / Tribunal des infractions mineures ☑ Serious offence court / Tribunal des infractions graves

For hearing a charge under Section 40 of the Corrections & Conditional Release Act. / Pour l'audition du chef d'accusation en vertu de l'article 40 de la Loi sur le système correctionnel et la mise en liberté sous condition. (Specify - Préciser) (See reverse side for offences - Voir la liste d'infractions au verso)

"i"

	Hour - Heure	Y-A M D-J	Title - Titre	Signature
Proposed date of hearing / Date prévue de l'audition	1000	01 12 11	S/O	[signature]
Delivered to inmate / Transmis au détenu	1000	01 12 05	CO2	[signature]

I have been advised of my right to retain and instruct counsel.

J'ai été informé de mon droit d'avoir recours aux services d'un avocat.

☒ Inmate refused to sign / Détenu à refusé de signer

Inmate - Signature - Détenu	Date (Y-A M D-J)	Time - Heure	Witnessing CSC official - Signature - Agent responsable témoin
	01 12 05	1000	[signature]

HEARING OF CHARGE - AUDITION DU CHEF D'ACCUSATION

Plea - Plaidoyer: ☐ Guilty / Coupable ☐ Not guilty / Non coupable ☐ Refused to plea / Refus de plaider

Remanded to - Audition ajourné à: Hour - Heure / Y-A / M / D-J

Reason - Motif

W/D

Copy to C. O'Connor 24 May 02 DA 23210

Correctional Service Canada — Service correctionnel Canada

PROTECTED / PROTÉGÉE A ☐ B ☒ C ☐ ONCE COMPLETED / UNE FOIS REMPLIE

PERSONAL INFORMATION BANK - FICHIER DE RENSEIGNEMENTS PERSONNELS

INMATE OFFENCE REPORT AND NOTIFICATION OF CHARGE — **RAPPORT DE L'INFRACTION D'UN DÉTENU ET AVIS DE L'ACCUSATION**

NOTE: Reference document CD 580. — NOTA: Document de référence DC 580.

PUT AWAY ON FILE / CLASSER AU DOSSIER — See reverse / Voir au verso

Institution - Établissement	MILLHAVEN
Resp. Centre Code - Code du centre de resp.	42100
Location of offence - Lieu de l'infraction	ECA/HEALTHCARE
Date and time of offence - Date et l'heure de l'infraction (Y-A M D-J / Time - Heure)	02 02 25 / 16:00
FPS number - Numéro SED	464271D
Family name - Nom de famille	THOMAS
Given name(s) - Prénom(s)	Shane
Date of birth - Date de naissance	

DESCRIPTION OF OFFENCE (including names of witnesses, unusual behaviour of offender, etc.)
DESCRIPTION DE L'INFRACTION (y compris le nom des témoins, comportement inhabituel du délinquant, etc.)

On the above date and time while escorting I/m THOMAS to health care, I/m THOMAS repeatedly threatened to "Kick my face off" and "Kick my head in" I/m THOMAS made these threats repeatedly during the escort to health care.

Date report written - Date de la rédaction du rapport (Y-A M D-J)	02 02 25
Name of witnessing officer - Nom de l'agent témoin	J. PELKEY
Signature	[signature]
Physical evidence - Preuve(s)	☐ Yes/Oui ☐ No/Non
If yes, provide a brief description - Dans l'affirmative, fournir une brève description	
Disposition	
Supervisor or officer in charge of the institution advised - Avis donné au surveillant ou à l'agent responsable de l'établ.	☒ Yes/Oui
Disposition of inmate - Mesure prise à l'égard du détenu	☐ Admin. seg. / Isolement préventif ☐ Confined to cell / Retenu dans sa cellule ☐ Normal association / Intégration normale
Other witnessing officer - Autre agent témoin	R. MARSHALL

DECISION TAKEN - DÉCISION PRISE

I have reviewed this report and determine that a charge is warranted under section 40 of the Corrections and Conditional Release Act.
J'ai lu ce rapport et décidé qu'une accusation est justifiée en vertu de l'article 40 de la Loi sur le système correctionnel et la mise en liberté sous condition

☒ Yes/Oui ☐ No/Non — Signature: [signature] — Position Title - Titre du poste: CCO — Date charge laid - Date l'accusation imposée (Y-A M D-J): 02 02 26

Offence category - Catégorie de l'infraction	☐ Minor/Mineure ☒ Serious/Grave
Referred to - Renvoyé au	☐ Minor offence court / Tribunal des infractions mineures ☒ Serious offence court / Tribunal des infractions graves
For hearing a charge under Section 40 of the Corrections & Conditional Release Act. Pour l'audition du chef d'accusation en vertu de l'article 40 de la Loi sur le système correctionnel et la mise en liberté sous condition (Specify - Préciser) (See reverse side for offences - Voir la liste d'infractions au verso)	& H
Proposed date of hearing - Date prévue de l'audition (Hour - Heure / Y-A M D-J)	1300 / 02 03 05
Title - Titre	CCO
Signature	[signature]
Delivered to inmate - Transmis au détenu (Hour - Heure / Y-A M D-J)	1255 / 02 03 01
Title - Titre	CX1
Signature	[signature]

I have been advised of my right to retain and instruct counsel. — J'ai été informé de mon droit d'avoir recours aux services d'un avocat.

☒ Inmate refused to sign / Détenu a refusé de signer

Inmate - Signature - Détenu: — Date (Y-A M D-J): 020301 — Time - Heure: 1255 — Witnessing CSC official - Signature - Agent responsable témoin: [signature]

HEARING OF CHARGE - AUDITION DU CHEF D'ACCUSATION

Plea - Plaidoyer: ☐ Guilty/Coupable ☐ Not guilty/Non coupable ☐ Refused to plea/Refus de plaider

Remanded to - Audition ajourné à: Hour - Heure / Y-A M D-J

Reason - Motif:
March 19/02 TBST (inmate detained attending March 12/02)
April 23/02 TBST. 1 May 7/02 ppt, to date + Atts (inmate refused)

Correctional Service Canada / Service correctionnel Canada

DA 23322 — 02 1203

PROTÉGÉE A ☐ B ☐ C ☒ — ONCE COMPLETED / UNE FOIS REMPLI

PERSONAL INFORMATION BANK - FICHIER DE RENSEIGNEMENTS PERSONNELS

INMATE OFFENCE REPORT AND NOTIFICATION OF CHARGE — **RAPPORT DE L'INFRACTION D'UN DÉTENU ET AVIS DE L'ACCUSATION**

NOTE: Reference document CD 580. — NOTA: Document de référence DC 580.

PUT AWAY ON FILE / CLASSER AU DOSSIER — See reverse / Voir au verso

FPS number / Numéro SED	46427 D
Family name / Nom de famille	THOMAS
Given name(s) / Prénom(s)	
Date of birth / Date de naissance	

Institution - Établissement: Millhaven — Resp. Centre Code - Code du centre de resp.: 4510

Location of offence - Lieu de l'infraction: Diss cell #8

Date and time of offence / Date et l'heure de l'infraction: Y-A M D-J 02 02 28 — Time - Heure 0930

DESCRIPTION OF OFFENCE (including names of witnesses, unusual behaviour of offender, etc.)
DESCRIPTION DE L'INFRACTION (y compris le nom des témoins, comportement inhabituel du délinquant, etc.)

During the above date and time, while conducting a routine search. This officer located a tooth brush with a razor blade melted to it. [redacted]

22(1)(c)

421-2002-119

Date report written / Date de la rédaction du rapport: 02 02 28 — Name of witnessing officer - Nom de l'agent témoin: A. Risto — Signature: A. Risto

Physical evidence - Preuve(s): ☒ Yes/Oui ☐ No/Non — If yes, provide a brief description - Dans l'affirmative, fournir une brève description: tooth brush with razor blade melted to it — Disposition: IPSO Locker #1

Supervisor or officer in charge of the institution advised / Avis donné au surveillant ou à l'agent responsable de l'étab.: ☒ Yes/Oui

Disposition of inmate - Mesure prise à l'égard du détenu: ☒ Admin. seg. / Isolement préventif ☐ Confined to cell / Retenu dans sa cellule ☐ Normal association / Intégration normale

Other witnessing officer - Autre agent témoin: K. McBride

DECISION TAKEN - DÉCISION PRISE

I have reviewed this report and determine that a charge is warranted under section 40 of the Corrections and Conditional Release Act.
J'ai lu ce rapport et décidé qu'une accusation est justifiée en vertu de l'article 40 de la Loi sur le système correctionnel et la mise en liberté sous condition

☒ Yes/Oui ☐ No/Non — Signature — Position Title - Titre du poste: CCO — Date charge laid / Date l'accusation imposée: 02 03 01

Offence category - Catégorie de l'infraction: ☐ Minor/Mineure ☒ Serious/Grave

Referred to - Renvoyé au: ☐ Minor offence court / Tribunal des infractions mineures ☒ Serious offence court / Tribunal des infractions graves

For hearing a charge under Section 40 of the Corrections & Conditional Release Act. / Pour l'audition du chef d'accusation en vertu de l'article 40 de la Loi sur le système correctionnel et la mise en liberté sous condition. (Specify - Préciser) (See reverse side for offences - Voir la liste d'infractions au verso): (i)

	Hour - Heure	Y-A M D-J	Title - Titre	Signature
Proposed date of hearing / Date prévue de l'audition	1300	02 03 12	CCO	
Delivered to inmate / Transmis au détenu	13:00	02 03 08	CX 2	

I have been advised of my right to retain and instruct counsel. — J'ai été informé de mon droit d'avoir recours aux services d'un avocat.

☒ Inmate refused to sign / Détenu a refusé de signer

Inmate - Signature - Détenu — Date Y-A M D-J — Time - Heure 13:00 — Witnessing CSC officer - Signature - Agent responsable témoin

HEARING OF CHARGE - AUDITION DU CHEF D'ACCUSATION

Plea - Plaidoyer: ☐ Guilty/Coupable ☒ Not guilty/Non coupable ☐ Refused to plea/Refus de plaider — Remanded to - Audition ajournée à: Hour - Heure, Y-A M D-J

Reason - Motif: March 19/02 TBSR (inmate delayed attending March 12/02) [illegible] March 22/02 TBSR [illegible] to [illegible]

Correctional Service Canada / Service correctionnel Canada

PROT A ☐ B ☒ C ☐ ONCE COMPLETED / UNE FOIS REMPLIE

PERSONAL INFORMATION BANK - FICHIER DE RENSEIGNEMENTS PERSONNELS

INMATE OFFENCE REPORT AND NOTIFICATION OF CHARGE / **RAPPORT DE L'INFRACTION D'UN DÉTENU ET AVIS DE L'ACCUSATION**

NOTE: Reference document CD 580. / NOTA: Document de référence DC 580.

PUT AWAY ON FILE / CLASSER AU DOSSIER — See reverse / Voir au verso — amended to:

FPS number / Numéro SED: [redacted] 464221C

Family name / Nom de famille: Thomas — May 9/02.

Given name(s) / Prénom(s):

Date of birth / Date de naissance:

Institution - Établissement: Millhaven

Resp. Centre Code - Code du centre de resp.: 421C

Location of offence - Lieu de l'infraction: Cell L225

Date and time of offence / Date et l'heure de l'infraction: Y-A 02 M 04 D-J 16 Time - Heure 10:20

DESCRIPTION OF OFFENCE (including names of witnesses, unusual behaviour of offender, etc.)
DESCRIPTION DE L'INFRACTION (y compris le nom des témoins, comportement inhabituel du délinquant, etc.)

On April 16, 2002 At Approx. 1020 hrs, myself (CX1 P Swanson) and CX1 A. Holmes were searching cell L225 belonging to I/m Thomas FPS [redacted] (amended to: 464221C). During the search, the following items were found in I/m Thomas' cell. Four (4) homemade weapons [redacted], 2 pieces of metal, A piece of rolled up carpet, A piece of sandpaper and [redacted]

Date report written / Date de la rédaction du rapport: 02 02 16

Name of witnessing officer - Nom de l'agent témoin: CX1 P. Swanson

Signature: [signature]

Physical evidence - Preuve(s): ☑ Yes / Oui ☐ No / Non

If yes, provide a brief description - Dans l'affirmative, fournir une brève description: Home made weapons, metal pieces, sand paper

Disposition: 421-2002-188 with I.P.S.O.

Supervisor or officer in charge of the institution advised / Avis donné au surveillant ou à l'agent responsable de l'établ.: ☑ Yes / Oui

Disposition of inmate - Mesure prise à l'égard du détenu: ☐ Admin. seg. / Isolement préventif ☐ Confined to cell / Retenu dans sa cellule ☑ Normal association / Intégration normale

Other witnessing officer - Autre agent témoin: CX1 Arthur Holmes

DECISION TAKEN - DÉCISION PRISE

I have reviewed this report and determine that a charge is warranted under section 40 of the Corrections and Conditional Release Act.
J'ai lu ce rapport et décidé qu'une accusation est justifiée en vertu de l'article 40 de la Loi sur le système correctionnel et la mise en liberté sous condition.

☑ Yes / Oui ☐ No / Non — Signature: [signature]

Position Title - Titre du poste: CCO

Date charge laid / Date l'accusation imposée: 02 04 17

Offence category - Catégorie de l'infraction: ☐ Minor / Mineure ☑ Serious / Grave

Referred to - Renvoyé au: ☐ Minor offence court / Tribunal des infractions mineures ☑ Serious offence court / Tribunal des infractions graves

For hearing a charge under Section 40 of the Corrections & Conditional Release Act. / Pour l'audition du chef d'accusation en vertu de l'article 40 de la Loi sur le système correctionnel et la mise en liberté sous condition. (Specify - Préciser) (See reverse side for offences - Voir au verso): (i) 26 22(1)(c)

Proposed date of hearing / Date prévue de l'audition: Hour - Heure 1300 Y-A M D-J 02 04 23 Title - Titre: CCO Signature: [signature]

Delivered to inmate / Transmis au détenu: Hour - Heure 1245 Y-A M D-J 02 04 18 Title - Titre: CX2 Signature: [signature]

I have been advised of my right to retain and instruct counsel. / J'ai été informé de mon droit d'avoir recours aux services d'un avocat.

Y-A M D-J 02 04 18 ☒ Inmate refused to sign / Détenu a refusé de signer [signature]

Inmate - Signature - Détenu | Date | Time - Heure | Witnessing CSC official - Signature - Agent responsable témoin

HEARING OF CHARGE - AUDITION DU CHEF D'ACCUSATION

Plea - Plaidoyer: ☐ Guilty / Coupable ☐ Not guilty / Non coupable ☑ Refused to plea / Refus de plaider — by being absent

Remanded to - Audition ajourné à: Hour - Heure Y-A M D-J

Reason - Motif: May 7/02 TBGS

025885

Correctional Service Canada / Service correctionnel Canada

PROTECTED / PROTÉGÉE A ☐ B ☐ C ☐ ONCE COMPLETED / UNE FOIS REMPLIE

PERSONAL INFORMATION BANK - FICHIER DE RENSEIGNEMENTS PERSONNELS

INMATE OFFENCE REPORT AND NOTIFICATION OF CHARGE

RAPPORT DE L'INFRACTION D'UN DÉTENU ET AVIS DE L'ACCUSATION

NOTE: Reference document CD 580. / NOTA: Document de référence DC 580.

PUT AWAY ON FILE / CLASSER AU DOSSIER — See reverse / Voir au verso

Institution - Établissement	MILLHAVEN
Resp. Centre Code - Code du centre de resp.	
Location of offence - Lieu de l'infraction	J-UNIT 2L RANGE
Date and time of offence / Date et l'heure de l'infraction (Y-A M D-J)	02 06 15
Time - Heure	1935
FPS number / Numéro SED	464 2710
Family name / Nom de famille	THOMAS
Given name(s) / Prénom(s)	
Date of birth / Date de naissance	

DESCRIPTION OF OFFENCE (including names of witnesses, unusual behaviour of offender, etc.)
DESCRIPTION DE L'INFRACTION (y compris le nom des témoins, comportement inhabituel du délinquant, etc.)

On the above date approximate time. I/m THOMAS did refuse to lock-up for the 1935 formal count. I/m THOMAS chose to stay out in his range and not lock-up in his cell.

Date report written / Date de la rédaction du rapport (Y-A M D-J)	02 06 15
Name of witnessing officer - Nom de l'agent témoin	BRAD SULLIVAN
Signature	B. Sullivan
Physical evidence - Preuve(s)	☐ Yes/Oui ☑ No/Non
If yes, provide a brief description - Dans l'affirmative, fournir une brève description	
Disposition	
Supervisor or officer in charge of the institution advised / Avis donné au surveillant ou à l'agent responsable de l'établ.	☑ Yes/Oui
Disposition of inmate - Mesure prise à l'égard du détenu	☐ Admin. seg. / Isolement préventif ☐ Confined to cell / Retenu dans sa cellule ☑ Normal association / Intégration normale
Other witnessing officer - Autre agent témoin	C. MARACLE

DECISION TAKEN - DÉCISION PRISE

I have reviewed this report and determine that a charge is warranted under section 40 of the Corrections and Conditional Release Act.
J'ai lu ce rapport et décidé qu'une accusation est justifiée en vertu de l'article 40 de la Loi sur le système correctionnel et la mise en liberté sous condition

☐ Yes/Oui ☐ No/Non Signature — Position Title - Titre du poste — Date charge laid / Date l'accusation imposée (Y-A M D-J)

Offence category - Catégorie de l'infraction: ☐ Minor/Mineure ☐ Serious/Grave

Referred to - Renvoyé au: ☐ Minor offence court / Tribunal des infractions mineures ☐ Serious offence court / Tribunal des infractions graves

For hearing a charge under Section 40 of the Corrections & Conditional Release Act. / Pour l'audition du chef d'accusation en vertu de l'article 40 de la Loi sur le système correctionnel et la mise en liberté sous condition. (Specify - Préciser) (See reverse side for offences - Voir la liste d'infractions au verso)

	Hour - Heure	Y-A M D-J	Title - Titre	Signature
Proposed date of hearing / Date prévue de l'audition			Rollover	
Delivered to inmate / Transmis au détenu	2045	02/06/18	COI	[signature]

I have been advised of my right to retain and instruct counsel. / J'ai été informé de mon droit d'avoir recours aux services d'un avocat.

Y-A M D-J ☐ Inmate refused to sign / Détenu a refusé de signer

Inmate - Signature - Détenu | Date | Time - Heure | Witnessing CSC official - Signature - Agent responsable témoin

HEARING OF CHARGE - AUDITION DU CHEF D'ACCUSATION

Plea - Plaidoyer: ☐ Guilty/Coupable ☐ Not guilty/Non coupable ☐ Refused to plea/Refus de plaider

Remanded to - Audition ajourné à: Hour - Heure | Y-A M D-J

Reason - Motif

Correctional Service Canada — Service correctionnel Canada

025885

PROTECTED / PROTÉGÉE A ☐ B ☐ C ☐ ONCE COMPLETED / UNE FOIS REMPLIE

PERSONAL INFORMATION BANK - FICHIER DE RENSEIGNEMENTS PERSONNELS

INMATE OFFENCE REPORT AND NOTIFICATION OF CHARGE — **RAPPORT DE L'INFRACTION D'UN DÉTENU ET AVIS DE L'ACCUSATION**

NOTE: Reference document CD 580. — NOTA: Document de référence DC 580.

PUT AWAY ON FILE / CLASSER AU DOSSIER — See reverse / Voir au verso

Institution - Établissement	Millhaven
Resp. Centre Code - Code du centre de resp.	
Location of offence - Lieu de l'infraction	2L Range
Date and time of offence / Date et l'heure de l'infraction (Y-A M D-J; Time - Heure)	02 06 15; 11:00
FPS number / Numéro SED	464271D
Family name / Nom de famille	THOMAS
Given name(s) / Prénom(s)	
Date of birth / Date de naissance	

DESCRIPTION OF OFFENCE (including names of witnesses, unusual behaviour of offender, etc.)
DESCRIPTION DE L'INFRACTION (y compris le nom des témoins, comportement inhabituel du délinquant, etc.)

At the above time and date I/M Thomas refused to lock-up in his cell after returning from recreation. He barricaded his cell and delayed the count by several hours.

Date report written / Date de la rédaction du rapport (Y-A M D-J)	Name of witnessing officer - Nom de l'agent témoin	Signature
02 06 15	CO II McMILLAN	[signature]

Physical evidence - Preuve(s): ☐ Yes / Oui ☑ No / Non — If yes, provide a brief description - Dans l'affirmative, fournir une brève description — Disposition

Supervisor or officer in charge of the institution advised / Avis donné au surveillant ou à l'agent responsable de l'établ.: ☑ Yes / Oui

Disposition of inmate - Mesure prise à l'égard du détenu: ☐ Admin. seg. / Isolement préventif ☐ Confined to cell / Retenu dans sa cellule ☑ Normal association / Intégration normale

Other witnessing officer - Autre agent témoin: [signature]

DECISION TAKEN - DÉCISION PRISE

I have reviewed this report and determine that a charge is warranted under section 40 of the Corrections and Conditional Release Act.
J'ai lu ce rapport et décidé qu'une accusation est justifiée en vertu de l'article 40 de la Loi sur le système correctionnel et la mise en liberté sous condition

☑ Yes / Oui ☐ No / Non — Signature: [signature] — Position Title - Titre du poste: IPSO — Date charge laid / Date l'accusation imposée (Y-A M D-J): 02 06 17

Offence category - Catégorie de l'infraction: ☑ Minor / Mineure ☐ Serious / Grave

Referred to - Renvoyé au: ☑ Minor offence court / Tribunal des infractions mineures ☐ Serious offence court / Tribunal des infractions graves

For hearing a charge under Section 40 of the Corrections & Conditional Release Act. Pour l'audition du chef d'accusation en vertu de l'article 40 de la Loi sur le système correctionnel et la mise en liberté sous condition. (Specify - Préciser) (See reverse side for offences - Voir la liste d'infractions au verso): "M"

	Hour - Heure	Y-A M D-J	Title - Titre	Signature
Proposed date of hearing / Date prévue de l'audition	1000	02 07 02	IPSO	[signature]
Delivered to inmate / Transmis au détenu	2045	02/06/18	CO1	[signature]

I have been advised of my right to retain and instruct counsel. — J'ai été informé de mon droit d'avoir recours aux services d'un avocat.

Y-A M D-J — ☐ Inmate refused to sign / Détenu a refusé de signer

Inmate - Signature - Détenu — Date — Time - Heure — Witnessing CSC official - Signature - Agent responsable témoin

HEARING OF CHARGE - AUDITION DU CHEF D'ACCUSATION

Plea - Plaidoyer: ☐ Guilty / Coupable ☐ Not guilty / Non coupable ☐ Refused to plea / Refus de plaider

Remanded to - Audition ajourné à: Hour - Heure Y-A M D-J

Reason - Motif

Correctional Service Canada / Service correctionnel Canada

PROTECTED / PROTÉGÉE A ☐ B ☒ C ☐ ONCE COMPLETED / UNE FOIS REMPLIE

2002026089

PERSONAL INFORMATION BANK - FICHIER DE RENSEIGNEMENTS PERSONNELS

IMATE OFFENCE REPORT ND NOTIFICATION OF HARGE — RAPPORT DE L'INFRACTION D'UN DÉTENU ET AVIS DE L'ACCUSATION

DTE: Reference document CD 580. — NOTA: Document de référence DC 580.

PUT AWAY ON FILE / CLASSER AU DOSSIER — See reverse / Voir au verso

stitution - Établissement	Millhaven
Resp. Centre Code - Code du centre de resp.	421
ocation of offence - Lieu de l'infraction	2L Landing
Date and time of offence / Date et l'heure de l'infraction (Y-A M D-J)	02-06-27
Time - Heure	0840
FPS number / Numéro SED	464271 D
Family name / Nom de famille	Thomas
Given name(s) / Prénom(s)	
Date of birth / Date de naissance	

DESCRIPTION OF OFFENCE (including names of witnesses, unusual behaviour of offender, etc.)
DESCRIPTION DE L'INFRACTION (y compris le nom des témoins, comportement inhabituel du délinquant, etc.)

On the above date + time the above I/M approached the control and stated to the reporting officer "What the fuck are you looking at you white faggot.

Date report written / Date de la rédaction du rapport: 02-06-27
Name of witnessing officer - Nom de l'agent témoin: G Daniels
Signature: G Daniels

Physical evidence - Preuve(s): ☐ Yes / Oui ☒ No / Non
If yes, provide a brief description - Dans l'affirmative, fournir une brève description
Disposition

Supervisor or officer in charge of the institution advised / Avis donné au surveillant ou à l'agent responsable de l'établ.: ☒ Yes / Oui

Disposition of inmate - Mesure prise à l'égard du détenu: ☐ Admin. seg. / Isolement préventif ☐ Confined to cell / Retenu dans sa cellule ☒ Normal association / Intégration normale

Other witnessing officer - Autre agent témoin: J. Cross

DECISION TAKEN - DÉCISION PRISE

I have reviewed this report and determine that a charge is warranted under section 40 of the Corrections and Conditional Release Act.
J'ai lu ce rapport et décidé qu'une accusation est justifiée en vertu de l'article 40 de la Loi sur le système correctionnel et la mise en liberté sous condition

☒ Yes / Oui ☐ No / Non — Signature: R Deslauriers — Position Title - Titre du poste: IPSO — Date charge laid / Date l'accusation imposée (Y-A M D-J): 02 06 28

Offence category - Catégorie de l'infraction: ☐ Minor / Mineure ☒ Serious / Grave

Referred to - Renvoyé au: ☐ Minor offence court / Tribunal des infractions mineures ☒ Serious offence court / Tribunal des infractions graves

For hearing a charge under Section 40 of the Corrections & Conditional Release Act. Pour l'audition du chef d'accusation en vertu de l'article 40 de la Loi sur le système correctionnel et la mise en liberté sous condition. (Specify - Préciser) (See reverse side for offences - Voir la liste d'infractions au verso)

"F"

	Hour - Heure	Y-A M D-J	Title - Titre	Signature
Proposed date of hearing / Date prévue de l'audition	1000	02 07 02	IPSO	R Deslauriers
Delivered to inmate / Transmis au détenu	1940	2 6 30	CX II	[signature]

I have been advised of my right to retain and instruct counsel. — J'ai été informé de mon droit d'avoir recours aux services d'un avocat.

☒ Inmate refused to sign / Détenu a refusé de signer

Inmate - Signature - Détenu: — Date: 2.6.30 — Time - Heure: 1940 — Witnessing CSC official - Signature - Agent responsable témoin: [signature]

HEARING OF CHARGE - AUDITION DU CHEF D'ACCUSATION

Plea - Plaidoyer: ☐ Guilty / Coupable ☐ Not guilty / Non coupable ☐ Refused to plea / Refus de plaider

Remanded to - Audition ajourné à: Hour - Heure, Y-A M D-J — Tues NOV 19/02. [illegible]

Correctional Service Canada — Service correctionnel Canada

026500

PROTECTED / PROTÉGÉE A [ ] B [X] C [ ] ONCE COMPLETED / UNE FOIS REMPLIE

PERSONAL INFORMATION BANK - FICHIER DE RENSEIGNEMENTS PERSONNELS

INMATE OFFENCE REPORT AND NOTIFICATION OF CHARGE

RAPPORT DE L'INFRACTION D'UN DÉTENU ET AVIS DE L'ACCUSATION

NOTE: Reference document CD 580. / NOTA: Document de référence DC 580.

PUT AWAY ON FILE / CLASSER AU DOSSIER — See reverse / Voir au verso

Institution - Établissement	MILLHAVEN
Resp. Centre Code - Code du centre de resp.	
Location of offence - Lieu de l'infraction	2L ~~2K~~ RANGE
Date and time of offence / Date et l'heure de l'infraction (Y-A M D-J)	02 07 19
Time - Heure	0800
FPS number / Numéro SED	464271D
Family name / Nom de famille	THOMAS
Given name(s) / Prénom(s)	
Date of birth / Date de naissance	

DESCRIPTION OF OFFENCE (including names of witnesses, unusual behaviour of offender, etc.)
DESCRIPTION DE L'INFRACTION (y compris le nom des témoins, comportement inhabituel du délinquant, etc.)

ON THE ABOVE DATE AND APPROXIMATE TIME, I/M THOMAS REFUSED TO LOCK UP UPON HIS RETURN FROM HEALTHCARE. A CALL WAS PLACED OVER THE INTERCOM FOR THOMAS TO "LOCK UP" TO NO AVAIL. FLOOR OFFICERS ATTENDED 2L RANGE BARRIER AND NOTICED THOMAS HIDING IN THE KITCHENETTE AREA. THOMAS WOULD STILL NOT LOCK UP.

Date report written / Date de la rédaction du rapport (Y-A M D-J)	02 07 19
Name of witnessing officer - Nom de l'agent témoin	R. DAVIS
Signature	[signature]
Physical evidence - Preuve(s)	Yes / Oui [ ] No / Non [X]
If yes, provide a brief description - Dans l'affirmative, fournir une brève description	
Disposition	
Supervisor or officer in charge of the institution advised / Avis donné au surveillant ou à l'agent responsable de l'établ.	Yes / Oui [ ]
Disposition of inmate - Mesure prise à l'égard du détenu	[ ] Admin. seg. / Isolement préventif [ ] Confined to cell / Retenu dans sa cellule [ ] Normal association / Intégration normale
Other witnessing officer - Autre agent témoin	SHIPMAN, M.

DECISION TAKEN - DÉCISION PRISE

I have reviewed this report and determine that a charge is warranted under section 40 of the Corrections and Conditional Release Act.
J'ai lu ce rapport et décidé qu'une accusation est justifiée en vertu de l'article 40 de la Loi sur le système correctionnel et la mise en liberté sous condition

Yes / Oui [✓] No / Non [ ]	Signature: [signature]
Position Title - Titre du poste	A/CCO
Date charge laid / Date l'accusation imposée (Y-A M D-J)	02 07 22
Offence category - Catégorie de l'infraction	Minor / Mineure [✓] Serious / Grave [ ]
Referred to - Renvoyé au	[✓] Minor offence court / Tribunal des infractions mineures [ ] Serious offence court / Tribunal des infractions graves
For hearing a charge under Section 40 of the Corrections & Conditional Release Act. Pour l'audition du chef d'accusation en vertu de l'article 40 de la Loi sur le système correctionnel et la mise en liberté sous condition. (Specify - Préciser) (See reverse side for offences - Voir la liste d'infractions au verso)	40 "a"
Proposed date of hearing / Date prévue de l'audition — Hour - Heure	13:00
Y-A M D-J	02 07 30
Title - Titre	A/CCO
Signature	[signature]
Delivered to inmate / Transmis au détenu — Hour - Heure	1015
Y-A M D-J	02 07 23
Title - Titre	CX2 D Simms
Signature	[signature]

I have been advised of my right to retain and instruct counsel. / J'ai été informé de mon droit d'avoir recours aux services d'un avocat.

Y-A M D-J

[ ] Inmate refused to sign / Détenu a refusé de signer

Inmate - Signature - Détenu | Date | Time - Heure | Witnessing CSC official - Signature - Agent responsable témoin

HEARING OF CHARGE - AUDITION DU CHEF D'ACCUSATION

Plea - Plaidoyer: [ ] Guilty / Coupable [ ] Not guilty / Non coupable [ ] Refused to plea / Refus de plaider

Remanded to - Audition ajourné à: Hour - Heure | Y-A | M | D-J

Reason - Motif

597 026600 JMS

Correctional Service Canada — Service correctionnel Canada

PROTECTED / PROTÉGÉE A ☐ B ☐ C ☐ ONCE COMPLETED / UNE FOIS REMPLIE

PERSONAL INFORMATION BANK - FICHIER DE RENSEIGNEMENTS PERSONNELS

INMATE OFFENCE REPORT AND NOTIFICATION OF CHARGE — **RAPPORT DE L'INFRACTION D'UN DÉTENU ET AVIS DE L'ACCUSATION**

NOTE: Reference document CD 580. — NOTA: Document de référence DC 580.

PUT AWAY ON FILE / CLASSER AU DOSSIER — See reverse / Voir au verso

Institution - Établissement	MILLHAVEN
Resp. Centre Code - Code du centre de resp.	42100 421
Location of offence - Lieu de l'infraction	CELL L225
Date and time of offence - Date et l'heure de l'infraction (Y-A M D-J, Time - Heure)	02 07 25 0930
FPS number - Numéro SED	464271D
Family name - Nom de famille	THOMAS
Given name(s) - Prénom(s)	
Date of birth - Date de naissance	

DESCRIPTION OF OFFENCE (including names of witnesses, unusual behaviour of offender, etc.)
DESCRIPTION DE L'INFRACTION (y compris le nom des témoins, comportement inhabituel du délinquant, etc.)

On the above date and time while searching the above inmates cell numerous items of contraband were found.

1 plastic purple toothbrush sharpened shank approx. 8 inches
1 metal shank approx 8 inches
1 12 inch steel rod sharpened
2 shanks sharpened at one end made from window frame.
1 inch flat bar sharpened at one end with a blue linen handle.
1 10 inch steel shank with taped handle

Date report written - Date de la rédaction du rapport	02 07 25
Name of witnessing officer - Nom de l'agent témoin	E. COSTA COI
Signature	[signature]
Physical evidence - Preuve(s)	☒ Yes / Oui ☐ No / Non
If yes, provide a brief description - Dans l'affirmative, fournir une brève description	See above list
Disposition	421-2002-346 Keepers HALL Locker #2
Supervisor or officer in charge of the institution advised - Avis donné au surveillant ou à l'agent responsable de l'établ.	☒ Yes / Oui
Disposition of inmate - Mesure prise à l'égard du détenu	☒ Admin. seg. / Isolement préventif ☐ Confined to cell / Retenu dans sa cellule ☐ Normal association / Intégration normale
Other witnessing officer - Autre agent témoin	CX2 DENNEY

DECISION TAKEN - DÉCISION PRISE

I have reviewed this report and determine that a charge is warranted under section 40 of the Corrections and Conditional Release Act.
J'ai lu ce rapport et décidé qu'une accusation est justifiée en vertu de l'article 40 de la Loi sur le système correctionnel et la mise en liberté sous condition.

☒ Yes / Oui ☐ No / Non — Signature: [signature] — Position Title - Titre du poste: A/CCO — Date charge laid - Date l'accusation imposée (Y-A M D-J): 02 07 26

Offence category - Catégorie de l'infraction	☐ Minor / Mineure ☒ Serious / Grave
Referred to - Renvoyé au	☐ Minor offence court / Tribunal des infractions mineures ☒ Serious offence court / Tribunal des infractions graves
For hearing a charge under Section 40 of the Corrections & Conditional Release Act. Pour l'audition du chef d'accusation en vertu de l'article 40 de la Loi sur le système correctionnel et la mise en liberté sous condition. (Specify - Préciser) (See reverse side for offences - Voir la liste d'infractions au verso)	40(i)
Proposed date of hearing - Date prévue de l'audition (Hour - Heure, Y-A M D-J)	12:00 02 08 06
Title - Titre	A/CCO
Signature	[signature]
Delivered to inmate - Transmis au détenu (Hour - Heure, Y-A M D-J)	13:18 02-07-29
Title - Titre	CX1
Signature	[signature]

I have been advised of my right to retain and instruct counsel. — J'ai été informé de mon droit d'avoir recours aux services d'un avocat.

☒ Inmate refused to sign / Détenu a refusé de signer

Inmate - Signature - Détenu: — Date (Y-A M D-J): 02-07-29 — Time - Heure: 13:18 — Witnessing CSC official - Signature - Agent responsable témoin: [signature]

HEARING OF CHARGE - AUDITION DU CHEF D'ACCUSATION

Plea - Plaidoyer: ☐ Guilty / Coupable ☒ Not guilty / Non coupable ☐ Refused to plea / Refus de plaider

Remanded to - Audition ajourné à: Hour - Heure / Y-A / M / D-J

– TRIAL IN ABSENTIA

Reason - Motif: [illegible] 2002 1001 [illegible]

OMS   PA DXI)

Correctional Service Canada / Service correctionnel Canada

PROTECTED / PROTÉGÉ A ☐ B ☒ C ☐ ONCE COMPLETED / UNE FOIS REMPLI

PERSONAL INFORMATION BANK – FICHIER DE RENSEIGNEMENTS PERSONNELS

INMATE OFFENCE REPORT AND NOTIFICATION OF CHARGE

RAPPORT DE L'INFRACTION D'UN DÉTENU ET AVIS DE L'ACCUSATION

NOTE: Reference document CD 580. / NOTA : Document de référence DC 580.

PUT AWAY ON FILE / CLASSER AU DOSSIER — See reverse / Voir au verso

Institution – Établissement	Kingston Pen
Resp. centre code – Code du centre de resp.	
Location of offence – Lieu de l'infraction	Reg Hosp cell #5
Date and time of offence / Date et heure de l'infraction (Y-A M D-J, Time – Heure)	02-07-25 2220
FPS number / Numéro SED	464271 D
Family name / Nom de famille	THOMAS
Given name(s) / Prénom(s)	
Date of birth / Date de naissance	

MILLHAVEN INSTITUTION — SEP 14 2003 — RECORDS MANAGEMENT / GESTION des DOCUMENTS

DESCRIPTION OF INCIDENT (including names of witnesses, unusual behaviour of offender, etc.)
DESCRIPTION DE L'INFRACTION (y compris le nom des témoins, le comportement inhabituel du délinquant, etc.)

At the above date and time inmate THOMAS FPS #464271D did tear down the cartain rod in cell #5 in the reginal hospital and used this rod to break the window in the outer door of his cell.

KINGSTON PENITENTIARY — SEP 2003 — OFFEN[illegible]

INFORMAL RESOLUTION ATTEMPTED – TENTATIVE DE RÈGLEMENT INFORMEL
☒ Yes / Oui ☐ No (provide a brief explanation) / Non (fournir une brève explication)

Date report written / Date de la rédaction du rapport (Y-A M D-J)	02-07-25
Name of witnessing officer (please print) – Nom de l'agent témoin (en lettres moulées)	R. Menard CX-1
Signature	R. [signature]
Physical evidence – Preuve(s)	☒ Yes / Oui ☐ No / Non
If yes, provide a brief description – Dans l'affirmative, fournir une brève description	metal rod approx. 2 feet in length
Test results – Résultats des tests	
Disposition of evidence – Disposition des preuves	Keepers hall
Supervisor or officer in charge of the institution advised / Avis donné au surveillant ou à l'agent responsable de l'établissement	☒ Yes / Oui
Disposition of inmate – Mesure prise à l'égard du détenu	☐ Admin. segregation / Isolement préventif ☒ Confined to cell / Retenu dans sa cellule ☐ Normal association / Intégration normale
Other witnessing officers – Autres agents témoins	1. R. Guertin 2.

DECISION TAKEN – DECISION PRISE

I have reviewed this report and determine that a charge is warranted under section 40(C) of the *Corrections and Conditional Release Act* (see reverse).

J'ai lu le présent rapport et décidé qu'une accusation est justifiée en vertu de l'article 40(____) de la *Loi sur le système correctionnel et la mise en liberté sous condition* (voir au verso).

☑ Yes / Oui ☐ No / Non

Offence category – Catégorie d'infraction: ☐ Minor / Mineur ☑ Serious / Grave

Referred to – Renvoyé au: ☐ Minor offence court / Tribunal des infractions mineures ☑ Serious offence court / Tribunal des infractions graves

Signature of person designated in Standing Order / Signature de la personne désignée dans l'ordre permanent	[signature]
Name and title – Nom et titre	T. FERRIS AUM
Date charge laid – Date de l'accusation (Y-A M D-J)	02 07 26
Proposed date of hearing / Date prévue de l'audience (Time – Heure; Y-A M D-J)	not before 1230 02 07 31
Name and title – Nom et titre	T. Ferris AUM
Signature	[signature]
Location of hearing / Lieu de l'audience	
Delivered to inmate / Transmis au détenu (Time – Heure; Y-A M D-J)	1015 02 07 26
Name and title – Nom et titre	Paul Bérubé CX1
Signature	Paul Bérubé

I acknowledge my right to retain and instruct counsel for the hearing of a serious charge.

Je suis au courant de mon droit d'avoir recours aux services d'un avocat pour l'audition d'une accusation d'infraction grave.

☐ Inmate refused to sign / Le détenu a refusé de signer

Inmate – Signature – Détenu ____ Date (Y-A M D-J) ____ Time – Heure ____ Witnessing CSC official – Signature – Agent responsable témoin ____

HEARING OF CHARGE – AUDITION DU CHEF D'ACCUSATION

Plea – Plaidoyer: ☐ Guilty / Coupable ☐ Not guilty / Non coupable ☐ Refused to plea / Refus de plaider

Hearing remanded to – Audience ajournée à (Y-A M D-J) | Remanded to – Ajournée à (Y-A M D-J) | Remanded to – Ajournée à (Y-A M D-J)

Reason for remand(s) – Motif de l'ajournement ou des ajournements

Correctional Service Canada | Service correctionnel Canada

026635

PROTÉGÉ / PROTÉGÉE A ☐ B ☒ C ☐ ONCE COMPLETED / UNE FOIS REMPLIE

PERSONAL INFORMATION BANK - FICHIER DE RENSEIGNEMENTS PERSONNELS

INMATE OFFENCE REPORT AND NOTIFICATION OF CHARGE / **RAPPORT DE L'INFRACTION D'UN DÉTENU ET AVIS DE L'ACCUSATION**

NOTE: Reference document CD 580. / NOTA: Document de référence DC 580.

PUT AWAY ON FILE / CLASSER AU DOSSIER — See reverse / Voir au verso

FPS number / Numéro SED	464271D
Family name / Nom de famille	Thomas
Given name(s) / Prénom(s)	
Date of birth / Date de naissance	
Institution - Établissement	MI
Resp. Centre Code - Code du centre de resp.	421
Location of offence - Lieu de l'infraction	ECA #8
Date and time of offence / Date et l'heure de l'infraction (Y-A M D-J / Time - Heure)	020726 / 2230

DESCRIPTION OF OFFENCE (including names of witnesses, unusual behaviour of offender, etc.)
DESCRIPTION DE L'INFRACTION (y compris le nom des témoins, comportement inhabituel du délinquant, etc.)

The above I/m had his cell window covered thus delaying the institutional count because extra staff had to come to assist with the count. This was the 2230 hour count.

Date report written / Date de la rédaction du rapport (Y-A M D-J)	020726
Name of witnessing officer - Nom de l'agent témoin	B Jones
Signature	B Jones
Physical evidence - Preuve(s)	☐ Yes / Oui ☒ No / Non
If yes, provide a brief description - Dans l'affirmative, fournir une brève description	
Disposition	
Supervisor or officer in charge of the institution advised / Avis donné au surveillant ou à l'agent responsable de l'établ.	☒ Yes / Oui
Disposition of inmate - Mesure prise à l'égard du détenu	☐ Admin. seg. / Isolement préventif ☐ Confined to cell / Retenu dans sa cellule ☒ Normal association / Intégration normale
Other witnessing officer - Autre agent témoin	M Shipman

DECISION TAKEN - DÉCISION PRISE

I have reviewed this report and determine that a charge is warranted under section 40 of the Corrections and Conditional Release Act.
J'ai lu ce rapport et décidé qu'une accusation est justifiée en vertu de l'article 40 de la Loi sur le système correctionnel et la mise en liberté sous condition

Yes / Oui – No / Non	☒ Yes / Oui ☐ No / Non
Signature	[signature]
Position Title - Titre du poste	A/CCO
Date charge laid / Date l'accusation imposée (Y-A M D-J)	02 07 29
Offence category - Catégorie de l'infraction	☒ Minor / Mineure ☐ Serious / Grave
Referred to - Renvoyé au	☒ Minor offence court / Tribunal des infractions mineures ☐ Serious offence court / Tribunal des infractions graves
For hearing a charge under Section 40 of the Corrections & Conditional Release Act. / Pour l'audition du chef d'accusation en vertu de l'article 40 de la Loi sur le système correctionnel et la mise en liberté sous condition (Specify - Préciser) (See reverse side for offences - Voir la liste d'infractions au verso)	R
Proposed date of hearing / Date prévue de l'audition — Hour - Heure	1300
Y-A M D-J	02 08 06
Title - Titre	A/CCO
Signature	[signature]
Delivered to inmate / Transmis au détenu — Hour - Heure	1350
Y-A M D-J	020731
Title - Titre	CX2
Signature	B Jones

I have been advised of my right to retain and instruct counsel. / J'ai été informé de mon droit d'avoir recours aux services d'un avocat.

Y-A M D-J ☐ Inmate refused to sign / Détenu a refusé de signer

Inmate - Signature - Détenu | Date | Time - Heure | Witnessing CSC official - Signature - Agent responsable témoin

HEARING OF CHARGE - AUDITION DU CHEF D'ACCUSATION

Plea - Plaidoyer: ☐ Guilty / Coupable ☐ Not guilty / Non coupable ☐ Refused to plea / Refus de plaider

Remanded to - Audition ajourné à: Hour - Heure | Y-A | M | D-J

25

Correctional Service Canada — Service correctionnel Canada

PROTECTED / PROTÉGÉE A ☐ B ☐ C ☒ ☐ ONCE COMPLETED / UNE FOIS REMPLIE   OMS   E48

PERSONAL INFORMATION BANK - FICHIER DE RENSEIGNEMENTS PERSONNELS

INMATE OFFENCE REPORT AND NOTIFICATION OF CHARGE
RAPPORT DE L'INFRACTION D'UN DÉTENU ET AVIS DE L'ACCUSATION

NOTE: Reference document CD 580. NOTA: Document de référence DC 580.

PUT AWAY ON FILE / CLASSER AU DOSSIER — See reverse / Voir au verso

Institution - Établissement	MI
Resp. Centre Code - Code du centre de resp.	421
Location of offence - Lieu de l'infraction	EcA #8
Date and time of offence / Date et l'heure de l'infraction (Y-A M D-J)	020726
Time - Heure	2242
FPS number / Numéro SED	464271D
Family name / Nom de famille	Thomas
Given name(s) / Prénom(s)	
Date of birth / Date de naissance	

DESCRIPTION OF OFFENCE (including names of witnesses, unusual behaviour of offender, etc.)
DESCRIPTION DE L'INFRACTION (y compris le nom des témoins, comportement inhabituel du délinquant, etc.)

While trying to conduct the count at 2230 hours the I/m had his window covered. Once the slot was open the I/m had a blue sheet tied around his neck and hooked onto the table. He was attempting to do self harm. Shortly after he unhooked the sheet and threw a liquid at this officer. The liquid hit the shield and got onto the officers uniform and arm. This I/m assaulted the writer.

Date report written / Date de la rédaction du rapport (Y-A M D-J)	020726
Name of witnessing officer - Nom de l'agent témoin	BCT Jones
Signature	B Jones
Physical evidence - Preuve(s)	☐ Yes / Oui ☒ No / Non
If yes, provide a brief description - Dans l'affirmative, fournir une brève description	
Disposition	
Supervisor or officer in charge of the institution advised / Avis donné au surveillant ou à l'agent responsable de l'établ.	☒ Yes / Oui
Disposition of inmate - Mesure prise à l'égard du détenu	☐ Admin. seg. / Isolement préventif ☐ Confined to cell / Retenu dans sa cellule ☒ Normal association / Intégration normale
Other witnessing officer - Autre agent témoin	M Shipman

DECISION TAKEN - DÉCISION PRISE

I have reviewed this report and determine that a charge is warranted under section 40 of the Corrections and Conditional Release Act.
J'ai lu ce rapport et décidé qu'une accusation est justifiée en vertu de l'article 40 de la Loi sur le système correctionnel et la mise en liberté sous condition

☒ Yes / Oui ☐ No / Non	Signature: H Cassidy
Position Title - Titre du poste	A/CCO
Date charge laid / Date l'accusation imposée (Y-A M D-J)	02 07 29
Offence category - Catégorie de l'infraction	☐ Minor / Mineure ☒ Serious / Grave
Referred to - Renvoyé au	☐ Minor offence court / Tribunal des infractions mineures ☒ Serious offence court / Tribunal des infractions graves
For hearing a charge under Section 40 of the Corrections & Conditional Release Act. / Pour l'audition du chef d'accusation en vertu de l'article 40 de la Loi sur le système correctionnel et la mise en liberté sous condition (Specify - Préciser) (See reverse side for offences - Voir la liste d'infractions au verso)	H

	Hour - Heure	Y-A M D-J	Title - Titre	Signature
Proposed date of hearing / Date prévue de l'audition	1300	02 08 06	A/CCO	H Cassidy
Delivered to inmate / Transmis au détenu	1555	020731	CX2	B Jones

I have been advised of my right to retain and instruct counsel. / J'ai été informé de mon droit d'avoir recours aux services d'un avocat.

☒ Inmate refused to sign / Détenu a refusé de signer

Inmate - Signature - Détenu	Date (Y-A M D-J)	Time - Heure	Witnessing CSC official - Signature - Agent responsable témoin
	020731	1555	B Jones

HEARING OF CHARGE - AUDITION DU CHEF D'ACCUSATION

Plea - Plaidoyer	☐ Guilty / Coupable ☒ Not guilty / Non coupable ☐ Refused to plea / Refus de plaider
Remanded to - Audition ajourné à	Hour - Heure: Y-A M D-J

Reason - Motif

Aug 20/02 TBD (inmate at RIC Aug 6/02) - Sept 3/02 [illegible] Nov 12/02 [illegible] to Oct 29/02)

ured from RP Hosp
23 Sept

02027253 OMS ECA1

Correctional Service Canada / Service correctionnel Canada

PROTECTED / PROTÉGÉE A [ ] B [X] C [ ] ONCE COMPLETED / UNE FOIS REMPLIE

PERSONAL INFORMATION BANK - FICHIER DE RENSEIGNEMENTS PERSONNELS

INMATE OFFENCE REPORT AND NOTIFICATION OF CHARGE

RAPPORT DE L'INFRACTION D'UN DÉTENU ET AVIS DE L'ACCUSATION

NOTE: Reference document CD 580.
NOTA: Document de référence DC 580.

PUT AWAY ON FILE / CLASSER AU DOSSIER — See reverse / Voir au verso

FPS number / Numéro SED	464271D
Family name / Nom de famille	Thomas
Given name(s) / Prénom(s)	
Date of birth / Date de naissance	

Institution - Établissement	Resp. Centre Code - Code du centre de resp.
MI	421

Location of offence - Lieu de l'infraction: MHU Cell 16

Date and time of offence / Date et l'heure de l'infraction: Y-A M D-J 02 08 30 — Time - Heure: 0955

DESCRIPTION OF OFFENCE (including names of witnesses, unusual behaviour of offender, etc.)
DESCRIPTION DE L'INFRACTION (y compris le nom des témoins, comportement inhabituel du délinquant, etc.)

The above I/m was moved from ECA #2 to MHU #16. Once the I/m was inside the cell he proceded to wet some toilet paper and cover the camera face with it. I am unable to view the I/m because of the obstruction. This I/m had interferred with the writers ability to perform his duties as a result of his actions.

Date report written / Date de la rédaction du rapport (Y-A M D-J)	Name of witnessing officer - Nom de l'agent témoin	Signature
02 08 30	B Jones	B Jones

Physical evidence - Preuve(s): Yes / Oui [ ] No / Non [X]
If yes, provide a brief description - Dans l'affirmative, fournir une brève description:
Disposition:

Supervisor or officer in charge of the institution advised / Avis donné au surveillant ou à l'agent responsable de l'établ.: Yes / Oui [X]

Disposition of inmate - Mesure prise à l'égard du détenu: Admin. seg. / Isolement préventif [ ] Confined to cell / Retenu dans sa cellule [ ] Normal association / Intégration normale [X]

Other witnessing officer - Autre agent témoin: PC Marcotte

DECISION TAKEN - DÉCISION PRISE

I have reviewed this report and determine that a charge is warranted under section 40 of the Corrections and Conditional Release Act.
J'ai lu ce rapport et décidé qu'une accusation est justifiée en vertu de l'article 40 de la Loi sur le système correctionnel et la mise en liberté sous condition.

Yes / Oui [X] No / Non [ ] Signature: [signature] — Position Title - Titre du poste: A/CCO — Date charge laid / Date l'accusation imposée (Y-A M D-J): 02 09 03

Offence category - Catégorie de l'infraction: Minor / Mineure [X] Serious / Grave [ ]

Referred to - Renvoyé au: Minor offence court / Tribunal des infractions mineures [X] Serious offence court / Tribunal des infractions graves [ ]

For hearing a charge under Section 40 of the Corrections & Conditional Release Act. / Pour l'audition du chef d'accusation en vertu de l'article 40 de la Loi sur le système correctionnel et la mise en liberté sous condition. (Specify - Préciser) (See reverse side for offences - Voir la liste d'infractions au verso): 40 "r"

	Hour - Heure	Y-A M D-J	Title - Titre	Signature
Proposed date of hearing / Date prévue de l'audition	12:00	02 09 10	A/CCO	[signature]
Delivered to inmate / Transmis au détenu	1230	02 09 24	CX-02	[signature]

I have been advised of my right to retain and instruct counsel. / J'ai été informé de mon droit d'avoir recours aux services d'un avocat.

[X] Inmate refused to sign / Détenu a refusé de signer

Inmate - Signature - Détenu	Date (Y-A M D-J)	Time - Heure	Witnessing CSC official - Signature - Agent responsable témoin
	02 09 24	1230	[signature]

HEARING OF CHARGE - AUDITION DU CHEF D'ACCUSATION

Plea - Plaidoyer: Guilty / Coupable [crossed out] Not guilty / Non coupable [X] Refused to plea / Refus de plaider [ ]

Remanded to - Audition ajourné à: Hour - Heure / Y-A / M / D-J

Inmate refusing to attend court. A plea of not guilty was entered on his behalf.

OMS

Correctional Service Canada | Service correctionnel Canada

PROTECTED / PROTÉGÉ A ☐ B ☐ C ☒ ☐ ONCE COMPLETED / UNE FOIS REMPLI

PERSONAL INFORMATION BANK – FICHIER DE RENSEIGNEMENTS PERSONNELS

INMATE OFFENCE REPORT AND NOTIFICATION OF CHARGE

RAPPORT DE L'INFRACTION D'UN DÉTENU ET AVIS DE L'ACCUSATION

PUT AWAY ON FILE / CLASSER AU DOSSIER — See reverse / Voir au verso

NOTE: Reference document CD 580 — NOTA : Document de référence DC 580

Institution – Établissement: R.T.C

Resp. centre code – Code du centre de resp.:

FPS number / Numéro SED: 464271 DV

Family name / Nom de famille: THOMAS

Given name(s) / Prénom(s): SHANE

Location of offence – Lieu de l'infraction: 1 D Range

Date and time of offence / Date et heure de l'infraction: Y-A M D-J 04-04-14 Time – Heure 15:00

Date of birth / Date de naissance:

DESCRIPTION OF INCIDENT (including names of witnesses, unusual behaviour of offender, etc.)
DESCRIPTION DE L'INFRACTION (y compris le nom des témoins, le comportement inhabituel du délinquant, etc.)

On the above date and time I/m Thomas FPS 464271I did assault inmate [redacted] in his cell [redacted]. I/m Thomas was interviewed by this writer and Correctional Supervisor L Murphy when he made an admission to assaulting [redacted] in his cell.

INFORMAL RESOLUTION ATTEMPTED – TENTATIVE DE RÈGLEMENT INFORMEL
☐ Yes / Oui ☒ No (provide a brief explanation) / Non (fournir une brève explication)

Date report written / Date de la rédaction du rapport: 04-4-15

Name of witnessing officer (please print) – Nom de l'agent témoin (en lettres moulées): C S L JUNG

Signature: [signature]

Physical evidence – Preuve(s) ☐ Yes / Oui ☐ No / Non — If yes, provide a brief description – Dans l'affirmative, fournir une brève description

Test results – Résultats des tests

Disposition of evidence – Disposition des preuves

Supervisor or officer in charge of the institution advised / Avis donné au surveillant ou à l'agent responsable de l'établissement: ☒ Yes / Oui

Disposition of inmate – Mesure prise à l'égard du détenu: ☒ Admin. segregation / Isolement préventif ☐ Confined to cell / Détenu dans sa cellule ☐ Normal association / Intégration normale

Other witnessing officers – Autres agents témoins: c/s Murphy was present for the interview, staff did not witness the assault

DECISION TAKEN – DÉCISION PRISE

I have reviewed this report and determine that a charge is warranted under section 40(h) of the Corrections and Conditional Release Act (see reverse).
J'ai lu le présent rapport et décidé qu'une accusation est justifiée en vertu de l'article 40 ___ de la Loi sur le système correctionnel et la mise en liberté sous condition (voir au verso).

☒ Yes / Oui ☐ No / Non

Offence category – Catégorie d'infraction: ☐ Minor / Mineure ☒ Serious / Grave

26

Referred to – Renvoyé au: ☐ Minor offence court / Tribunal des infractions mineures ☒ Serious offence court / Tribunal des infractions graves

Signature of person designated in Standing Order / Signature de la personne désignée dans l'ordre permanent: [signature]

Name and title – Nom et titre: Lisa murphy, a/unit manager

Date charge laid – Date de l'accusation: 04/04/16

Proposed date of hearing / Date prévue de l'audience: Time – Heure 0900 Y-A M D-J 04/04/23

Name and title – Nom et titre: Lisa murphy, a/u.m.

Signature: [signature]

Location of hearing / Lieu de l'audience: RTC COS

Delivered to inmate / Transmis au détenu: Time – Heure 15:30 Y-A M D-J 0404-16

Name and title – Nom et titre: [signature]

Signature: [signature]

I acknowledge my right to retain and instruct counsel for the hearing of a serious charge.

Je suis au courant de mon droit d'avoir recours aux services d'un avocat pour l'audition d'une accusation d'infraction grave.

☐ Inmate refused to sign / Le détenu a refusé de signer

Y-A M D-J 0404 16 — 15:30 — [signature]

Inmate – Signature – Détenu | Date | Time – Heure | Witnessing CSC official – Signature – Agent responsable témoin

HEARING OF CHARGE – AUDITION DU CHEF D'ACCUSATION

Plea – Plaidoyer: ☒ Guilty / Coupable ☐ Not guilty / Non coupable ☐ Refused to plea / Refus de plaider

Hearing remanded to – Audience ajournée à (Y-A M D-J): FA 04 05 25

Remanded to – Ajournée à (Y-A M D-J):

Remanded to – Ajournée à (Y-A M D-J):

Reason for remand(s) – Motif de l'ajournement ou des ajournements

[illegible]

Correctional Service Canada — Service correctionnel Canada

PROTECTED / PROTÉGÉ A ☐ B ☒ C ☐ ONCE COMPLETED / UNE FOIS REMPLI

PERSONAL INFORMATION BANK – FICHIER DE RENSEIGNEMENTS PERSONNELS

INMATE OFFENCE REPORT AND NOTIFICATION OF CHARGE
RAPPORT DE L'INFRACTION D'UN DÉTENU ET AVIS DE L'ACCUSATION

NOTE: Reference document CD 580. / NOTA: Document de référence DC 580

PUT AWAY ON FILE / CLASSER AU DOSSIER — See reverse / Voir au verso

Institution – Établissement	41500 RTC(O)
Resp. centre code – Code du centre de resp.	41500
Location of offence – Lieu de l'infraction	unit 1CD
Date and time of offence – Date et heure de l'infraction (Y-A M D-J / Time – Heure)	04 04 14 / 15:00
FPS number – Numéro SED	464271D
Family name – Nom de famille	Thomas
Given name(s) – Prénom(s)	Shane
Date of birth – Date de naissance	

DESCRIPTION OF INCIDENT (including names of witnesses, unusual behaviour of offender, etc.)
DESCRIPTION DE L'INFRACTION (y compris le nom des témoins, le comportement inhabituel du délinquant, etc.)

At the above time I/m Thomas was seen assaulting I/m [redacted] inside cell [redacted]

INFORMAL RESOLUTION ATTEMPTED – TENTATIVE DE RÈGLEMENT INFORMEL
☐ Yes / Oui ☑ No (provide a brief explanation) / Non (fournir une brève explication)

Date report written – Date de la rédaction du rapport	Name of witnessing officer – Nom de l'agent témoin	Signature
04 04 14	P. Brick	[signature]

Physical evidence – Preuve(s): ☐ Yes / Oui ☑ No / Non — If yes, provide a brief description – Dans l'affirmative, fournir une brève description — Test results – Résultats des tests — Disposition of evidence – Disposition des preuves

Supervisor or officer in charge of the institution advised – Avis donné au surveillant ou à l'agent responsable de l'établissement: ☑ Yes / Oui

Disposition of inmate – Mesure prise à l'égard du détenu: ☐ Admin. segregation / Isolement préventif ☑ Confined to cell / Retenu dans sa cellule ☐ Normal association / Intégration normale

Other witnessing officers – Autres agents témoins: L. Sharpe

DECISION TAKEN – DÉCISION PRISE

I have reviewed this report and determine that a charge is warranted under section 40(h) of the *Corrections and Conditional Release Act* (see reverse).
J'ai lu le présent rapport et décidé qu'une accusation est justifiée en vertu de l'article 40( ) de la *Loi sur le système correctionnel et la mise en liberté sous condition* (voir au verso).
☑ Yes / Oui ☐ No / Non

Offence category – Catégorie: ☐ Minor / Mineure ☑ Serious / Grave

26

Referred to – Renvoyé au: ☐ Minor offence court / Tribunal des infractions mineures ☑ Serious offence court / Tribunal des infractions graves

Signature of person designated in Standing Order	Name and title – Nom et titre	Date charge laid – Date de l'accusation
[signature]	Lisa Murphy A/Unit manager	04/04/15

	Time – Heure	Y-A M D-J	Name and title	Signature
Proposed date of hearing – Date prévue de l'audience	0900 (not before)	04/04/20	Lisa Murphy A/UM	[signature]
Location of hearing – Lieu de l'audience	RTC (O)			
Delivered to inmate – Transmis au détenu	2000	04-04-15	Stephane Gravelle	[signature]

I acknowledge my right to retain and instruct counsel for the hearing of a serious charge.
Je suis au courant de mon droit d'avoir recours aux services d'un avocat pour l'audition d'une accusation d'infraction grave.

☐ Inmate refused to sign / Le détenu a refusé de signer

Inmate – Signature – Détenu	Date	Time – Heure	Witnessing CSC official – Signature – Agent responsable témoin
[signature]	04-04-15	20:02	

HEARING OF CHARGE – AUDITION DU CHEF D'ACCUSATION

Plea – Plaidoyer: ☑ Guilty / Coupable ☐ Not guilty / Non coupable ☐ Refused to plea / Refus de plaider

Hearing remanded to – Audience ajournée à: FA 04 04 20 — Remanded to – Ajournée à — Remanded to – Ajournée à

Reason for remand(s) – Motif de l'ajournement ou des ajournements

Third party representation requested by inmate – Représentation par un tiers requise par le détenu: ☐ Yes / Oui ☐ No / Non
Representation – Représentation: ☐ Accepted / Acceptée ☐ Refused / Refusée
Name of representative – Nom du représentant

D40 398

Name of witness – Nom du témoin — Name of witness – Nom du témoin

Finding – Décision: ☑ Guilty / Coupable ☐ Dismissed / Rejeté ☐ Withdrawn / Retrait

SANCTION AWARDED – SANCTION IMPOSÉE

Sanction awarded – Sanction imposée	Suspended	Sanction awarded – Sanction imposée	Suspended
☐ Warning or reprimand / Avertissement ou réprimande	☐	☑ Fine / Amende	☐
☐ Loss of privileges / Perte de privilèges	☐	☐ Extra duties / Travaux supplémentaires	☐
☐ Order for restitution / Ordre de restitution	☐	☐ Disciplinary segregation / Isolement disciplinaire	☐

Particulars of sanction – Détails sur la sanction:
$30.00
$10.00 to withdraw
$20.00 suspended for 90 days only if no further charge

Date of hearing – Date de l'audience	Name of presiding officer – Nom du président	Signature of presiding officer – Signature du président
04 04 20	J. J. MENARD	[signature]

CSC/SCC 222 (R-01-09) 7530-21-036-4518

DISTRIBUTION: SEE INSTRUCTIONS ON REVERSE – VOIR LES INSTRUCTIONS AU VERSO

Correctional Service Canada / Service correctionnel Canada

PROTECTED / PROTÉGÉ A ☐ B ☒ C ☐ ONCE COMPLETED / UNE FOIS REMPLI

PUT AWAY ON FILE – CLASSER AU DOSSIER
See distribution – Voir la distribution
(See instruction page – Voir la page d'instructions)

Steve Poporski
Judy Kelly

OFFICER'S STATEMENT/ OBSERVATION REPORT

RAPPORT D'OBSERVATION OU DÉCLARATION D'UN AGENT

NOTE: Completion and handling instructions on last page.

NOTA : Instructions pour remplir et classer ce formulaire à la dernière page.

Institution – Établissement	Date and time of report / Date et heure du rapport — Time – Heure	YY-AA M D-J	Reporting officer's name and rank (print) / Nom et niveau du signataire du rapport (en lettres moulées)
KEELE CCC	1600	2005-01-05	RAYMOND LUNG

Subject – Objet	Date and time of incident/observation / Date et heure de l'incident ou l'observation — Time – Heure	YY-AA M D-J
Resident Thomas FPS 464271D Failed to comply with sign in procedures	1600	2005-01-05

**Statement/Observation – Déclaration ou observation

On above date and time, resident Thomas failed to sign in as required. He was seen within the center. Please be advised that such resident had problems to comply with above procedures during the past. Five reports of similar nature had been submitted on the month of December.

☐ I understand officers are to complete this report independently. Any collusion in the preparation of this report will be subject to disciplinary action. Je sais que les agents doivent remplir ce rapport indépendamment. Toute collusion dans la préparation du rapport entraînera des mesures disciplinaires.

Officer – Signature – Agent	Post – Poste	Date (YY-AA M D-J)
Raymond Lung	COII. Evening Shift	05 01 05

Supervisor – Signature – Surveillant	Post – Poste	Date (YY-AA M D-J)

Page 1

Correctional Service
Canada

PROTECTED ONCE COMPLETED
[ ]A [X]B [ ]C
PERSONAL INFORMATION BANK

REVIEW OF OFFENDER'S
SEGREGATED STATUS
INSTITUTIONAL REVIEW

PUT AWAY ON FILE > See Distribution

Decision Number 7
Decision Date 2000/12/04

FPS Number
464271D
Family Name
THOMAS
Given Name(s)
SHANE

Completing Operational Unit
COLLINS BAY INSTITUTION

Current Institution or Address
COLLINS BAY INSTITUTION

Date of Birth
1979/07/19

Type of segregation	Date admitted into segregation (Y M D)	Date of last review (Y M D)
INVOLUNTARY	2000/11/09	2000/11/16

Accumulated days in segregation 24

Reason: CCRA 31(3-A) JEP INST/OTH IND

Rationale:
You have been identified as an aggressor in the assault against another inmate. You are being placed in Segregation pending a further investigation by the IPSO. As part of his investigation the IPSO will be talking with Committee members. A unit or range change is not considered feasible at this time. Segregation is the only viable option at this time.

Amended Reason (if applicable): Effective Date:

Comment:

SEGREGATED STATUS UPDATE

MILLHAVEN INSTITUTION
DEC 20..
Records Management
Gestion des Documents

Synopsis of segregated status
SRD - May 2003
Parole Officer - Wendy Robinson

30 Day Institutional Review - December 04, 2000
Val Whitton, Unit Manager (A)
Wendy Robinson, A/Parole Officer
Brenda Giff, Segregation Clerk

Thomas did attend SRB. He was told that due to illness Mr. Tait is no longer his Parole Officer and that Wendy Robinson is. All the transfer papers have been completed, Thomas was presented with these and given his 48 hours notice to complete his rebuttal. His PO will ensure that legal aid is contacted on his behalf.
Thomas is still experiencing health care digestive problems, which he feels are a result of stress, lack of exercise and his diabetes. He was asked if he felt he needs to see a psychologist, but said he did not. Thomas will be maintained in segregation pending the outcome of the involuntary transfer decision.
~~~~~~
~~~~~~

5 Day Segregation Review - November 16, 2000
Segregation Review Board
Val Whitton, Unit Manager
Chris Tsatsakis, CS
Brenda Giff, Unit Clerk

Thomas did attend Seg Review. Thomas has been placed in Segregation due to concerns of his involvement in the assault on an inmate from 3

REVIEW OF OFFENDER'S SEGREGATION STATUS
INSTITUTIONAL REVIEW
Ce formulaire existe aussi en français

Date and Time Locked 2000/12/04 13:29

DISTRIBUTION
Original = Inmate DD file
Copy = Inmate

..../02

HERE IS ... KS

PROTECTED ONCE COMPLETED
[ ]A [X]B [ ]C

FPS 464271D	NAME THOMAS , SHANE
DOB 1979/07/19	LOC. COLLINS BAY INSTITUTION

Synopsis of segregated status

Block Oct. 22. This investigation is still ongoing. Thomas was informed that his Parole Officer has been advised to write him up for Maximum Security. Situation has caused him to have headaches and nausea. Health Care will be notified. At this time, no alternative but to maintain segregaton.

~~~~~~

1ST. WORKING DAY REVIEW

I have reviewed the placement information for offender Thomas and agree to maintain him in segregation pending another recommendation by the Five-Day Segregation Review Board.

Y M D

00 12 4

Signature
WHITTON , VAL R
UNIT MANAGER/A

Date

ADDITIONAL RECOMMENDATIONS

Comment:

Recommendation:

Date
Y M D

REFUSED TO LEAVE SEGREGATION/REBUTTAL INFORMATION

Refused to Leave Segregation NO

Reason

Rebuttal Received from Offender: NO
Date Received

Type of Rebuttal
Date Recorded

Dated

Synopsis

ADMINISTRATIVE SEGREGATION REVIEW BOARD

Review Board Date 2000/12/04 Time 9:30
Offender Appeared in Person YES

Recommendation MAINTAIN IN SEGREGATION

Rationale:
SEGREGATION REVIEW BOARD MEMBERS
Val Whitton, Unit Manager (A)
Brenda Giff- Segregation Unit Clerk

REVIEW OF OFFENDER'S SEGREGATION STATUS
INSTITUTIONAL REVIEW
Ce formulaire existe aussi en français
CSC 2019-1 (R-97-08) OMS VERS (1)
Date and Time Locked 2000/12/04 13:29

DISTRIBUTION
Original = Inmate DD file
Copy = Inmate

DW-39

..../03
~~~~~~

PROTECTED ONCE COMPLETED
[ ]A [X]B [ ]C

FPS 464271D	NAME THOMAS , SHANE
DOB 1979/07/19	LOC. COLLINS BAY INSTITUTION

Rationale:

Offender
-INTERVIEWED_yes____

Consideration of the state of health of the segregated inmate:
Thomas is still experiencing health care digestive problems, which he feels are a result of stress, lack of exercise and his diabetes. He was asked if he felt he needs to see a psychologist, but said he did not.

OVERALL ASSESSMENT, REINTEGRATION PLAN AND RECOMMENDATIONS:

Thomas did attend SRB. He was told that due to illness Mr. Tait is no longer his Parole Officer and that Wendy Robinson is. All the transfer papers have been completed, Thomas was presented with these and given his 48 hours notice to complete his rebuttal. His PO will ensure that legal aid is contacted on his behalf.
Thomas will be maintained in segregation pending the outcome of the involuntary transfer decision.

SCHEDULE OF ACTIVITIES
1. CASE MANAGEMENT
The Case Management Team for offender THOMAS is keeping in contact.

2. SPIRITUALITY
As requested, the spiritual leader/mentor for offender THOMAS is available to him.

3. ACCESS TO PROGRAMS
All program requirements of the CCRA and CCRR are available to offender THOMAS .

4. CONTACT WITH OTHER INMATES
Offender THOMAS is allowed contact with the inmate committee, a minimum of twice weekly, and at any other time that he requests it pending approval by Unit Manager.

CHAIRPERSON - SIGNATURE

Signature
WHITTON , VAL X
UNIT MANAGER/A

Y	M	D
00	12	4

Date

FINAL DECISION

Your status as a segregated offender has been reviewed and the decision has been made to:

MAINTAIN IN SEGREGATION

Rationale

After having reviewed the recommendations of the Segregation Review Board, it is the Institutional Head's decision that the Offender

REVIEW OF OFFENDER'S SEGREGATION STATUS

DISTRIBUTION

Copy = Inmate

Ce formulaire existe aussi en français
CSC 2019-1 (R-97-08) OMS VERS (1)
Date and Time Locked 2000/12/04 13:29

DHB 30

..../04

PROTECTED ONCE COMPLETED
[ ]A [X]B [ ]C

FPS 464271D DOB 1979/07/19	NAME THOMAS , SHANE LOC. COLLINS BAY INSTITUTION

Rationale

should be
'MAINTAINED IN ADMINISTRATIVE SEGREGATION'.

Decision Date
2000/12/04

Effective Date

DECISION MAKER - SIGNATURE

DeLaat, Janet
~~Warden / Acting~~

STEVENSON , A M
WARDEN

Y	M	D
00	12	4

Date

I hereby acknowledge receipt of the above mentioned document.

Offender's Signature

Y	M	D

Date

Staff Member's signature who informed the information.
Witnessed Offender sign this document

Staff Member's Signature

Y	M	D

Date

The inmate refuses to acknowledge receipt of the above mentioned document. His/Her copy was nevertheless given to him/her.

Signature of two (2) witnesses.

Witness' Signature

Y	M	D
00	12	04

Date

Witness' Signature

Y	M	D
00	12	04

Date

REVIEW OF OFFENDER'S SEGREGATION STATUS
INSTITUTIONAL REVIEW
Ce formulaire existe aussi en français
CSC 2019-1 (R-97-08) OMS VERS (1)
Date and Time Locked 2000/12/04 13:29

DISTRIBUTION
Original = Inmate DD file
Copy = Inmate

1HB37

..../05

Correctional Service
Canada

Page 1

PROTECTED ONCE COMPLETED
[ ]A [X]B [ ]C
PERSONAL INFORMATION BANK

INVOLUNTARY
SEGREGATION
PLACEMENT

PUT AWAY ON FILE > See Distribution

FPS Number
464271D
Family Name
THOMAS
Given Name(s)
SHANE
Date of Birth
1979/07/19

Completing Operational Unit
MILLHAVEN INSTITUTION

Current Institution or Address
MILLHAVEN INSTITUTION

Date/Time admitted into segregation 2001/04/04 09:30

PART A:
You are being placed in administrative segregation according to subsection 31 (3)(a) of the Corrections and Conditional Release Act because there are reasonable grounds to believe:"that (i) the inmate has acted, has attempted to act or intends to act in a manner that jeopardizes the security of the penitentiary or the safety of any person, and (ii) the continued presence of the inmate in the general inmate population would jeopardize the security of the penitentiary or the safety of any person".

Rationale:
DETAILS OF INCIDENT LEADING TO SEGREGATION:
The Subject was returning from the Institutional Hospital to the MSU. The Subject after entering the MSU allegedly struck the glass with his hand on J control window, proceeded to the barrier leading to 1K range and pushed it open. An offence report has been submitted.

COUNSELLING: Due to the Warden's policy in this institution that offenders will not in any way impeded the operation of security barriers, counseling was not an option in this case.

AGGRESSORS: The Subject.

RANGE CHANGES: Due to the Warden's policy in this institution that offenders will not in any way impeded the operation of security barriers, counseling was not an option in this case.

THERE WERE NO IDENTIFIED ALTERNATIVES TO SEGREGATION

THE INSTITUTIONAL HEAD WILL REVIEW YOUR CASE WITHIN TWENTY-FOUR WORKING HOURS AND YOU WILL BE NOTIFIED, IN WRITING, OF THE DECISION.

TOILETRIES AND BEDDING ISSUED: YES

ADMINISTRATION SEGREGATION HANDBOOK ISSUED: YES

OFFENDER SEEN BY HEALTH CARE OFFICER Stewart 00-04-04 @ 09:45hr.

CELL DEADLOCKED AT 09:35hr BY OFFICER CX 2 Bouchard.

Amended Reason (if applicable) : Effective Date:

Comment:

INVOLUNTARY SEGREGATION PLACEMENT
Ce formulaire existe aussi en français

DISTRIBUTION
Original = Inmate

Date and Time Produced 2001/04/04 09:55

TIME IS BASED ON A 24-HOUR CLOCK PERIOD. ..../02

Page 1

Correctional Service
Can.

PROTECTED ONCE COMPLETED
[ ]A [X]B [ ]C
PERSONAL INFORMATION BANK

DISCIPLINARY
SEGREGATION
PLACEMENT

PUT AWAY ON FILE : See Distribution

FPS Number
464271D

Family Name
THOMAS

Given Name(s)
SHANE

Completing Operational Unit
MILLHAVEN INSTITUTION

Current Institution or Address
MILLHAVEN INSTITUTION

Date of Birth
1979/07/19

Date/Time admitted into segregation 2001/06/19 13:50

PART A:
You are being placed in administrative segregation according to subsection 44 (1)(f) of the Corrections and Conditional Release Act because "An inmate who is found guilty of a disciplinary offence is liable, in accordance with the regulations made under paragraphs 96(i) and (j),to one or more of the following: (f) in the case of a serious disciplinary offence, segregation from other inmates for a maximum of thirty days."

Rationale:
DETAILS OF INCIDENT LEADING TO SEGREGATION:
The subject was awarded 5 days disciplinary segregation after being found guilty of a serious infraction. The independent chairperson authorized this award to be served without privileges. The subject's disciplinary segregation will be completed 01/06/23.

TOILETRIES AND BEDDING ISSUED: Yes.

ADMINISTRATION SEGREGATION HANDBOOK ISSUED: Yes.

OFFENDER SEEN BY HEALTH CARE OFFICER Stairs at 15:15 hours, 2001-06-19.

CELL DEADLOCKED AT 15:00 hours, 2001-06-19, BY OFFICER Mitchell.

CONFINEMENT AUTHORIZED BY - INDEPENDENT CHAIRPERSON

Denser for

LAFRANCE , MARK

Y	M	D
01	06	19

Date

I hereby acknowledge receipt of this document

X REFUSED

Offender - Signature

Y	M	D
01	06	19

Date

DYD-72

DISCIPLINARY SEGREGATION PLACEMENT
Ce formulaire existe aussi en français
CSC 2017-2 (R-00-10) OMS VERS (3)

DISTRIBUTION
Original = Inmate
Copy = Inmate DD file

Date and Time Produced 2001/06/20 08:37

TIME IS BASED ON A 24-HOUR CLOCK PERIOD.

..../02

Correctional Service
anada

PROTECTED ONCE COMPLETED
[ ]A [X]B [ ]C
PERSONAL INFORMATION BANK

REVIEW OF OFFENDER'S
SEGREGATED STATUS
FIRST WORKING DAY REVIEW

PUT AWAY ON FILE > See Distribution

Decision Number 12
Decision Date 2001/06/25

FPS Number
464271D
Family Name
THOMAS
Given Name(s)
SHANE

Completing Operational Unit
MILLHAVEN INSTITUTION

Current Institution or Address
MILLHAVEN INSTITUTION

Date of Birth
1979/07/19

Type of segregation
INVOLUNTARY

Date admitted into segregation
Y M D
2001/06/23

Accumulated days in segregation 1

Reason: CCRA 31(3-A) JEP INST/OTH IND

Rationale:
DETAILS OF INCIDENT LEADING TO SEGREGATION: You have been placed in segregation following your refusal to obey direct orders, by staff, to return to your cell. Further, you pushed past an officer who was attempting to direct you to return to your range/cell. Your behaviour and failure to obey direct orders resulted in a delay to the unit routine.

COUNSELLING: Counselling was not deemed to be appropriate as you blatantly refused to comply with staff direction.

AGGRESSORS: offender aggressive toward staff

RANGE CHANGES: Not appropriate as you were just released from segregation in the morning and had been placed on 2K.

THERE WERE NO IDENTIFIED ALTERNATIVES TO SEGREGATION

THE INSTITUTIONAL HEAD WILL REVIEW YOUR CASE WITHIN TWENTY-FOUR WORKING HOURS AND YOU WILL BE NOTIFIED, IN WRITING, OF THE DECISION.

TOILETRIES AND BEDDING ISSUED: yes

ADMINISTRATION SEGREGATION HANDBOOK ISSUED: yes

OFFENDER SEEN BY HEALTH CARE: yes, RN Heroux

CELL DEADLOCKED AT 1635 BY OFFICER Stewart.

Amended Reason (if applicable): Effective Date:

Comment:

SEGREGATED STATUS UPDATE

Synopsis of segregated status
2001-06-25, First Work Review.
The subject was segregated from the maximum security unit because of your refusal to obey direct orders to return to your cell. The subject allegedly pushed past an officer who was attempting to direct the subject to return to your range/cell. The subject's behaviour was deemed to be aggressive. The subject was finally escorted to

REVIEW OF OFFENDER'S SEGREGATION STATUS
FIRST WORKING DAY REVIEW

DISTRIBUTION
Original = Inmate DD file

CSC 2019 (R-97-08) OMS VERS (1)
Date and Time Locked 2001/06/25 13:22

TIME IS BASED ON A 24-HOUR CLOCK PERIOD. ..../02

PROTECTED ONCE COMPLETED
[ ]A [X]B [ ]C

FPS 464271D	NAME THOMAS , SHANE
DOB 1979/07/19	LOC. MILLHAVEN INSTITUTION

Synopsis of segregated status

segregation without further incident.

Signature
JENSEN , CHRISTOPHER K
CORRECTIONAL SUPERVISOR

Y M D
01 06 25
Date

REFUSED TO LEAVE SEGREGATION/REBUTTAL INFORMATION

Refused to Leave Segregation NO

Reason

Rebuttal Received from Offender: NO Type of Rebuttal Dated
Date Received Date Recorded

Synopsis

FINAL DECISION

Your status as a segregated offender has been reviewed and the decision has been made to:

RELEASE FROM SEGREGATION

Rationale

I have reviewed the information concerning this case and I am directing that the subject be released from segregation.

Decision Date 2001/06/25 Effective Date 2001/06/25

DECISION MAKER - SIGNATURE

SNYDER , PAUL
WARDEN/A

Y M D
01 06 25
Date

I hereby acknowledge receipt of the above mentioned document.

X

Offender's Signature

Y M D
01 06 25
Date

REVIEW OF OFFENDER'S SEGREGATION STATUS
FIRST WORKING DAY REVIEW
Ce formulaire existe aussi en français
CSC 2019 (R-97-08) OMS VERS (1)
Date and Time Locked 2001/06/25 13:22

DISTRIBUTION
Original = Inmate DO file
Copy = Inmate

TIME IS BASED ON A 24-HOUR CLOCK PERIOD.

..../03

DD

Correctional Service
nada

PROTECTED ONCE COMPLETED
[ ]A [X]B [ ]C
PERSONAL INFORMATION BANK

SHARING OF INFORMATION
FIFTH WORKING DAY REVIEW

PUT AWAY ON FILE > See Distribution

FPS Number
464271D

Family Name
THOMAS

Given Name(s)
SHANE

Completing Operational Unit
MILLHAVEN INSTITUTION

Current Institution or Address
MILLHAVEN INSTITUTION

Date of Birth
1979/07/19

This is to advise you that in accordance with article 33 of the Corrections and Conditional Release Act, you will be met by the Review Board Committee chairperson on 2001/07/05 at approximately 09:45 hours. At that time, a recommendation to the Institutional Head will be made for either your release to the general population (unless you are serving a disciplinary sentence imposed by the Independent Chairperson) or to continue your current segregated status. The following information will be considered in reviewing your case:

The subject was segregated from the general population range within the maximum security unit for refusing to comply with direction to return to his cell and becoming verbally abusive towards staff. While in segregation the subject remained verbally abusive to staff and threw his food tray. The subject claims he committed this action because he meals were not correct. The subject was informed that a continuation of this inappropriate behaviour would result in his continued segregation. The subject was also informed that a decision regarding his segregated status would be reviewed on or before the next scheduled review.

SEGREGATED STATUS UPDATE

Synopsis of segregated status

2001-06-28, First Working Day Review.

The subject was segregated from the maximum security unit because he refused to return to his cell when asked and ordered to do so at the end of the evening routine. The subject began by being verbally aggressive with staff; this escalated into arguing with staff as they attempted to gain his compliance by talking and counseling finally the subject did become physically aggressive with staff to the point O/C spray was used. While in segregation the subject remained argumentative he refused his prescribed diet claiming in was not a diabetic diet, the food service officer check the meal to ensure in was correct. The inmate still claimed that the meal was not correct and refused to take it. Health care officer Olhmann attended segregation in order to give the subject an insulin needle because of his refusal to go to the institutional hospital, the subject refused to take this medicine. The subject remains non-compliant.

2001-07-03, Fifth Working Day Review.
The subject was segregated from the general population range within the maximum security unit for refusing to comply with direction to return to his cell and becoming verbally abusive towards staff. While in segregation the subject remained verbally abusive to staff and threw his food tray. The subject claims he committed this action because his meals were not correct. The subject was informed that a continuation of this inappropriate behaviour would result in his continued segregation. The subject has been informed of the appropriate manner in which to address his concerns regarding his displeasure with his meals/diet. The subject was informed that a repeat of this action would result in his re-admittance to segregation and internal charges. The subject has committed to

SHARING OF INFORMATION

DISTRIBUTION

Ce formulaire existe aussi en français
CSC 2020 (R-97-08) OHS VERS (1)
Date and Time Produced 2001/07/03 11:47

Copy - Inmate

TIME IS BASED ON A 24-HOUR CLOCK PERIOD. ..../02

[ ]A [X]B [ ]C

FPS 464271D DOB 1979/07/19	NAME THOMAS , SHANE LOC. MILLHAVEN INSTITUTION

Synopsis of segregated status

abiding by the program and rules of this facility. The subject claims that he intends to comply and re-enter the population by acting in a pro-social manner on the general population range.

Synopsis Completed by
JENSEN , CHRISTOPHER K
CORRECTIONAL SUPERVISOR

Date
Y M D
2001/07/03

INMATE'S STATEMENT

[ ] I acknowledge receipt of the present notice, as well as the itemized documents listed above, which will be considered in the decision making process and I do not wish to be present at the Review Committee meeting.

[✓] I acknowledge receipt of the present notice, as well as the itemized documents listed above, which will be considered in the decision making process and I do wish to be present at the Review Committee meeting.

[ ] I did not receive this written notice 3 working days prior to the hearing; however, I waive my right to this delay and accept to be present at the hearing at the designated date.

[ ] I request a postponement of the review committee for a period of ______ days.

X ______________________ at Date (Y M D) ______ Hour ______

Offender Signature

[ ] Offender refuses to acknowledge receipt of the above mentioned document. His/Her copy was nevertheless given to him/her.

[ ] Offender refuses to accept the above mentioned document.

Signature of two (2) witnesses.

Witness' Signature	Date (Y M D)	Hour
[signature]	01 07 03	12 05
[signature]	01 07 03	12.05

SHARING OF INFORMATION
FIFTH WORKING DAY REVIEW
Ce formulaire existe aussi en français
CSC 2020 (R-97-08) OMS VERS (1)
Date and Time Produced 2001/07/03 11:47

DISTRIBUTION
Original = Inmate DD file
Copy = Inmate

TIME IS BASED ON A 24-HOUR CLOCK PERIOD. ..../END

Correctional Service
Canada

PROTECTED ONCE COMPLETED
[ ]A [X]B [ ]C
PERSONAL INFORMATION BANK

DD

SHARING OF
INFORMATION
INSTITUTIONAL REVIEW

PUT AWAY ON FILE > See Distribution

FPS Number
464271D
Family Name
THOMAS
Given Name(s)
SHANE

Completing Operational Unit
MILLHAVEN INSTITUTION

Current Institution or Address
MILLHAVEN INSTITUTION

Date of Birth
1979/07/19

This is to advise you that in accordance with article 33 of the Corrections and Conditional Release Act, you will be met by the Review Board Committee chairperson on 2001/07/26 at approximately 10:30 hours. At that time, a recommendation to the Institutional Head will be made for either your release to the general population (unless you are serving a disciplinary sentence imposed by the Independent Chairperson) or to continue your current segregated status. The following information will be considered in reviewing your case:

The subject was segregated from the general population range within the maximum security unit of this facility because he participated in a range disruption/destruction of government property, refused direct orders to stop his unlawful actions and threatened staff. These threats resulted in the use of [redacted] in order to bring the situation under control and escort the subject to segregation. Subject has continued to demonstrate an uncooperative attitude, setting fires in his cell, being disrespectful to staff, and threatening. The subject will be informed of any changes or new information on or before the next review date.

SEGREGATED STATUS UPDATE

Synopsis of segregated status

2001/07/09, First Working Day Review.
The subject was segregated from the general population range within the maximum security unit of this facility because he participated in a range disruption, refused direct orders to stop his unlawful actions and threaten staff. These threats resulted in the use of [redacted] in order to bring the situation under control and escort the subject to segregation.

2001-07-13, Fifth Working Day Review
The subject was segregated from the general population range within the maximum security unit of Millhaven because he participated in a range disruption and destruction of government property, refused direct orders to stop his unlawful actions and threaten staff. These actions resulted in [redacted] being deployed in order to bring the situation under control and escort the subject to segregation. The subject has been recently involved in similar events.

2001-07-26, Institutional Review
The subject has continued to demonstrate inappropriate behaviours and has been uncooperative. He has set fires in his cell, banged on his cell door, and threatened staff since his admission to segregation. He has not demonstrated a willingness to abide by the rules and regulations of segregation or the institution.

Synopsis Completed by
FREDERICK , BART
UNIT MANAGER

Date
Y M D
2001/07/26

22(1)(c)

SHARING OF INFORMATION
INSTITUTIONAL REVIEW

CSC 2020 (R-97-08) OMS VERS (1)
Date and Time Produced 2001/07/26 10:20

DISTRIBUTION
Original = Inmate DD file
Copy = Inmate

TIME IS BASED ON A 24-HOUR CLOCK PERIOD.

..../02

Correctional Service
Can.

PROTECTED ONCE COMPLETED
[ ]A [X]B [ ]C
PERSONAL INFORMATION BANK

INVOLUNTARY
SEGREGATION
PLACEMENT

PUT AWAY ON FILE > See Distribution

FPS Number
464271D

Family Name
THOMAS

Completing Operational Unit
MILLHAVEN INSTITUTION

Given Name(s)
SHANE

Current Institution or Address
MILLHAVEN INSTITUTION

Date of Birth
1979/07/19

Date/Time admitted into segregation 2001/08/18 15:10

PART A:
You are being placed in administrative segregation according to subsection 31 (3)(a) of the Corrections and Conditional Release Act because there are reasonable grounds to believe:"that (i) the inmate has acted, has attempted to act or intends to act in a manner that jeopardizes the security of the penitentiary or the safety of any person, and (ii) the continued presence of the inmate in the general inmate population would jeopardize the security of the penitentiary or the safety of any person".

Rationale:

DETAILS OF INCIDENT LEADING TO SEGREGATION:

When the subject was being cleared from the visiting area he was found to be in possession of cigarettes. Staff present advised the offender that he could not take this item back to the unit as it was considered to be an unauthorized item. The subject was not happy with this decision and he became argumentative with staff. The subject departed the V & C area and returned to N area. Staff followed the offender as he was still in an agitated state. Once in N area the offender again became argumentative and refused to return to 2F range in E unit. The subject was advised that if he continued to argue and not return to his cell he would be placed in segregation. The subject started towards E unit, but again became argumentative with staff. The subject refused to comply with staff direction to be handcuffed so he could be escorted to the segregation unit. Staff attempted to handcuff the offender, but he locked his hands together; physical force was used by staff to separate the offender's hands and a physical altercation ensues. Once the offender was handcuffed he was escorted to segregation without further incident. Once the subject was placed in a cell in the segregation unit he refused to produce his hands so that staff could remove the handcuffs. The subject did eventually comply and allowed the staff to remove the handcuffs.

COUNSELLING:

Staff in V& C and N area attempted to gain the subject's compliance with verbal interaction to no avail.

AGGRESSORS:

The subject was deemed to be the aggressor and presented a non-compliant attitude.

RANGE CHANGES:

Due to the subject's aggressive and non-complaint behaviour, and the fact that he was housed on the MSU orientation range this was not a viable option.

THERE WERE NO IDENTIFIED ALTERNATIVES TO SEGREGATION

INVOLUNTARY SEGREGATION PLACEMENT
Ce formulaire existe aussi en français
CSC 2017 (R-00-10) OMS VERS. (4)

DISTRIBUTION
Original = Inmate
Copy = Inmate DD file

OTA-14

Date and Time Produced 2001/08/19 21:45

TIME IS BASED ON A 24-HOUR CLOCK PERIOD. ..../02

Page 1

Correctional Service
Can.

PROTECTED ONCE COMPLETED
[ ]A [X]B [ ]C
PERSONAL INFORMATION BANK

INVOLUNTARY
SEGREGATION
PLACEMENT

PUT AWAY ON FILE > See Distribution

FPS Number
464271D

Family Name
THOMAS

Given Name(s)
SHANE

Completing Operational Unit
MILLHAVEN INSTITUTION

Current Institution or Address
MILLHAVEN INSTITUTION

Date of Birth
1979/07/19

Date/Time admitted into segregation 2001/11/30 14:10

PART A:
You are being placed in administrative segregation according to subsection 31 (3)(a) of the Corrections and Conditional Release Act because there are reasonable grounds to believe:"that (i) the inmate has acted, has attempted to act or intends to act in a manner that jeopardizes the security of the penitentiary or the safety of any person, and (ii) the continued presence of the inmate in the general inmate population would jeopardize the security of the penitentiary or the safety of any person".

Rationale:
DETAILS OF INCIDENT LEADING TO SEGREGATION:

You have been placed in Administrative Segregation for your refusal to be frisked by an officer as well as possession of a weapon. Your actions drew the suspicion of the "J" unit control officer's who directed an officer to frisk you. At the officer's request for you to halt and allow him to frisk you in the 2"K" common room you ran. You were cornered at the 2"L" barrier where you were observed to throw a weapon into the kitchenette on 2"L". The weapon was of the homemade variety,

COUNSELLING: Not an option at this time.

AGGRESSORS: None identified.

RANGE CHANGES: Not an option at this time.

THERE WERE NO IDENTIFIED ALTERNATIVES TO SEGREGATION

THE INSTITUTIONAL HEAD WILL REVIEW YOUR CASE WITHIN TWENTY-FOUR WORKING HOURS AND YOU WILL BE NOTIFIED, IN WRITING, OF THE DECISION.

TOILETRIES AND BEDDING ISSUED: Yes.

ADMINISTRATION SEGREGATION HANDBOOK ISSUED: Yes.

OFFENDER SEEN BY HEALTH CARE: R.N. J. Lecombe at 1500-1530hrs.

CELL DEADLOCKED AT___ 1415hrs___ BY OFFICER___
CoI T.Wright

22(1)(c)

Amended Reason (if applicable) :

Effective Date:

Comment:

INVOLUNTARY SEGREGATION PLACEMENT
Ce formulaire existe aussi en français

DISTRIBUTION
Original - Inmate

Date and Time Produced 2001/11/30 14:50

TIME IS BASED ON A 24-HOUR CLOCK PERIOD.

..../02

(A/57)

Page 1

Correctional Service Canada

PROTECTED ONCE COMPLETED
[ ]A [X]B [ ]C
PERSONAL INFORMATION BANK

DISCIPLINARY SEGREGATION PLACEMENT

PUT AWAY ON FILE > See Distribution

FPS Number
464271D

Family Name
THOMAS

Given Name(s)
SHANE

Completing Operational Unit
MILLHAVEN INSTITUTION

Current Institution or Address
MILLHAVEN INSTITUTION

Date of Birth
1979/07/19

Date/Time admitted into segregation 2002/01/08 16:00

PART A:
You are being placed in administrative segregation according to subsection 44 (1)(f) of the Corrections and Conditional Release Act because "An inmate who is found guilty of a disciplinary offence is liable, in accordance with the regulations made under paragraphs 96(i) and (j), to one or more of the following: (f) in the case of a serious disciplinary offence, segregation from other inmates for a maximum of thirty days."

Rationale:
DETAILS OF INCIDENT LEADING TO SEGREGATION:

The subject was found guilty by the IPC during major court. The subject was awarded 20 days disciplinary segregation. This sentence is to be served with a loss of privileges (no TV, no radio). The sentence will be completed on 2002/01/27.

THERE WERE NO IDENTIFIED ALTERNATIVES TO SEGREGATION

TOILETRIES AND BEDDING ISSUED: yes

ADMINISTRATION SEGREGATION HANDBOOK ISSUED: Yes

OFFENDER SEEN BY HEALTH CARE: Yes

CELL DEADLOCKED AT 1615.

CONFINEMENT AUTHORIZED BY - INDEPENDENT CHAIRPERSON

For [signature]
LAFRANCE , MARK

Y	M	D
02	01	08

Date

I hereby acknowledge receipt of this document

X
Offender - Signature

Y	M	D
02	01	08

Date

DISCIPLINARY SEGREGATION PLACEMENT
Ce formulaire existe aussi en français
CSC 2017-2 (R-00-10) OMS VERS (3)

DISTRIBUTION
Original = Inmate
Copy = Inmate DD file

Date and Time Produced 2002/01/09 07:59

TIME IS BASED ON A 24-HOUR CLOCK PERIOD.

...../02

Correctional Service
Canada

PROTECTED ONCE COMPLETED
[ ]A [X]B [ ]C
PERSONAL INFORMATION BANK

REVIEW OF OFFENDER'S
SEGREGATED STATUS
INSTITUTIONAL REVIEW

PUT AWAY ON FILE > See Distribution

Decision Number 26
Decision Date 2002/03/01

FPS Number
464271D
Family Name
THOMAS
Given Name(s)
SHANE

Completing Operational Unit
MILLHAVEN INSTITUTION

Current Institution or Address
MILLHAVEN INSTITUTION

Date of Birth
1979/07/19

Type of segregation	Date admitted into segregation (Y M D)	Date of last review (Y M D)
INVOLUNTARY	2002/02/01	2002/02/08

Accumulated days in segregation 31

Reason: CCRA 31(3-B) INTERF W/INVEST

Rationale:
DETAILS OF INCIDENT LEADING TO SEGREGATION:
You have been identified as being involved in an altercation where weapons were utilized. Segregation appears to be the only viable option to ensure the integrity of the OPP Pen. Squad investigation. There was no force required in your placement to segregation.

COUNSELLING: Not attempted at this juncture.

AGGRESSORS: You have been identified as one of the aggressors.

RANGE CHANGES: Not a reasonable alternative at this juncture.

THERE WERE NO IDENTIFIED ALTERNATIVES TO SEGREGATION

THE INSTITUTIONAL HEAD WILL REVIEW YOUR CASE WITHIN TWENTY-FOUR WORKING HOURS AND YOU WILL BE NOTIFIED, IN WRITING, OF THE DECISION.

TOILETRIES AND BEDDING ISSUED: At the time of admittance

ADMINISTRATION SEGREGATION HANDBOOK ISSUED: At the time of admittance.

OFFENDER SEEN BY HEALTH CARE: Seen by HCO Layman

CELL DEADLOCKED at 1030 BY OFFICER Teeple.

Amended Reason (if applicable): Effective Date:

Comment:

SEGREGATED STATUS UPDATE

Synopsis of segregated status
2002-02-04 First Working Day Review
The subject has been identified as being involved in an altercation where weapons were utilized. The incident is under investigation by both the IPSO and OPP pen squad.

2002-02-08 Fifth Working Day Review
The subject was segregated because he was allegedly involved in an assaulted in the yard. The subject did not suffer and notable wounds during the incident. An investigation into this event is on going at

REVIEW OF OFFENDER'S SEGREGATION STATUS
INSTITUTIONAL REVIEW

DISTRIBUTION
Original = Inmate DO file

CSC 2019-1 (R-97-08) OMS VERS (1)
Date and Time Locked 2002/03/05 13:38

TIME IS BASED ON A 24-HOUR CLOCK PERIOD. ..../02

PROTECTED ONCE COMPLETED
[ ]A [X]B [ ]C

FPS 464271D	NAME THOMAS , SHANE
DOB 1979/07/19	LOC. MILLHAVEN INSTITUTION

Synopsis of segregated status

this time by both the IPSO and OPP pen squad.

2002-03-01 Institutional Review
The subject was segregated because he was allegedly involved in an assault in the yard. The subject did not suffer any notable wounds during the incident. The subject's CMT has reviewed the subject's case to determine if he can be safely managed in the open MSU population. At this time it is felt that the subject can be safely managed if returned to the open population.

Y M D
02 03 01

Signature
SNEDDEN , KEVIN J A/UM
~~CORRECTIONAL SUPERVISOR~~

Date

ADDITIONAL RECOMMENDATIONS

Comment:

Recommendation:

Date
Y M D

REFUSED TO LEAVE SEGREGATION/REBUTTAL INFORMATION

Refused to Leave Segregation NO

Reason

Rebuttal Received from Offender: NO
Type of Rebuttal
Dated
Date Received
Date Recorded

Synopsis

ADMINISTRATIVE SEGREGATION REVIEW BOARD

Review Board Date 2002/03/01 Time 09:30
Offender Appeared in Person YES

Recommendation RELEASE FROM SEGREGATION

Rationale:
Segregation Review Board members are A/UM Snedden and CS Jensen.

The subject appeared in person before the board. The subject appears to be in good health and is provided the opportunity to see a Registered Nurse on a daily basis.

The subject's schedule of activities for the next review period, his access to programs, and contact with other offenders will be in

REVIEW OF OFFENDER'S SEGREGATION STATUS
INSTITUTIONAL REVIEW
Ce formulaire existe aussi en français
CSC 2019-1 (R-57-08) OMS VERS (1)
Date and Time Locked 2002/03/05 13:38

DISTRIBUTION
Original = Inmate DD file
Copy = Inmate

TIME IS BASED ON A 24-HOUR CLOCK PERIOD.

..../03

PROTECTED ONCE COMPLETED
[ ]A [X]B [ ]C

FPS 464271D	NAME THOMAS , SHANE
DOB 1979/07/19	LOC. MILLHAVEN INSTITUTION

Rationale:

accordance with the operational routine of the Millhaven Segregation Unit.

The subject was segregated because he was allegedly involved in an assault in the yard. The subject did not suffer any notable wounds during the incident. The subject's CMT has reviewed the subject's case to determine if he can be safely managed in the open MSU population. At this time it is felt that the subject can be safely managed if returned to the open population. The subject has been cautioned as to the possible consequences of any further non-compliance with his correctional plan. Given that the CMT review indicates the subject can be safely returned to the unit it is the recommendation of the board that the subject be released from segregation.

CHAIRPERSON - SIGNATURE

Y	M	D
02	03	01

Signature
SNEDDEN , KEVIN J
~~CORRECTIONAL SUPERVISOR~~

Date

FINAL DECISION

Your status as a segregated offender has been reviewed and the decision has been made to:

RELEASE FROM SEGREGATION

Rationale

I have reviewed the information in this case and concur with the recommendation of the board to release the subject from segregation.

Decision Date
2002/03/01

Effective Date
2002/03/05

DECISION MAKER - SIGNATURE

Y	M	D
02	03	01

MARSHALL , JIM G
WARDEN

Date

DHD-253

REVIEW OF OFFENDER'S SEGREGATION STATUS
INSTITUTIONAL REVIEW
Ce formulaire existe aussi en français

DISTRIBUTION
Original = Inmate DD file
Copy = Inmate

Date and Time Locked 2002/03/05 13:38

TIME IS BASED ON A 24-HOUR CLOCK PERIOD.

..../04

Correctional Service
anada

PROTECTED ONCE COMPLETED
[ ]A [X]B [ ]C
PERSONAL INFORMATION BANK

REVIEW OF OFFENDER'S
SEGREGATED STATUS
FIFTH WORKING DAY REVIEW

PUT AWAY ON FILE > See Distribution

Decision Number 28
Decision Date 2002/04/23

FPS Number
464271D
Family Name
THOMAS
Given Name(s)
SHANE

Completing Operational Unit
MILLHAVEN INSTITUTION

Current Institution or Address
MILLHAVEN INSTITUTION

Date of Birth
1979/07/19

Type of segregation	Date admitted into segregation (Y M D)	Date of last review (Y M D)
INVOLUNTARY	2002/04/16	2002/04/17

Accumulated days in segregation 6

Reason: CCRA 31(3-A) JEP INST/OTH IND

Rationale:
DETAILS OF INCIDENT LEADING TO SEGREGATION:
As a result of an assault that has occurred on your range (2L), the Warden has authorised an exceptional search of that range to find evidence relating to this assault. When the unit staff searched your cell they did find four (4) homemade weapons, two (2) pieces of metal [redacted]. After completing an individual risk assessment on this discovery the warden has ordered that you be placed in segregation due to the amount of weapons. It has been determined that this matter has to be investigated further to ensure the security of the institution and the safety of all persons therein.
No force was required to place in you in segregation.
The placement in segregation was video-taped even though you were compliant.

COUNSELLING: At the time of admittanec but not an applicable alternative at this time.

AGGRESSORS: None identified.

RANGE CHANGES: Not an appropriate alternative until the risk can be ascertained.

THERE WERE NO IDENTIFIED ALTERNATIVES TO SEGREGATION

THE INSTITUTIONAL HEAD WILL REVIEW YOUR CASE WITHIN TWENTY-FOUR WORKING HOURS AND YOU WILL BE NOTIFIED, IN WRITING, OF THE DECISION.

TOILETRIES AND BEDDING ISSUED: At the time of admittance

ADMINISTRATION SEGREGATION HANDBOOK ISSUED:At the time of admittance

OFFENDER SEEN BY HEALTH CARE: At the time of admittance by HCO Hicks.

CELL DEADLOCKED AT_1230BY OFFICER Stewart.

Amended Reason (if applicable): Effective Date:

Comment:

REVIEW OF OFFENDER'S SEGREGATION STATUS
FIFTH WORKING DAY REVIEW
Ce formulaire existe aussi en français
CSC 2019-1 (R-97-08) OMS VERS (1)
Date and Time Locked 2002/04/23 10:32

DISTRIBUTION
Original = Inmate DD file
Copy = Inmate

B40-370

TIME IS BASED ON A 24-HOUR CLOCK PERIOD.

..../02

Correctional Service
Canada

PROTECTED ONCE COMPLETED
[ ]A [X]B [ ]C
PERSONAL INFORMATION BANK

DISCIPLINARY
SEGREGATION
PLACEMENT

PUT AWAY ON FILE > See Distribution

FPS Number
464271D
Family Name
THOMAS
Given Name(s)
SHANE

Completing Operational Unit
MILLHAVEN INSTITUTION

Current Institution or Address
MILLHAVEN INSTITUTION

Date of Birth
1979/07/19

Date/Time admitted into segregation 2002/05/07 15:00

PART A:
You are being placed in administrative segregation according to subsection 44 (1)(f) of the Corrections and Conditional Release Act because "An inmate who is found guilty of a disciplinary offence is liable, in accordance with the regulations made under paragraphs 96(i) and (j), to one or more of the following: (f) in the case of a serious disciplinary offence, segregation from other inmates for a maximum of thirty days."

Rationale:
On conviction of offence(s) contrary to the CCRA the subject was awarded twenty-five days disciplinary segregation on this date by the Independent Chairperson.
This award includes a loss of privileges, (no TV - no radio).
This award will be completed on 2002-05-31.

CONFINEMENT AUTHORIZED BY - INDEPENDENT CHAIRPERSON

For LAFRANCE, MARK

Date Y 02 M 05 D 07

I hereby acknowledge receipt of this document

X
Offender - Signature

Date Y M D

Staff Member's signature who shared the information:

Staff Member - Signature

Date Y 02 M 05 D 08

DISCIPLINARY SEGREGATION PLACEMENT
Ce formulaire existe aussi en français
CSC 2017-2 (R-00-10) OMS VERS (3)

DISTRIBUTION
Original = Inmate
Copy = Inmate DD file

Date and Time Produced 2002/05/07 15:44

TIME IS BASED ON A 24-HOUR CLOCK PERIOD.

..../02

Correctional Service
Cana

PROTECTED ONCE COMPLETED
[ ]A [X]B [ ]C
PERSONAL INFORMATION BANK

INVOLUNTARY
SEGREGATION
PLACEMENT

PUT AWAY ON FILE > See Distribution

FPS Number
464271D

Family Name
THOMAS

Given Name(s)
SHANE

Date of Birth
1979/07/19

Completing Operational Unit
MILLHAVEN INSTITUTION

Current Institution or Address
MILLHAVEN INSTITUTION

Date/Time admitted into segregation 2002/07/25 11:00

PART A:
You are being placed in administrative segregation according to subsection 31 (3)(a) of the Corrections and Conditional Release Act because there are reasonable grounds to believe:"that (i) the inmate has acted, has attempted to act or intends to act in a manner that jeopardizes the security of the penitentiary or the safety of any person, and (ii) the continued presence of the inmate in the general inmate population would jeopardize the security of the penitentiary or the safety of any person".

Rationale:
DETAILS OF INCIDENT LEADING TO SEGREGATION: During a search of cell L225 which is occupied by offender Thomas, seven(7) homemade weapons were discovered. These weapons were made of various materials, heavy flat metal, plastic, steel rod and aluminum. Given the excessive number of weapons the decision was taken to segregate Thomas pending further investigation.

COUNSELLING: Thomas has an institutional history of possession of weapons, he has been counseled concerning this. Given the excessive number counseling was not seen as an alternative to segregation.

AGGRESSORS: the subject the only identified aggressor

RANGE CHANGES: given the number of weapons found in the cell which is located in the maximum security unit a range change within the unit was not deemed appropriate.

THERE WERE NO IDENTIFIED ALTERNATIVES TO SEGREGATION

THE INSTITUTIONAL HEAD WILL REVIEW YOUR CASE WITHIN TWENTY-FOUR WORKING HOURS AND YOU WILL BE NOTIFIED, IN WRITING, OF THE DECISION.

TOILETRIES AND BEDDING ISSUED: yes

ADMINISTRATION SEGREGATION HANDBOOK ISSUED: yes

OFFENDER SEEN BY HEALTH CARE: yes RN Stout

CELL DEADLOCKED AT 1115 BY OFFICER Denney.

Amended Reason (if applicable):

Effective Date:

Comment:

INVOLUNTARY SEGREGATION PLACEMENT
Ce formulaire existe aussi en français
CSC 2017 (R-00-10) OMS VERS (4)

DISTRIBUTION
Original = Inmate
Copy = Inmate DO file

Date and Time Produced 2002/07/25 12:56

TIME IS BASED ON A 24-HOUR CLOCK PERIOD.

..../02

Canada

INTERIM REPORT

PERSONAL INFORMATION BANK

PUT AWAY ON FILE > See distribution

INCIDENT REPORT FOR IPSO/RHQ/NHQ

INCIDENT No. 2002028871

THIS DOCUMENT CONTAINS INFORMATION WHICH IS EXEMPT UNDER THE PRIVACY ACT. DISCLOSURE OF THAT INFORMATION TO A PERSON NOT HAVING A NEED TO KNOW IS PROHIBITED. MATTERS RELATED TO ITS EXEMPTION MUST BE REFERRED TO THE PREVENTIVE SECURITY DIVISION OF CSC.

Notified - Police? YES Media? NO Support Agencies? NO

FACILITY
MILLHAVEN INSTITUTION

INCIDENT DATE & TIME: (Y M D Time) 2002/11/15 12:00

LOCK-DOWN? NO

USE OF FORCE? YES

INCIDENT TYPE
CELL EXTRACTION

CONTRIBUTING FACTORS
NONE

INDIVIDUALS INVOLVED

FPS: 404240D Name: THOMAS, SHANE Role: INSTIGATOR

LOCATION: CELL

PROPERTY DAMAGE: NOT APPLICABLE

COMMENT
Seg Cell.

METHOD
OTHER METHOD

WEAPONS

SYNOPSIS
Refused to comply with transfer to RTC. IERT activated. I/M extracted and decontaminated and transferred to RTC. No injuries reported.

CURRENT SITUATION
Inmate transferred without problems.

SUMMARY NARRATIVE
Negotiations were attempted without results. I/M refused to comply.

USE OF FORCE INFORMATION

Videotaped? YES

IERT Used? YES

Force - Type Force Quantity Measure

Comment

Force - Type Force Quantity Measure

Comment

Description - Force Used

Completed By: DESLAU[...]ERS, YVES

22(1)(c)

INCIDENT REPORT FOR IPSO/RHQ/NHQ
Ce formulaire existe aussi en français.
CSC 1083 (01-07) ONS VERS (5)

DISTRIBUTION
[Or]iginal - IPSO
Copy - RHQ
Copy - NHQ

DS-31

Date and Time Produced 2002/11/16

TIME IS BASED ON A 24-HOUR CLOCK PERIOD.

..../02

Page 1

Government of
Canada

PROTECTED ONCE COMPLETED
[ ]A [X]B [ ]C
PERSONAL INFORMATION BANK

PUT AWAY ON FILE > See distribution

INCIDENT REPORT FOR IPSO/RHQ/NHQ INCIDENT No. 2003029915

THIS DOCUMENT CONTAINS INFORMATION WHICH IS EXEMPT UNDER THE PRIVACY ACT. DISCLOSURE OF THAT INFORMATION TO A PERSON NOT HAVING A NEED TO KNOW IS PROHIBITED. MATTERS RELATED TO ITS EXEMPTION MUST BE REFERRED TO THE PREVENTIVE SECURITY DIVISION OF CSC.

Notified - Police? NO Media? NO Support Agencies? NO

FACILITY
REG. TREATMENT CENTRE - ONT

INCIDENT DATE & TIME: (Y M D) 2002/12/27 (Time) 10:00

LOCK-DOWN? NO

USE OF FORCE? NO

INCIDENT TYPE
OTHER INCIDENTS

CONTRIBUTING FACTORS
OTHER

INDIVIDUALS INVOLVED

FPS: 464271D THOMAS, SHANE Role: INSTIGATOR

LOCATION: CELL

PROPERTY DAMAGE: NOT APPLICABLE

COMMENT
Unit 1CD

METHOD

WEAPONS

SYNOPSIS
Inmate demanded to be transferred and said he would do anything to get out of RTC.

CURRENT SITUATION
Information has been disseminated to appropriate areas.

SUMMARY NARRATIVE
On December 27, 2002, at approximately 10:00 hrs. the inmate demanded to be transferred and was ranting. He said that he would do anything to get out of here.

INCIDENT REPORT FOR IPSO/RHQ/NHQ
Ce formulaire existe aussi en français.
CSC 1083 (01-07) OMS VERS (X)

DISTRIBUTION
Original - IPSO
Copy - RHQ
Copy - NHQ

PS-36

Date and Time Produced 2003/01/09 11:28

TIME IS BASED ON A 24-HOUR CLOCK PERIOD.

.../02

PROTECTED ONCE COMPLETED
[ ]A [X]B [ ]C
PERSONAL INFORMATION BANK
DESLAURIERS , YVES

CONTRABAND/UNAUTHORIZED ITEMS

Contraband/Unauthorized Item Group	Contraband/Unauthorized Items	Quantity	Measure

Comment

ROLE(S) IN THE INCIDENT

FPS: 464271D Name: THOMAS, SHANE

Offender Situation: SEGREGATION

Role	Type Category	Instigator Involvement
INSTIGATOR	OFFENDER	COMMIT
Injury	**Serious Bodily Injury**	**Injury From**
NONE	NO	NOT APPLICABLE

Description of Injury and Treatment Provided

INCIDENT RELATED INFORMATION

Report/Incident	Reference Number
OTHER	SMEAC
OTHER	I/C CHECKLIST
OTHER	USE OF FORCE
OTHER	ONT INCID REPORT

INCIDENT REPORT FOR IPSO/RHQ/NHQ
Ce formulaire existe aussi en français.
CSC 1083 (01-07) ONS VERS (5)

DISTRIBUTION
Original = IPSO Copy = NHQ
Copy = RHQ

Date and Time Produced 2002/11/16 17:46

TIME IS BASED ON A 24-HOUR CLOCK PERIOD. PJ-30.003

Correctional Service Canada · Service correctionnel Canada

RTC

PROTECTED / PROTÉGÉE A B C ONCE COMPLETED / UNE FOIS REMPLIE

PERSONAL INFORMATION BANK - FICHIER DE RENSEIGNEMENTS PERSONNELS

NOTICE OF INTERCEPTION OF COMMUNICATIONS / AVIS D'INTERCEPTION DES COMMUNICATIONS

PUT AWAY ON FILE / CLASSER AU DOSSIER Ü	See distribution / Voir la distribution
FPS number / Numéro SED Ü	184271D
Family name / Nom de famille Ü	Thomas
Given name(s) / Prénom(s) Ü	Shane
Date of birth / Date de naissance Ü	

Completing operational unit - Unité opérationnelle ayant rédigé le rapport: Preventive Security

Current institution or address - Adresse ou établissement actuel: Millhaven Institution

This is to advise you on the / La présente est pour vous aviser que le

Date (Y-A M D-J): 2002-07-24

authority was given to intercept your private communications because there were reasonable grounds to believe that your communications would contain evidence of:

i) √ an act that would jeopardize the security of the Penitentiary or safety of any person; or,

ii) a criminal offense or a plan to commit a criminal offense,

based on the following information:

Une autorisation a été donné dans le but d'intercepter vos communications car il existait des motifs raisonnables de croire que vos communications contiendraient des évidences de:

i) un acte qui compromettrait la sécurité du pénitencier ou quiconque; ou,

ii) une infraction criminelle ou un plan en vue de commettre une infraction criminelle,

Basé sur les renseignements suivants:

Interception of your communications was requested and authorized due to the concerns for the security of the Penitentiary and the safety of any person.

Your communications provided insufficient information to confirm any threat to the security of the institution or the safety of any person.

It has been determined that your safety is still in jeopardy in the unit.

The lack of resources to commit to the interception of communications, the intermittent ability to conduct the actual intercept resulted in a decision to terminate the interception on 02-08-31.

According to section 94(3) of the Corrections and Conditional Release Regulations, you may make representation to the Institutional Head concerning this matter.

D'après la section 94(3) des Règlements sur le système correctionnel et de la mise en liberté sous condition, vous pouvez soumettre vos observations à ce sujet au directeur de l'établissement.

Signature: Yves Deslauriers

Date (Y-A M D-J): 2002-12-08

CSC/SCC 1135 (95-12)

DISTRIBUTION

Original – Offender CM File - Dossier GC du/de la délinquant(e)

Page 1

Correctional Service
nada

PROTECTED ONCE COMPLETED
[ ] A [X] B [ ] C
PERSONAL INFORMATION BANK

NOTICE OF PUNISHMENT
OR ADMINISTRATIVE ACTION-
DISCIPLINARY COURT/
MINOR OFFENCE COURT

PUT AWAY ON FILE > See Distribution List

FPS Number
464271D
Family Name
THOMAS
Given Name(s)
SHANE

Completing Operational Unit
MILLHAVEN INSTITUTION

Current Institution or Address
MILLHAVEN INSTITUTION

Date of Birth
1979/07/19

Date of Offence
2001/07/08

The above offender was found guilty under Section 40 (DAMAGE/DESTROY) of the Corrections and Conditional Release Act at (SERIOUS) Court held on (2001/11/13) and was awarded the following punishment:

PUNISHMENT AWARDED

Punishment Type	Number of days	Effective Date Y M D	Suspended Num. of Days	Monetary Amount
RESTITUTION	0	2001/11/13	0	$ 55.00

Punishment Type	Number of days	Effective Date Y M D	Suspended Num. of Days	Monetary Amount
FINE	0	2001/11/13	30	$ 15.00

NOTE: Please take appropriate action to ensure that repayment is carried out.

Signature

NOTICE OF PUNISHMENT OR ADMINISTRATIVE ACTION
CSC 233 (R-93-05) OMS VERS (4)
7530-21-036-4519
Date and Time Produced 2001/11/14 15:22

Ce formulaire existe aussi en Français.

TIME IS BASED ON A 24-HOUR CLOCK PERIOD.

..../02

Correctional Service
Canada

Page 1

PROTECTED ONCE COMPLETED
[ ] A [X] B [ ] C
PERSONAL INFORMATION BANK

NOTICE OF PUNISHMENT
OR ADMINISTRATIVE ACTION-
DISCIPLINARY COURT/
MINOR OFFENCE COURT

PUT AWAY ON FILE > See Distribution List

FPS Number
464271D
Family Name
THOMAS
Given Name(s)
SHANE

Completing Operational Unit
MILLHAVEN INSTITUTION

Current Institution or Address
MILLHAVEN INSTITUTION

Date of Birth
1979/07/19

Date of Offence
2001/10/26

The above offender was found guilty under Section 40 (DISRESPECT/ABUSIVE TO STAFF) of the Corrections and Conditional Release Act at (MINOR) Court held on (2001/12/05) and was awarded the following punishment:

PUNISHMENT AWARDED

Punishment Type	Number of days	Effective Date Y M D	Suspended Num. of Days	Monetary Amount
FINE	0	2001/12/05	0	$ 3.00

NOTE: Please take appropriate action to ensure that repayment is carried out.

Signature Bray A/CS

DISTRIBUTION:

1. [ ] Witnessing Officer
2. [ ] Unit Manager
3. [X] Discipline and dissociation file
4. [ ] Clerk to the Institutional Boards
5. [ ] Officer in charge of institution recreation
6. [ ] Offender pay clerk (segregation and/or payment of damages)
7. [ ] Hobby Officer (Loss of hobby privileges)
8. [ ] Supervisor of visits and correspondence (Loss of visiting privileges)
9. [ ] Librarian (Loss of library privileges)
10. [ ] Work supervisor (Segregation)

DH-03

NOTICE OF PUNISHMENT OR ADMINISTRATIVE ACTION
CSC 233 (R-93-05) OMS VERS (4)
7530-21-036-4519
Date and Time Produced 2001/12/18 15:05

Ce formulaire existe aussi en Français.

TIME IS BASED ON A 24-HOUR CLOCK PERIOD. ..../END

OR ADMINISTRATIVE ACTION-
DISCIPLINARY COURT/
MINOR OFFENCE COURT

PUT AWAY ON FILE > See Distribution List

FPS Number
464271D
Family Name
THOMAS
Given Name(s)
SHANE

Completing Operational Unit
MILLHAVEN INSTITUTION

Current Institution or Address
MILLHAVEN INSTITUTION

Date of Birth
1979/07/19

Date of Offence
2001/10/26

The above offender was found guilty under Section 40 (DISOBEYS WRITTEN RULE) of the Corrections and Conditional Release Act at (MINOR) Court held on (2001/12/05) and was awarded the following punishment:

PUNISHMENT AWARDED

Punishment Type	Number of days	Effective Date Y M D	Suspended Num. of Days	Monetary Amount
FINE	0	2001/12/05	0	$ 4.00

NOTE: Please take appropriate action to ensure that repayment is carried out.

Signature

DISTRIBUTION:

1. [ ] Witnessing Officer
2. [ ] Unit Manager
3. [X] Discipline and dissociation file
4. [ ] Clerk to the Institutional Boards
5. [ ] Officer in charge of institution recreation
6. [ ] Offender pay clerk (segregation and/or payment of damages)
7. [ ] Hobby Officer (Loss of hobby privileges)
8. [ ] Supervisor of visits and correspondence (Loss of visiting privileges)
9. [ ] Librarian (Loss of library privileges)
10. [ ] Work supervisor (Segregation)

NOTICE OF PUNISHMENT OR ADMINISTRATIVE ACTION
CSC 233 (R-93-05) OMS VERS (4)
7530-21-036-4519
Date and Time Produced 2001/12/18 15:09

Ce formulaire existe aussi en Français.

DTD-201.

TIME IS BASED ON A 24-HOUR CLOCK PERIOD. ..../END

NOTICE OF PUNISHMENT
OR ADMINISTRATIVE ACTION-
DISCIPLINARY COURT/
MINOR OFFENCE COURT

PUT AWAY ON FILE > See Distribution List

FPS Number
464271D
Family Name
THOMAS
Given Name(s)
SHANE

Completing Operational Unit
MILLHAVEN INSTITUTION

Current Institution or Address
MILLHAVEN INSTITUTION

Date of Birth
1979/07/19

Date of Offence
2001/10/03

The above offender was found guilty under Section 40 (POSS./DEALS IN CONTRABAND) of the Corrections and Conditional Release Act at (SERIOUS) Court held on (2002/01/08) and was awarded the following punishment:

PUNISHMENT AWARDED

Punishment Type	Number of days	Effective Date Y M D	Suspended Num. of Days	Monetary Amount
FINE	0	2002/01/08	0	$ 20.00

Punishment Type	Number of days	Effective Date Y M D	Suspended Num. of Days	Monetary Amount
SEGREGATION	10	2002/01/08	60	$ 0.00

TO BE CONSECUTIVE IN NATURE AND IN RELATION TO ANY OTHER SUSPENDED PENALTY

Punishment Type	Number of days	Effective Date Y M D	Suspended Num. of Days	Monetary Amount
LOSS OF PRIVILEGES	10	2002/01/08	60	$ 0.00

TV AND RADIO

NOTE: Please take appropriate action to ensure that repayment is carried out.

Signature

NOTICE OF PUNISHMENT OR ADMINISTRATIVE ACTION
CSC 233 (R-93-05) OMS VERS (4)
7530-21-036-4519
Date and Time Produced 2002/01/09 14:19

Ce formulaire existe aussi en Français.

TIME IS BASED ON A 24-HOUR CLOCK PERIOD. ..../02

PA/DSD
Page 1

Correctional Service
nada

PROTECTED ONCE COMPLETED
[ ] A [X] B [ ] C
PERSONAL INFORMATION BANK

NOTICE OF PUNISHMENT
OR ADMINISTRATIVE ACTION-
DISCIPLINARY COURT/
MINOR OFFENCE COURT

PUT AWAY ON FILE > See Distribution List

FPS Number
464271D
Family Name
THOMAS
Given Name(s)
SHANE

Completing Operational Unit
MILLHAVEN INSTITUTION

Current Institution or Address
MILLHAVEN INSTITUTION

Date of Birth
1979/07/19

Date of Offence
2001/06/26

The above offender was found guilty under Section 40 (DISOBEY ORDER) of the Corrections and Conditional Release Act at (SERIOUS) Court held on (2002/01/08) and was awarded the following punishment:

PUNISHMENT AWARDED

Punishment Type	Number of days	Effective Date Y M D	Suspended Num. of Days	Monetary Amount
FINE	0	2002/01/08	0	$ 15.00

NOTE: Please take appropriate action to ensure that repayment is carried out.

Signature

DISTRIBUTION:

1. [ ] Witnessing Officer
2. [ ] Unit Manager
3. [ ] Discipline and dissociation file
4. [ ] Clerk to the Institutional Boards
5. [ ] Officer in charge of institution recreation
6. [ ] Offender pay clerk (segregation and/or payment of damages)
7. [ ] Hobby Officer (Loss of hobby privileges)
8. [ ] Supervisor of visits and correspondence (Loss of visiting privileges)
9. [ ] Librarian (Loss of library privileges)
10. [ ] Work supervisor (Segregation)

NOTICE OF PUNISHMENT OR ADMINISTRATIVE ACTION
CSC 233 (R-93-05) OMS VERS (4)
7530-21-036-4519
Date and Time Produced 2002/01/09 14:13

Ce formulaire existe aussi en Français.

TIME IS BASED ON A 24-HOUR CLOCK PERIOD.

010-018

..../END

CONTRABAND SEIZURE TAG

BORDEREAU DE SAISIE

☐ Visitor / Visiteur ☐ Other / Autre ☐ ▶ FPS No. - Nº SED 744421D

Name - Nom

THOMAS

Register Serial No. - Nº de registre

421 - 2002 - 188

Item description - Nature de l'article

2 pieces of metal

Location - Endroit

L225

Seizure - Saisie Time - Heure	Date Y-A	M	D-J
1030	02	04	16

Seizing officer - Agent ayant effectuée la saisie
Name (Print) - Nom (lettres moulées)

[signature]

Signature

A. HOLMES

0040-379

Correctional Service Canada — Service correctionnel Canada

CSC/SCC 482 (R-92-10) 7530-21-895-1068

CONTRABAND SEIZURE TAG / **BORDEREAU DE SAISIE**

☐ Visitor / Visiteur ☐ Other / Autre ☐ ▶ FPS No. - Nº SED 744421D

Name - Nom: THOMAS

Register Serial No. - Nº de registre: 421-2002-188

Item description - Nature de l'article: piece of carpet, 2 food trays, 1 piece sandpaper, body armour & homemade weapons

Location - Endroit: L225

Seizure - Saisie Time - Heure: 1020

Date Y-A: 02 M: 04 D-J: 16

Seizing officer - Agent ayant effectuée la saisie
Name (Print) - Nom (lettres moulées): [signature]

Signature: P. SAMSON

DHD-280

Correctional Service Canada / Service correctionnel Canada

CSC/SCC 482 (R-92-10) 7530-21-895-1068

CONTRABAND SEIZURE TAG — **BORDEREAU DE SAISIE**

☐ Visitor / Visiteur ☐ Other / Autre ☐ ▶ FPS No. - Nº SED 464271D

Name - Nom
THOMAS

Register Serial No. - Nº de registre
421-2002-119

Item description - Nature de l'article
tooth brush with razor blade melted to it.

Location - Endroit
DISSCELL #8

Seizure - Saisie
Time - Heure 0930 Date Y-A 02 M 02 D-J 28

Seizing officer - Agent ayant effectuée la saisie
Name (Print) - Nom (lettres moulées)
A. RISTO

Signature
A. Risto

DHA-283

Correctional Service Canada — Service correctionnel Canada

CSC/SCC 482 (R-92-10) 7530-21-895-1068

CONTRABAND SEIZURE TAG — **BORDEREAU DE SAISIE**

☐ Visitor / Visiteur ☐ Other / Autre ☐ FPS No. - Nº SED 464271D

Name - Nom
Thomas

Register Serial No. - Nº de registre
421-2002-238

Item description - Nature de l'article
body armour

Location - Endroit
L225

Seizure - Saisie
Time - Heure: 1020.
Date: Y-A 02 | M 05 | D-J 05

Seizing officer - Agent ayant effectuée la saisie
Name (Print) - Nom (lettres moulées)
Day

Signature
[signature]

OTO-299

Correctional Service Canada — Service correctionnel Canada

CSC/SCC 482 (R-92-10) 7530-21-895-1068

CONTRABAND SEIZURE TAG — **BORDEREAU DE SAISIE**

☐ Visitor / Visiteur ☐ Other / Autre ☐ ▶ FPS No. - Nº SED

Name - Nom: THOMAS 464271D

Register Serial No. - Nº de registre:

Item description - Nature de l'article:
1 Plastic shank approx 8 inches
1 Metal shank approx 8 inches

Location - Endroit: under the pillow

Seizure - Saisie
Time - Heure: 09:45 am
Date Y-A / M / D-J: 02 / 07 / 25

Seizing officer - Agent ayant effectué la saisie
Name (Print) - Nom (lettres moulées): Keith McBride

Signature: Keith McBride

BHO-368

Correctional Service Canada — Service correctionnel Canada

CSC/SCC 482 (R-92-10) 7530-21-895-1068

CONTRABAND SEIZURE TAG | **BORDEREAU DE SAISIE**

☐ Visitor / Visiteur ☐ Other / Autre ☐ ▶ FPS No. - Nº SED

Name - Nom
THOMAS #464271D

Register Serial No. - Nº de registre
421-2002-346

Item description - Nature de l'article
1 12 inch steel rod sharpened
2 shanks - sharpened - made from window frame
1 inch flat bar sharpened + 1 10 inch steel shank with taped handle

Location - Endroit
CELL L225

Seizure - Saisie

Time - Heure: 0930

Date: Y-A 02 | M 07 | D-J 25

Seizing officer - Agent ayant effectuée la saisie

Name (Print) - Nom (lettres moulées)
Keith McBride

Signature
Keith McBride

DHD-369

Correctional Service Canada / Service correctionnel Canada

CSC/SCC 482 (R-92-10) 7530-21-895-1066

CONTRABAND SEIZURE TAG — **BORDEREAU DE SAISIE**

☐ Visitor / Visiteur ☐ Other / Autre ☐ ▶ FPS No. - Nº SED 464271 D

Name - Nom
THOMAS

Register Serial No. - Nº de registre

Item description - Nature de l'article
2 BROKEN FOOD TRAYS

Location - Endroit
J-K208

Seizure - Saisie
Time - Heure: 10:00
Date: Y-A 01 | M 07 | D-J 11

Seizing officer - Agent ayant effectué la saisie
Name (Print) - Nom (lettres moulées)
D. VELLA

Signature

BMM136

Correctional Service Canada — Service correctionnel Canada

CSC/SCC 482 (R-92-10) 7530-21-895-1068

CONTRABAND SEIZURE TAG | **BORDEREAU DE SAISIE**

☐ Visitor / Visiteur ☐ Other / Autre ☐ ▶ FPS No. - Nº SED 464571D

Name - Nom
Thomas ECA#12

Register Serial No. - Nº de registre
421-2001-202

Item description - Nature de l'article
Home-made alcohol substance (approx. 3 L)

Location - Endroit
ECA#12 housed by Thomas

Seizure - Saisie Time - Heure	Date Y-A	M	D-J
15:20 hrs	01	07	30

Seizing officer - Agent ayant effectuée la saisie
Name (Print) - Nom (lettres moulées)
GALLIMORE L. CX-01

Signature
[illegible]

DM-172

Correctional Service Canada | Service correctionnel Canada

CSC/SCC 482 (R-92-10) 7530-21-895-1068

CONTRABAND SEIZURE TAG | **BORDEREAU DE SAISIE**

☐ Visitor / Visiteur ☐ Other / Autre ☐ ▶ FPS No. - Nº SED 4642710.

Name - Nom
Thomas

Register Serial No. - Nº de registre
2001-139

Item description - Nature de l'article
Brew sample, Sandpaper.
Homemade weapon

Location - Endroit

Seizure - Saisie
Time - Heure: 0950
Date: Y-A 01 | M 06 | D-J 13.

Seizing officer - Agent ayant effectuée la saisie
Name (Print) - Nom (lettres moulées)
S Frydenburgl

Signature

DHM-174

Correctional Service Canada / Service correctionnel Canada

CSC/SCC 482 (R-92-10) 7530-21-895-1068

CONTRABAND SEIZURE TAG | **BORDEREAU DE SAISIE**

☐ Visitor / Visiteur ☐ Other / Autre ☐ FPS No. - Nº SED 464271D

THOMAS

Register Serial No. - Nº de registre

421 2001 - 221

Item description - Nature de l'article

1 DISPOSABLE LIGHTER

18 EXPORT A CIGARETTES

Location - Endroit

Seizure - Saisie

Time - Heure	Date Y-A	M	D-J
1450	01	08	18

Seizing officer - Agent ayant effectuée la saisie

Name (Print) - Nom (lettres moulées)

R. E. GOODWIN

Signature

RE Goodwin

DTD177

Correctional Service Canada / Service correctionnel Canada

CSC/SCC 482 (R-92-10) 7530-21-895-1068

CONTRABAND SEIZURE TAG — **BORDEREAU DE SAISIE**

☐ Visitor / Visiteur ☐ Other / Autre ☐ ▶ FPS No. - Nº SED

Name - Nom: Thomas #464271D

Register Serial No. - Nº de registre: 421-2001-360

Item description - Nature de l'article: homemade weapon approx. 7 8 inches

Location - Endroit: 2L Kitchen area

Seizure - Saisie

Time - Heure	Date Y-A	M	D-J
14:00	01	11	30

Seizing officer - Agent ayant effectuée la saisie

Name (Print) - Nom (lettres moulées): Chris Birchall CX1

Signature: [signature]

[signature]

Correctional Service Canada — Service correctionnel Canada

CSC/SCC 482 (R-92-10) 7530-21-895-1068

CONTRABAND SEIZURE TAG / **BORDEREAU DE SAISIE**

☐ Visitor / Visiteur ☐ Other / Autre ☐ ▶ FPS No. - Nº SED 464271D

Name - Nom
THOMAS

Register Serial No. - Nº de registre
4[illegible]-2001-210

Item description - Nature de l'article
(1) 1L bottle containing alcohol

Location - Endroit
ECH #11

Seizure - Saisie Time - Heure	Date Y-A	M	D-J
10:06	01	08	06

Seizing officer - Agent ayant effectuée la saisie
Name (Print) - Nom (lettres moulées)
J. PELKEY

Signature

Correctional Service Canada / Service correctionnel Canada

CSC/SCC 482 (R-92-10) 7530-21-895-1068

CONTRABAND SEIZURE TAG

BORDEREAU DE SAISIE

☐ Visitor Visiteur ☐ Other Autre ☐ ▶ FPS No. - Nº SED 4640

Name - Nom

Thomas

Register Serial No. - Nº de registre

421-2001-589

Item description - Nature de l'article

3x9 pointed piece of plexiglass

Location - Endroit

J-UNIT K227

Seizure - Saisie

Time - Heure	Date Y-A	M	D-J
17:10	01	10	03

Seizing officer - Agent ayant effectuée la saisie
Name (Print) - Nom (lettres moulées)

M. MONTGOMERY

Signature

040-215

Correctional Service Canada — Service correctionnel Canada

CSC/SCC 482 (R-92-10) 7530-21-895-1068

CONTRABAND SEIZURE TAG | **BORDEREAU DE SAISIE**

☐ Visitor / Visiteur ☐ Other / Autre

☐ ▶ FPS No. - Nº SED 464371 D

Name - Nom
Wm THOMAS

Register Serial No. - Nº de registre
421-2001-028

Item description - Nature de l'article
10" "Shiv" shaped like icepick.

Location - Endroit
K117

Seizure - Saisie
Time - Heure
1750 hrs

Date Y-A	M	D-J
01	01	30

Seizing officer - Agent ayant effectuée la saisie
Name (Print) - Nom (lettres moulées)
M. Bouchard

Signature
M. Bouchard

[illegible] 221(b)

Correctional Service Canada | Service correctionnel Canada

CSC/SCC 482 (R-92-10) 7530-21-895-1666

CONTRABAND SEIZURE TAG | BORDEREAU DE SAISIE

☐ Visitor / Visiteur ☐ Other / Autre ☐ ▶ FPS No. - Nº SED 464271D

Thomas

Register Serial No. - Nº de registre
421-2001-141

Item description - Nature de l'article
home made knife 8" steel (shank) to look like approx length / a knife

Location - Endroit
17-1K

Seizure - Saisie
Time - Heure 1420
Date Y-A 01 M 06 D-J 18

Seizing officer - Agent ayant effectuée la saisie
Name (Print) - Nom (lettres moulées)
B Jones

Signature
B Jones

Correctional Service Canada / Service correctionnel Canada

CSC/SCC 482 (R-92-10) 7530-21-895-1068

CONTRABAND SEIZURE TAG

BORDEREAU D' J

☐ Visitor Visiteur ☒ Other Autre ☐ ▶ FPS No. - N° 464271D

Name - Nom

THOMAS

Register Serial No. - N° de registre

2001-186

Item description - Nature de l'article

1 HOME-made Weapon

Approx. 22cm Long

Location - Endroit

SEGREGATION

Seizure - Saisie

Time - Heure

09:30

Date Y-A	M	D-J
2001	07	16

Seizing officer - Agent ayant effectuée la saisie

Name (Print) - Nom (lettres moulées)

JOHN PELKEY

Signature

Correctional Service Canada — Service correctionnel Canada

CSC/SCC 482 (R-92-10) 7530-21-895-10

CONTRABAND SEIZURE TAG | **BORDEREAU DE SAISIE**

☐ Visitor / Visiteur ☐ Other / Autre ☐ ▶ FPS No. - Nº SED 464271D

Name - Nom
THOMAS

Register Serial No. - Nº de registre
411-2001-270

Item description - Nature de l'article
HOMEMADE ICEPICK Approx 8"

Location - Endroit
Hall between 5 ... + ...

Seizure - Saisie
Time - Heure: 1800 HRS.

Date		
Y-A	M	D-J
01	09	04

Seizing officer - Agent ayant effectuée la saisie
Name (Print) - Nom (lettres moulées)
L.C. LEMAIRE

Signature
[illegible]

DHD-226

Correctional Service Canada | Service correctionnel Canada

CSC/SCC 482 (R-92-10) | 7530-21-895-1066

Ontario Secondary School Diploma
Diplôme d'études secondaires de l'Ontario

This Diploma is granted to
Ce diplôme est décerné à

Shane Anthony Thomas

a student of
élève de

GARY ALLAN HIGH SCHOOL

who has fulfilled the requirements for the Ontario Secondary School Diploma
in accordance with the provisions of the Ministry of Education, Ontario
qui a rempli les exigences prescrites pour l'obtention du diplôme d'études secondaires de l'Ontario,
en vertu des dispositions du ministère de l'Éducation de l'Ontario

Dated at
Délivré à **Burlington, Ontario**

Minister of Education/Ministre de l'Éducation

the ce **20th** day of jour de **AUGUST** **2007**

Principal of School/Directeur ou directrice de l'école

Starting at St. Leonards Place
Mon. 9th Nov 2009

Computer Workshop Basics

Mondays 7:00-9:00pm

Upon successful completion you will receive a Computer Basics Certificate which will help your job search effort

Please register prior to start of workshop
Talk to Carmen
Or
call Munaf: 416-629-8289

I have completed my cognitive skills program while I was incarcerated in Collins Bay institution. However, I have misplaced the certificate.

Certificate of Achievement

Awarded to

SHANE THOMAS

for attending the

ANGER AND EMOTIONAL SELF-REGULATION GROUP

delivered at the Secure Treatment Unit
St. Lawrence Valley Correctional & Treatment Centre

Sarah Clarke, Social Worker

RN
Program Nurse

June 24, 2008
Date

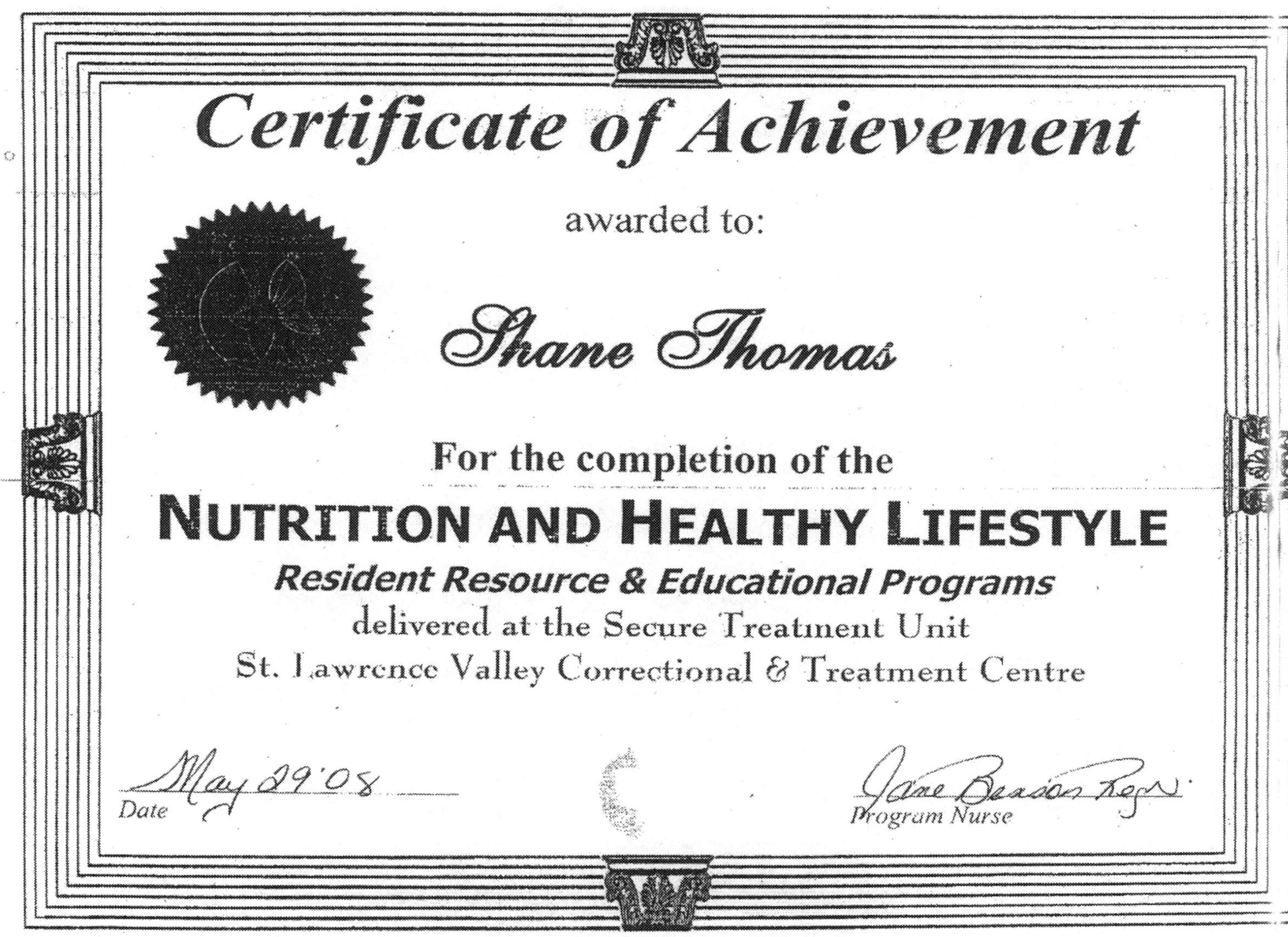

Certificate of Achievement

awarded to:

Shane Thomas

For the completion of the

NUTRITION AND HEALTHY LIFESTYLE

Resident Resource & Educational Programs

delivered at the Secure Treatment Unit

St. Lawrence Valley Correctional & Treatment Centre

May 09'08

Date

Program Nurse

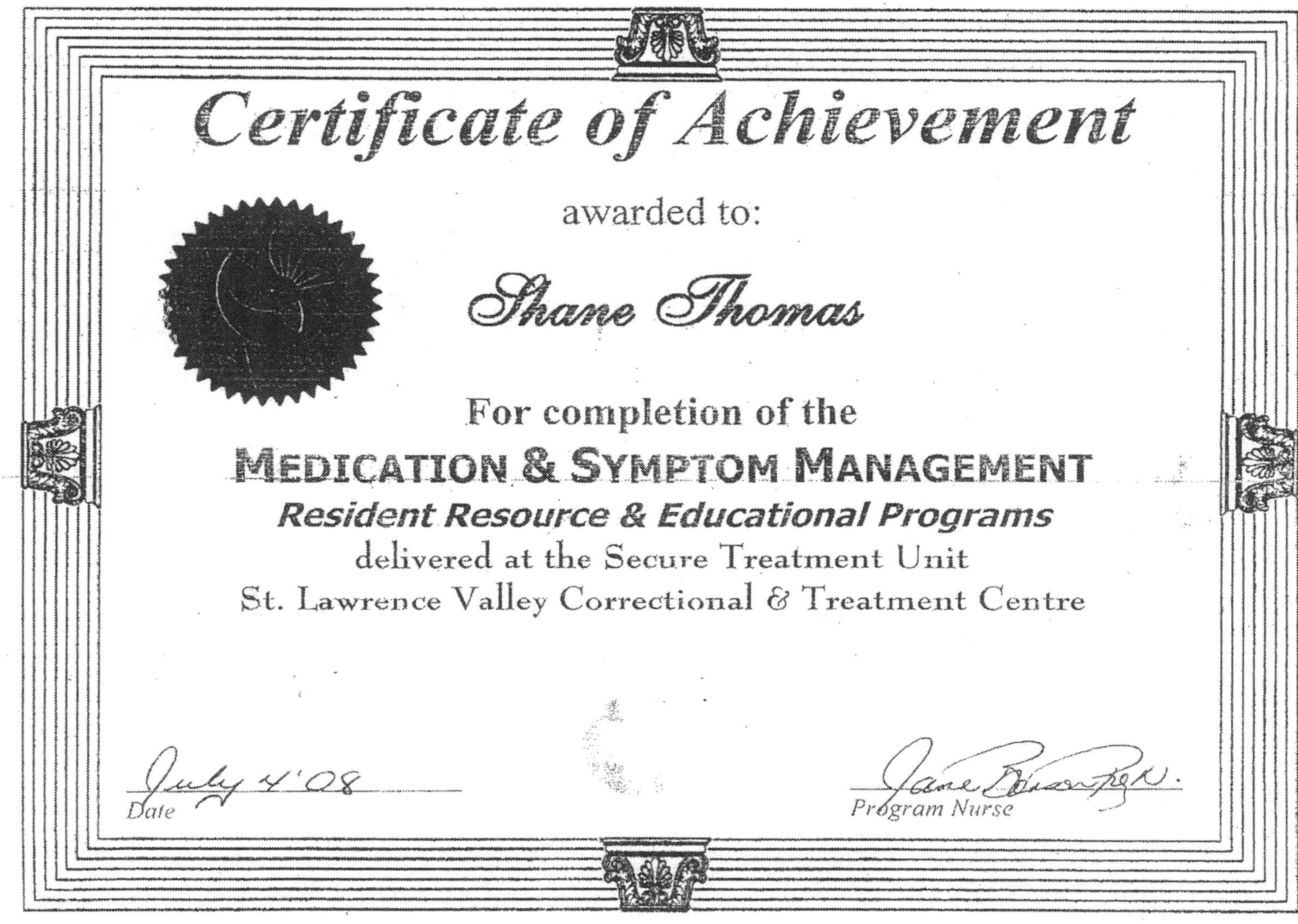

Certificate of Achievement

awarded to:

Shane Thomas

For completion of the

MEDICATION & SYMPTOM MANAGEMENT

Resident Resource & Educational Programs

delivered at the Secure Treatment Unit

St. Lawrence Valley Correctional & Treatment Centre

July 4 '08

Date

Program Nurse

Certificate of Achievement

awarded to:

Shane Thomas

for participation in the

EXERCISE/WEIGHT TRAINING ACTIVITY

(20 HOURS)

delivered at the Secure Treatment Unit
St. Lawrence Valley Correctional & Treatment Centre

Date

Tim Seed, Recreational Therapist

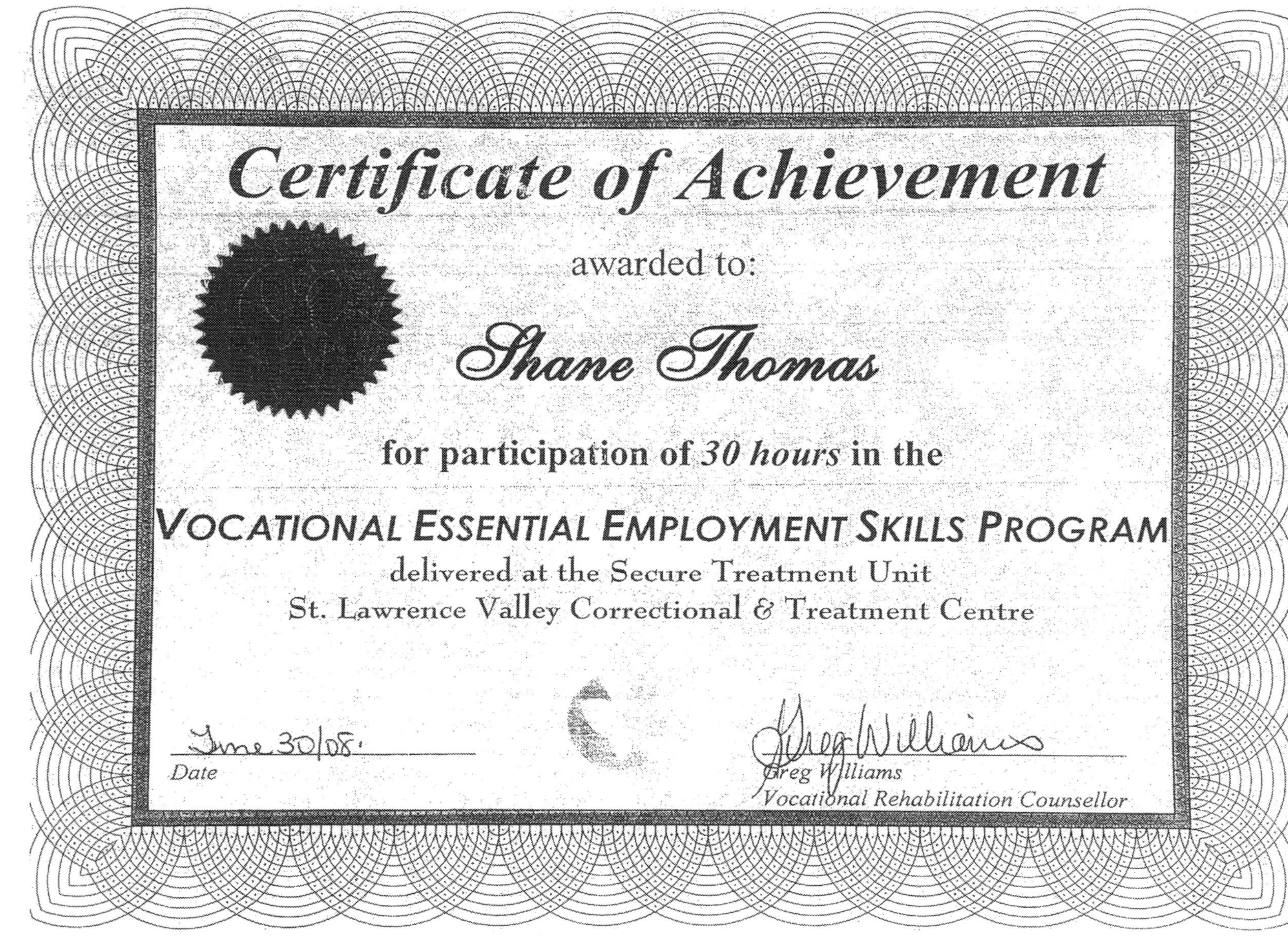

Certificate of Achievement

awarded to:

Shane Thomas

for participation of *30 hours* in the

VOCATIONAL ESSENTIAL EMPLOYMENT SKILLS PROGRAM

delivered at the Secure Treatment Unit

St. Lawrence Valley Correctional & Treatment Centre

June 30/08.

Date

Greg Williams

Greg Williams

Vocational Rehabilitation Counsellor

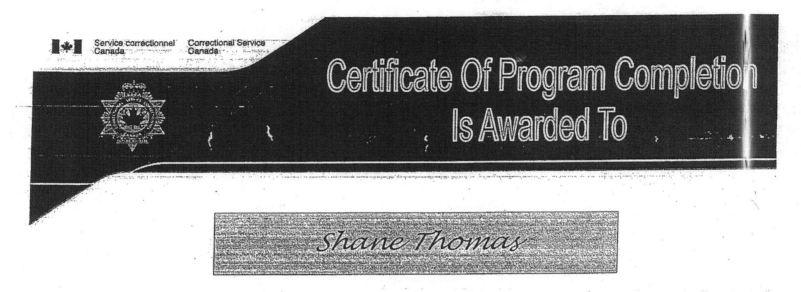

Service correctionnel Canada   Correctional Service Canada

Certificate Of Program Completion Is Awarded To

Shane Thomas

In Recognition of His Participation in

The Moderate Intensity Violence Prevention Program

November 30, 2009 – March 31, 2010

Program Delivery Staff

Manager of Programs

Canada

THESE ARE MY MENTAL ILLNESS'

PSYCHOTIC DISORDER NOT OTHERWISE SPECIFIED: Psychosis is a symptom or feature of mental illness typically characterized by radical changes in personality, impaired functioning, and a distorted or nonexistent sense of objective reality.

SCHIZOPHRENIA: is a mental disorder characterized by a breakdown of thought processes and by poor emotional responsiveness.[1] It most commonly manifests itself as auditory hallucinations, paranoid or bizarre delusions, or disorganized speech and thinking, and it is accompanied by significant social or occupational dysfunction. The onset of symptoms typically occurs in young adulthood, with a global lifetime prevalence of about 0.3–0.7%.[2] Diagnosis is based on observed behavior and the patient's reported experiences.

SCHIZOAFFECTIVE DISORDER: is a mental condition that causes both a loss of contact with reality (psychosis) and mood problems.

SUBSTANCE INDUCED PYSCHOTIC DISORDER: A substance-induced psychotic disorder is subtyped or categorized based on whether the prominent feature is delusions or hallucinations. Delusions are fixed, false beliefs. Hallucinations are seeing, hearing, feeling, tasting, or smelling things that are not there

PSYCHOTIC DISORDER DUE TO A GENERAL MEDICAL CONDITION: The essential features of Psychotic Disorder Due to a General Medical Condition are prominent hallucinations or delusions that are judged to be due to the direct physiological effects of a general medical condition (Criterion A).

SCHIZOPHRENIA PROVISIONAL: Because of the variability of symptom expression, diagnostic requirements of chronicity, and lack of pathognomonic features, an ED diagnosis of schizophrenia should be provisional at best. As a diagnosis-by-exclusion, schizophrenia must be distinguished from the numerous psychiatric and organic disorders that also can lead to psychotic disturbances in thinking and behavior.

When an individual goes to prison seventy dollars is taken from their account to pay for a body bag. It is then given back to you if you get out alive. While I was confined I got caught for a lot of things and I got away with a lot of things such as contraband and serious assaults against other convicts and correctional officers. I also made it on the local Kingston news for some of my crazy antics. When I look back into my life it is clear that I was very problematic and was in need of professional assistance in which I got and I myself wanted to change in which I am successful. I am now a new man, a productive and pro-social man.

I took a serious look at my life, and got seriously concerned, I wanted to change. I needed to get motivated, make crime, and violence a thing of the past and drop my anti-social tendencies. The last time I was in jail, I observed 40-60 year old men living happily and comfortably. I quickly realized that I don't want to fall into that statistic. I want my freedom back, and I want responsibilities out in the community. I get Ontario Disability Pension Monthly, in which I am saving up. I want a house, nice car, wife, and twelve children, which will bring great joy to my heart. While I am residing at St Leonard's Place Peel, a halfway house in Brampton, Ontario, Canada. I visit my family every weekend. I do volunteer work to give back to the community, I have bills to pay, and I take advantage of my community access time. I volunteer to complete programs, and I started to interact with staff, and other residents. I go to church every Sunday with uncle Corl. I have been a resident at St. Leonard's since May 06/09, and get along with my parole officer, and the case management team in the halfway house. My parole officer informed me that I am doing extremely well, and if I continue to do so for the next 2 years, she will support in her report to the National Parole Board, to get my residency condition lifted. This will enable me to reside out in the community independently on my own

While at St. Leonard's Place Peel Halfway House, I participated in the Violence Prevention Program, which I attended 3 times a week, for 3 hours, each day. This was imposed on me by my Parole Officer, to better address my issues of crime and violence. I did well in this program, according to my program instructor and Parole Officer. I really benefited from it and learned different skills, which I now use in my everyday life. My favourite skill is self talk, I learned to look at options and analyze situations well, from this skill. For example, is crime worth it, could it hurt me in the long run, will anyone get hurt, can I loose my family or end up in jail. All of these are concerns which make me not want to commit crime. My mental Illnesses prevent me from working, so I am grateful that I now get ODSP, as an income. I learned to be satisfied with the little I have, because crime does not pay.

My journey was long and hard, I wouldn't want to do it again, but if I had to I would because of my reward which is riches, power, kingdom, glory, and dominion forever and ever. None can walk in my shoes, which proves that I am above all. Only the fittest of the fittest shall survive, I am He. Perfection means no limitations I will forever walk with my head high, because I love myself. The world leaders are fully aware of my presence, because I sent some of them a copy of my book. In 2012 I will rise up perfectly to rule the world, because my journey is done, in which I will make trillions of dollars, generated from the sales of this book. You also need to purchase my three music CD's, which are also advertised in this book which will also generate trillions of dollars. I will request, and get riches from the world leaders, in which they will be responsible for I to live comfortably, I am really looking forward to that. The choicest of women the choicest of foods, and material things. My book, and my music possess' perfect powers, and perfect visuals, which is perfect truth, and will go to the media via satellite on television for the world to purchase. If you purchase my book, and my three albums, you will get saved and your reward is with me. If you don't purchase them, then you will surely burn in the fire for eternity, along with the hopeless sinners, and that's what they want. Something spectacular will happen after the world buys my book, along with my three CD's, I will start exercising my powers. Everyone will be rich, everyone will be free, everyone will have perfect health, everyone will be good looking, everyone will have eternal life, and much more.

GREETINGS PEOPLE

I LOVE MUSIC

I HAVE THREE ALBUMS IN ITUNE STORES

WORLDWIDE

<u>MY THREE ALBUMS ARE CALLED:</u>

1. THE REBIRTH OF SHANE THOM
2. THE WRATH OF SHANE THOM
3. SPIRIT SHANE THOM

MY MUSIC NAME IS SHANE THOM
CLICK ON REGGAE
SEARCH FOR SHANE THOM
TO PURCHASE MY THREE ALBUMS.

24th Psalm

1 A Psalm of David. The earth is the LORD's and the fulness thereof, the world and those
who dwell therein; 2 for he has founded it upon the seas, and established it upon the
rivers. 3 Who shall ascend the hill of the LORD? And who shall stand in his holy place?
4 He who has clean hands and a pure heart, who does not lift up his soul to what is false,
and does not swear deceitfully. 5 He will receive blessing from the LORD, and
vindication from the God of his salvation. 6 Such is the generation of those who seek
him, who seek the face of the God of Jacob. [Selah] 7 Lift up your heads, O gates! and be
lifted up, O ancient doors! that the King of glory may come in. 8 Who is the King of
glory? The LORD, strong and mighty, the LORD, mighty in battle! 9 Lift up your heads,
O gates! and be lifted up, O ancient doors! that the King of glory may come in. 10 Who is
this King of glory? The LORD of hosts, he is the King of glory! [Selah]